thinking
science
through

teacher's book

3
RED

Hodder Murray

A MEMBER OF THE HODDER HEADLINE GROUP

Arthur Cheney
Howard Flavell
Chris Harrison
George Hurst
Carolyn Yates

Although every effort has been made to ensure that website addresses are correct at time of going to press, Hodder Murray cannot be held responsible for the content of any website mentioned in this book. It is sometimes possible to find a relocated web page by typing in the address of the home page for a website in the URL window of your browser.

Papers used in this book are natural, renewable and recyclable products. They are made from wood grown in sustainable forests. The logging and manufacturing processes conform to the environmental regulations of the country of origin.

Orders: Please contact Bookpoint Ltd, 130 Milton park, Abingdon, Oxon OX14 4SB. Telephone: (44) 01235 827720. Fax: (44) 01235 400454. Lines are open from 9.00a.m. – 6.00p.m., Monday to Saturday, with a 24 hour message answering service. Visit our website at www.hoddereducation.co.uk.

First published in 2005
by Hodder Murray, a member of the Hodder Headline Group
338 Euston Road
London NW1 3BH

Impression number   10 9 8 7 6 5 4 3 2 1
Year   2010 2009 2008 2007 2006 2005

Typeset in 10/13 pt Lucida by DC Graphic Design Ltd., Swanley, Kent
Printed in Great Britain by Hobbs the Printers, Totton, Hampshire

A catalogue entry for this title is available from the British Library
ISBN-10 0 7195 7858 2
ISBN-13 978 0 719 57858 8
CD-ROM 3 0 7195 7859 0
Pupil's Book 3 Red 0 7195 7857 4

Contents

Thinking skills audit

The following skills are explicitly addressed in the Pupil's Book, and other opportunities to include thinking and reasoning skills are suggested within the teacher's notes.

QCA thinking skills	Investigative skills	Chapter coverage
Enquiry (planning)	a) Devise questions to be investigated b) Use of secondary sources c) Make predictions/preliminary work d) Controlling variables e) Decide extent and range of data f) Choose equipment and materials – accuracy and safety g) Choose sample size/repeat measurements	Introduction, 8, 9 2, 3, 4, 6 1, 4, 5 4, 5, 9 7, 9 1, 3, 8, 9 5, 6, 7, 9
Obtaining evidence	h) Collect evidence to appropriate precision	6, 9
Information processing	i) Present data – tables and graphs j) Interpret data – patterns	2, 4, 5, 7 1, 3, 4, 6
Reasoning	k) Draw conclusions l) Explain conclusions	Introduction, 2, 4, 7 Introduction, 2, 4, 5, 7
Evaluation	m) Conclusions support prediction? n) Anomalous results – explanation o) Evidence supports conclusions? – fair test; accurate; reliable; sample size p) Improvements to the investigation?	2, 4, 7 3, 8, 9 1, 4, 5, 6, 7, 8 2, 6

CASE reasoning pattern	Chapter coverage
Control of variable, exclusion of irrelevant variables, combinations of variables	4, 5, 6, 9
Classification	1, 5, 9
Ratios, scaling and inverse proportionality	1, 3, 4, 8
Compound variables and equilibrium	3, 4, 8
Probability and correlation	2, 6, 7
Formal modelling	1, 2, 3, 4, 6, 8, 9

General skills audit

General skills	Chapter coverage
Literacy	
Key words – Etymology, usage	1, 2, 3, 4, 5, 6, 7, 8, 9
Text types – Recount	2
Information	1, 2, 3, 4, 5, 6 7, 8, 9
Instructions	7, 8
Explanation	Introduction, 1, 2, 3, 4, 5, 6, 7, 8, 9
Discursive	2, 3, 7
Persuasion	2, 4, 7
Analysis	1, 2, 3, 4, 5, 6, 7, 8, 9
Evaluation	2, 3, 7
Numeracy	
Estimating	7
Units	3, 8
Application of number	1, 3, 4, 6, 8
ICT	
Finding out (e.g. CD-ROM, internet)	1, 2, 3, 4, 5, 6, 7
Capturing data (e.g. datalogging)	2, 4
Visualising (e.g. simulations, animations)	7
Interpreting (e.g. spreadsheets, graphing, databases)	2, 4, 8
Modelling (e.g. spreadsheets, 'Croc Clips')	4, 7
Communicating (e.g. 'Word', 'PowerPoint')	2, 6, 7
Graphs	
Interpreting – Pie	5, 6
Bar	2, 6, 7
Scatter	2, 6
Line	2, 4, 6, 7
Plotting – Bar	2, 7
Scatter	2, 7
Line	2, 4, 6, 7, 8
Ideas and evidence	1, 3, 4, 5, 6, 7, 8, 9
Spiritual, moral, social, cultural	2, 7, 9
Creative thinking	2, 3, 6, 7, 8, 9
Investigations	
Fair testing	2, 3, 7, 8
Pattern seeking (survey or record)	1, 2, 4, 5, 6, 7, 8, 9
Identifying/classifying	2, 5
Exploring (observing over time)	6
Technology (design to solve a problem)	
Test out an explanation	5, 9
Reference (look up)	1, 2, 7

Key Stage 3 Programme of Study

During Key Stage 3 pupils build on their scientific knowledge and understanding and make connections between different areas of science. They use scientific ideas and models to explain phenomena and events, and to understand a range of familiar applications of science. They think about the positive and negative effects of scientific and technological developments on the environment and in other contexts. They take account of others' views and understand why opinions may differ. They do more quantitative work, carrying out investigations on their own and with others. They evaluate their work, in particular the strength of the evidence they and others have collected. They select and use a wide range of reference sources. They communicate clearly what they did and its significance. They learn how scientists work together on present-day scientific developments and about the importance of experimental evidence in supporting scientific ideas.

Knowledge, skills and understanding
Teaching should ensure that scientific enquiry is taught through contexts taken from the sections on life processes and living things, materials and their properties, and physical processes.

Sc1 Scientific enquiry

Ideas and evidence in science

1 Pupils should be taught:

		Chapter coverage		
		Book 1	**Book 2**	**Book 3**
a)	about the interplay between empirical questions, evidence and scientific explanations using historical and contemporary examples (for example, Lavoisier's work on burning, the possible causes of global warming)	1, 3, 6, 7, 11	1, 4, 6, 11	4, 6, 7, 8, 9
b)	that it is important to test explanations by using them to make predictions and by seeing if evidence matches the predictions	Introduction, 10,11, 12	8	4, 6, 7, 9
c)	about the ways in which scientists work today and how they worked in the past, including the roles of experimentation, evidence and creative thought in the development of scientific ideas.	Introduction, 2, 4, 7, 8, 10	Introduction, 1, 4, 6, 9, 11	1, 4, 6, 7, 8, 9

Investigative skills

2 Pupils should be taught to:

Planning

a)	use scientific knowledge and understanding to turn ideas into a form that can be investigated, and to decide on an appropriate approach	9, 10, 11, 12	2, 3, 5, 6, 7, 8, 9, 11, 12	Introduction, 2, 3, 5, 7, 8
b)	decide whether to use evidence from first-hand experience or secondary sources	1, 11, 12	4	5, 6
c)	carry out preliminary work and make predictions, where appropriate	6, 7, 10, 11	2, 3, 5, 10, 11, 12	1, 3, 5, 6, 7, 8

	Book 1	Book 2	Book 3
d) consider key factors that need to be taken into account when collecting evidence, and how evidence may be collected in contexts (for example, fieldwork, surveys) in which the variables cannot readily be controlled	1, 9, 12	5, 10, 12	2, 3, 5, 7, 8
e) decide the extent and range of data to be collected and the techniques, equipment and materials to use (for example, appropriate sample size for biological work)	1, 5, 8, 10, 11, 12	2, 6, 12	2, 3, 5, 7, 8

Obtaining and presenting evidence

	Book 1	Book 2	Book 3
f) use a range of equipment and materials appropriately and take action to control risks to themselves and to others	3, 5, 7, 10, 11, 12	3, 12	2, 3, 5, 7, 8
g) make observations and measurements, including the use of ICT for datalogging (for example, variables changing over time) to an appropriate degree of precision	1, 9, 10, 11, 12	3, 12	2, 3, 5, 7, 8
h) make sufficient relevant observations and measurements to reduce error and obtain reliable evidence	1, 10, 11, 12	9, 12	2, 3, 5, 7, 8
i) use a wide range of methods, including diagrams, tables, charts, graphs and ICT, to represent and communicate qualitative and quantitative data	1, 3, 6, 7, 10, 12	1, 5, 11, 12	2, 3, 5, 7, 8

Considering evidence

	Book 1	Book 2	Book 3
j) use diagrams, tables, charts and graphs, including lines of best fit, to identify and describe patterns or relationships in data	1, 2, 6, 7, 8, 9, 10, 11, 12	Introduction, 1, 3, 6, 12	Introduction, 1, 2, 3, 4, 5, 7, 8
k) use observations, measurements and other data to draw conclusions	1, 2, 3, 5, 6, 7, 10, 11, 12	Introduction, 4, 6, 7, 9, 12	1, 2, 3, 4, 6, 7, 8
l) decide to what extent these conclusions support a prediction or enable further predictions to be made	4, 10, 11	9	1, 2, 3, 5, 7, 8
m) use their scientific knowledge and understanding to explain and interpret observations, measurements or other data, and conclusions	1, 2, 4, 5, 10, 11, 12	Introduction, 4, 6, 7, 9, 10, 12	2, 3, 4, 5, 7, 8

Evaluating

	Book 1	Book 2	Book 3
n) consider anomalies in observations or measurements and try to explain them	3, 9, 10	Introduction, 1, 12	2, 3, 7, 8
o) consider whether the evidence is sufficient to support any conclusions or interpretations made	3, 7	Introduction, 4, 9	2, 3, 7, 8
p) suggest improvements to the methods used, where appropriate.	5, 7, 9, 11	1, 6, 7, 9, 11, 12	5, 7, 8

Sc2 Life processes and living things

Chapter coverage

Cells and cell functions

	Book 1	Book 2	Book 3
1 Pupils should be taught:			
a) that animal and plant cells can form tissues, and tissues can form organs	7		
b) the functions of chloroplasts and cell walls in plant cells and the functions of the cell membrane, cytoplasm and nucleus in both plant and animal cells	7		

c) ways in which some cells, including ciliated epithelial cells, sperm, ova, and root hair cells, are adapted to their functions   7   7

d) that fertilisation in humans and in flowering plants is the fusion of a male and a female cell   8

e) to relate cells and cell functions to life processes in a variety of organisms.   7   6

Humans as organisms

2 Pupils should be taught:

Nutrition

a) about the need for a balanced diet containing carbohydrates, proteins, fats, minerals, vitamins, fibre and water, and about foods that are sources of these   1   2

b) the principles of digestion, including the role of enzymes in breaking down large molecules into smaller ones   1

c) that the products of digestion are absorbed into the bloodstream and transported throughout the body, and that waste material is egested   1

d) that food is used as a fuel during respiration to maintain the body's activity and as a raw material for growth and repair   12   6

Movement

e) the role of the skeleton and joints and the principle of antagonistic muscle pairs (for example, biceps and triceps) in movement   2

Reproduction

f) about the physical and emotional changes that take place during adolescence   8

g) about the human reproductive system, including the menstrual cycle and fertilisation   8

h) how the foetus develops in the uterus, including the role of the placenta   8

Breathing

i) the role of lung structure in gas exchange, including the effect of smoking   2

Respiration

j) that aerobic respiration involves a reaction in cells between oxygen and food, in which glucose is broken down into carbon dioxide and water   7   6   2

k) to summarise aerobic respiration in a word equation   6

l) that the reactants and products of respiration are transported throughout the body in the bloodstream   6

Health

m) that the abuse of alcohol, solvents and other drugs affects health   2

n) how the growth and reproduction of bacteria and the replication of viruses can affect health, and how the body's natural defences may be enhanced by immunisation and medicines.   9   2

Green plants as organisms
3 Pupils should be taught:

Nutrition and growth
a) that plants need carbon dioxide, water and light for photosynthesis, and produce biomass and oxygen   6
b) to summarise photosynthesis in a word equation   6
c) that nitrogen and other elements, in addition to carbon, oxygen and hydrogen, are required for plant growth   6
d) the role of root hairs in absorbing water and minerals from the soil   6

Respiration
e) that plants carry out aerobic respiration.   6

Variation, classification and inheritance
4 Pupils should be taught:

Variation
a) about environmental and inherited causes of variation within a species   2   7

Classification
b) to classify living things into the major taxonomic groups   2

Inheritance
c) that selective breeding can lead to new varieties.   2   7

Living things in their environment
5 Pupils should be taught:

Adaptation and competition
a) about ways in which living things and the environment can be protected, and the importance of sustainable development   6
b) that habitats support a diversity of plants and animals that are interdependent   1
c) how some organisms are adapted to survive daily and seasonal changes in their habitats   1   12
d) how predation and competition for resources affect the size of populations (for example, bacteria, growth of vegetation)   1

Feeding relationships
e) about food webs composed of several food chains, and how food chains can be quantified using pyramids of numbers   1   12
f) how toxic materials can accumulate in food chains.   12

Sc3 Materials and their properties

Classifying materials

1 Pupils should be taught:

	Chapter coverage		
	Book 1	Book 2	Book 3
Solids, liquids and gases			
a) how materials can be characterised by melting point, boiling point and density		7	
b) how the particle theory of matter can be used to explain the properties of solids, liquids and gases, including changes of state, gas pressure and diffusion	4, 9	3, 7	
Elements, compounds and mixtures			
c) that the elements are shown in the periodic table and consist of atoms, which can be represented by symbols		4	
d) how elements vary widely in their physical properties, including appearance, state at room temperature, magnetic properties, and thermal and electrical conductivity, and how these properties can be used to classify elements as metals or non-metals		4	
e) how elements combine through chemical reactions to form compounds (for example, water, carbon dioxide, magnesium oxide, sodium chloride, most minerals) with a definite composition	11	7	
f) to represent compounds by formulae and to summarise reactions by word equations	11	4, 7	
g) that mixtures (for example, air, sea water and most rocks) are composed of constituents that are not combined		7	
h) how to separate mixtures into their constituents using distillation, chromatography and other appropriate methods.	9	7	

Changing materials

2 Pupils should be taught:

	Book 1	Book 2	Book 3
Physical changes			
a) that when physical changes (for example, changes of state, formation of solutions) take place, mass is conserved	9		
b) about the variation of solubility with temperature, the formation of saturated solutions, and the differences in solubility of solutes in different solvents	9		
c) to relate changes of state to energy transfers		7	
Geological changes			
d) how forces generated by expansion, contraction and the freezing of water can lead to the physical weathering of rocks		2	6
e) about the formation of rocks by processes that take place over different timescales, and that the mode of formation determines their texture and the minerals they contain		10	

f) how igneous rocks are formed by the cooling of magma, sedimentary rocks by processes including the deposition of rock fragments or organic material, or as a result of evaporation, and metamorphic rocks by the action of heat and pressure on existing rocks   10

Chemical reactions

g) how mass is conserved when chemical reactions take place because the same atoms are present, although combined in different ways   1

h) that virtually all materials, including those in living systems, are made through chemical reactions, and to recognise the importance of chemical change in everyday situations (for example, ripening fruit, setting superglue, cooking food)   11

i) about possible effects of burning fossil fuels on the environment (for example, production of acid rain, carbon dioxide and solid particles) and how these effects can be minimised.   11   6

Patterns of behaviour

3 Pupils should be taught:

Metals

a) how metals react with oxygen, water, acids and oxides of other metals, and what the products of these reactions are   11   5

b) about the displacement reactions that take place between metals and solutions of salts of other metals   5

c) how a reactivity series of metals can be determined by considering these reactions, and used to make predictions about other reactions   5

Acids and bases

d) to use indicators to classify solutions as acidic, neutral or alkaline, and to use the pH scale as a measure of the acidity of a solution   5

e) how metals and bases, including carbonates, react with acids, and what the products of these reactions are   11   1

f) about some everyday applications of neutralisation (for example, the treatment of indigestion, the treatment of acid soil, the manufacture of fertiliser)   5

g) how acids in the environment can lead to corrosion of some metals and chemical weathering of rock (for example, limestone)   11

h) to identify patterns in chemical reactions.   11

Sc4 Physical processes	Chapter coverage		
Electricity and magnetism	**Book 1**	**Book 2**	**Book 3**
1 Pupils should be taught:			

Circuits

	Book 1	Book 2	Book 3
a) how to design and construct series and parallel circuits, and how to measure current and voltage	3		3
b) that the current in a series circuit depends on the number of cells and the number and the nature of other components, and that current is not 'used up' by components	3		
c) that energy is transferred from batteries and other sources to other components in electrical circuits	3		

Magnetic fields

	Book 1	Book 2	Book 3
d) about magnetic fields as regions of space where magnetic materials experience forces, and that like magnetic poles repel and unlike poles attract		11	

Electromagnets

	Book 1	Book 2	Book 3
e) that a current in a coil produces a magnetic field pattern similar to that of a bar magnet		11	
f) how electromagnets are constructed and used (for example, relays, lifting magnets).		11	

Forces and motion
2 Pupils should be taught:

Force and linear motion

	Book 1	Book 2	Book 3
a) how to determine the speed of a moving object and to use the quantitative relationship between speed, distance and time	6		4
b) that the weight of an object on Earth is the result of the gravitational attraction between its mass and that of the Earth	6		4
c) that unbalanced forces change the speed or direction of movement of objects and that balanced forces produce no change in the movement of an object	6		
d) ways in which frictional forces, including air resistance, affect motion (for example, streamlining cars, friction between tyre and road)	6		

Force and rotation

	Book 1	Book 2	Book 3
e) that forces can cause objects to turn about a pivot			8
f) the principle of moments and its application to situations involving one pivot			8

Force and pressure

	Book 1	Book 2	Book 3
g) the quantitative relationship between force, area and pressure, and its application (for example, the use of skis and snowboards, the effect of sharp blades, hydraulic brakes).			8

Light and sound
3 Pupils should be taught:

The behaviour of light
a) that light travels in a straight line at a finite speed in a uniform medium   8
b) that non-luminous objects are seen because light scattered from them enters the eye   8
c) how light is reflected at plane surfaces   8
d) how light is refracted at the boundary between two different materials   8
e) that white light can be dispersed to give a range of colours   8
f) the effect of colour filters on white light and how coloured objects appear in white light and in other colours of light   8

Hearing
g) that sound causes the eardrum to vibrate and that different people have different audible ranges   5
h) some effects of loud sounds on the ear (for example, temporary deafness)   5

Vibration and sound
i) that light can travel through a vacuum but sound cannot, and that light travels much faster than sound   5
j) the relationship between the loudness of a sound and the amplitude of the vibration causing it   5
k) the relationship between the pitch of a sound and the frequency of the vibration causing it.   5

The Earth and beyond
4 Pupils should be taught:

The Solar System
a) how the movement of the Earth causes the apparent daily and annual movement of the Sun and other stars   10
b) the relative positions of the Earth, Sun and planets in the Solar System   10
c) about the movements of planets around the Sun and to relate these to gravitational forces   10   4
d) that the Sun and other stars are light sources and that the planets and other bodies are seen by reflected light   10
e) about the use of artificial satellites and probes to observe the Earth and to explore the Solar System.   4

Energy resources and energy transfer
5 Pupils should be taught:

Energy resources
a) about the variety of energy resources, and the distinction between renewable and non-renewable resources   12   3

b) about the Sun as the ultimate source of most of the Earth's energy resources and to relate this to how coal, oil and gas are formed	12		
c) that electricity is generated by means of a variety of energy resources	12		3

Conservation of energy

d) the distinction between temperature and heat, and that differences in temperature can lead to transfer of energy		3	
e) ways in which energy can be usefully transferred and stored		3	3
f) how energy is transferred by the movement of particles in conduction, convection and evaporation, and that energy is transferred directly by radiation		3	3
g) that although energy is always conserved, it may be dissipated, reducing its availability as a resource.		3	3

Sc5 Breadth of study

Chapter coverage

	Book 1	Book 2	Book 3
1 During the Key Stage, pupils should be taught the knowledge, skills and understanding through:			
a) a range of domestic, industrial and environmental contexts		2, 4, 9	2, 3, 4, 6, 7, 8, 9
b) considering ways in which science is applied in technological developments		3, 5, 8	3, 4, 5, 8, 9
c) considering the benefits and drawbacks of scientific and technological developments, including those related to the environment, health and quality of life		5, 7, 9	2, 3, 4, 6, 7, 8, 9
d) using a range of sources of information, including ICT-based sources		4, 6, 9	1, 2, 3, 4, 5, 6, 7, 8, 9
e) using first-hand and secondary data to carry out a range of scientific investigations, including complete investigations		5, 6, 12	2, 3, 5, 7, 8
f) using quantitative approaches where appropriate, including calculations based on simple relationships between physical quantities.		3, 5, 7	2, 3, 4, 6, 7, 8
2 During the Key Stage, pupils should be taught to:			
Communication			
a) use scientific language, conventions and symbols, including SI units, word equations and chemical symbols, formulae and equations, where appropriate, to communicate scientific ideas and to provide scientific explanations based on evidence		Introduction, 1, 2, 3, 4, 5, 6, 7, 8, 9, 10, 11, 12	1, 2, 3, 4, 5, 6, 7, 8, 9
Health and safety			
b) recognise that there are hazards in living things, materials and physical processes, and assess risks and take action to reduce risks to themselves and others.		Introduction, 1, 2, 3, 4, 5, 6, 7, 8, 9, 10, 11, 12	

Preface

Thinking Through Science is a set of textbooks and resources produced by experienced science educators and practising teachers for delivery of the Key Stage 3 Science curriculum through innovative activities, reading and study. *Thinking Through Science* activities are designed to promote better thinking in learners so that they become more adept and effective in their studies. While this textbook is intended for average to high ability pupils in Year 9, there is some differentiation within the activities, and the suggested teaching style enables less able pupils to access the work through collaborative group work. The intention of the activities is to encourage children to think and articulate their thinking in an environment that provides both challenge and support.

The textbook activities are built on the strong foundation produced by Michael Shayer, Philip Adey and Carolyn Yates in the Cognitive Acceleration through Science Education (CASE) project developed at King's College London. This project is well known for its effectiveness in raising achievement and developing logical thinking. The curriculum materials for the CASE project, called *Thinking Science*, are available from Nelson Thornes Ltd. While it is not essential for you and your classes to take on CASE in order to use this textbook course, those schools who do CASE intervention lessons will recognise the reasoning patterns and questioning style associated with CASE within many of the activities. *Thinking Through Science* therefore provides useful bridging of the CASE methodology throughout the Key Stage 3 curriculum.

While we have elected to follow the topics suggested in the QCA Scheme of Work for each year, there is some switching round of topics within the year to ensure that the type of reasoning and thinking that pupils are involved in fits with the CASE scheme and provides progression and coherence for all pupils.

Thinking

The basis for *Thinking Through Science* lies in a belief that pupils must construct knowledge for themselves. To do this they need to be set challenges that are ahead of where their current learning is, as well as to articulate and consolidate what they think they know and understand already. This idea is based on the work of the psychologist, Lev Vygotsky, whose interest lay in the interaction between people learning together. Vygotsky described the importance of mediation within learning. This refers to the role of one person who encourages others in the group to talk out loud their ideas and thoughts, so that others can hear and comment on these thoughts, enabling the speaker to modify his/her ideas. Clearly, at the same time, this also sparks off ideas and thoughts in the listeners' heads so they too challenge or consolidate their own understanding. While in many classroom situations the teacher will take on the role of mediator, there are advantages in allowing peers to take on this role for some of the time. It is far more likely that a pupil will question what has been said and comment on ideas in a small group consisting of his/her peers than in the public arena of whole class situations, where the teacher is looked on as the expert. In this way, pupils can build their knowledge base through social interaction. For you, as the teacher, it means honing your classroom management skills to maximise the interactions between pupils. This may need some initial work with groups, to enhance their listening and cooperating skills, so that they make the most use of the times that they interact with one another.

A child's thinking capacity develops, just as their bodies do, throughout childhood and adolescence. It is a teacher's role to aid that development. In order to do that it helps to understand cognitive development. Jean Piaget and Barbel Inhelder, psychologists interested in describing cognitive development, proposed stages of cognitive development which learners go through. The rate of an individual person's cognitive development varies and is unique, but each stage has broadly similar characteristics for most people. While Piagetian psychology is criticised by some researchers, most education researchers accept that their stage descriptions give insights into types of thinking and can help to design effective learning opportunities. The earliest stage of development is preoperational and is typical of children in the early years of primary school. From about 7 years old, most pupils will begin to develop what is called 'concrete thinking'. Thinkers in this stage are only able to think about two or three variables at a time. They can make simple 'cause and effect' predictions based on previous experience, for example, they will predict that 'heavy objects sink while light objects float'. They cannot yet grasp the concept of density, where both heaviness and size determine whether something sinks or floats.

At around the time pupils begin secondary school, they are starting to think in more complex ways and are able to apply rules that will predict events, for example, they will recognise that 'small, heavy objects will sink but large, light objects can float'. This is the concrete generalisation stage. Pupils in this stage will tend to describe investigations more easily than they will offer explanations based on scientific knowledge and understanding. Many pupils are still in this stage by the time they reach GCSE exams. By Year 9, however, some pupils will start to build quite complex mental models of the world around them and will be able to use these to make predictions and test their hypothesis. They understand that you have to think about two variables at the same time, mass and volume, to predict whether something can sink or float. This is 'early formal' or 'abstract thinking'. Sometimes this is called 'high order thinking' or 'HOT stuff'. Formal operational thinkers can think about and manipulate more than three variables at a time and have a 'feel' for mathematical relationships, using symbolic language. The CASE project was designed to help more pupils acquire these formal thinking abilities.

This Year 9 book promotes formal operational thought by providing activities which help pupils look for general principles, make predictions, explain anomalies, look for mathematical relationships and use models to explain scientific ideas. To help pupils form scientific concepts, their classifying skills are extended so that they can look for logical similarities and differences to form groups and sub-groups. Much of Key Stage 4 Science requires formal operational thinking, in particular formal modelling. If we can develop this kind of thinking through Key Stage 3 then more pupils will find that they can handle the transition to Key Stage 4. The reasoning patterns identified by CASE are developed through the chapters listed in the table on page iv.

CASE utilises a number of thinking processes to enhance the movement from concrete to formal operational thinking.

- Cognitive conflict – creating a challenge to an idea or previous experience that causes the learner to seek new ways of thinking.
- Construction – allowing learners to pursue ideas and reform thoughts.
- Metacognition – persuading learners to think about their thinking and be aware of their new ideas.
- Bridging – linking newly formed ways of thinking in other contexts both in science and everyday life.

The Scheme of Work for Key Stage 3 Science lists five types of thinking skills:

- information-processing skills
- reasoning skills
- enquiry skills
- creative-thinking skills
- evaluation skills.

Information-processing skills

Information-processing skills require learners to locate and collect relevant information from a variety of sources. In Red Book 3 this is particularly encouraged through the use of internet searches. Learners sort, classify, sequence, compare and contrast, and analyse part/whole relationships to organise information into a form that either aids thinking or presents the information for analysis. In science, information is often in the form of data sets, so mathematical skills are required to process these. This includes making tally charts, ranking data sets or constructing tables for data so that relationships between variables can be seen. It also includes reading and constructing line graphs, bar charts and pie charts. In general most pupils will have consolidated these skills through Years 7 and 8. In Year 9, the emphasis is on linking these graph-related skills to whole investigations. Learners will make decisions about the way to process information and data, using appropriate tables and graphs. They will be able to identify and explain any anomalies in the information in a variety of contexts, and will have strategies for re-analysing and collecting new information and data to look for relationships. The 2004 SATs showed that graphing skills (Level 5) were clearly a weakness in both Maths and Science.

By the start of Year 9, learners using this textbook will be able to transform data sets into all kinds of graphs, although they may still find selecting appropriate scales difficult. Red Book 3 gives practice in selecting the most appropriate way of processing data, deciding on the range of scales, plotting complex sets of data and how to include several sets of data on one graph to make comparisons. It also aims to develop a deeper understanding of correlation and lines of best fit as a means of looking for relationships.

Reasoning skills

Reasoning skills enable pupils to give reasons for opinions and actions. Most learners are confident to do this by the end of Year 8. Teachers can reinforce the importance of justifying and giving reasons by using questions such as, 'Why do you think that?' or 'Does everyone in the class think that?'. By Year 9, pupils are learning to draw inferences and make deductions in order to make judgements and decisions informed by reason or evidence. This requires the ability to identify assumptions they may be making and to examine these to see if they are reasonable in a specific science context. 'Ideas and evidence' sections in most chapters provide opportunities for developing this skill. The skill of using precise language to explain what they think will still be developing through Year 9, as this is a difficult skill to use in a scientific context. It requires a good understanding of technical vocabulary and logical sequencing, i.e. the 'development metacognition'. This is when the learner reflects by verbalising their thinking processes. Teachers can encourage pupils to become more metacognitve by asking the following sort of questions:

> 'How did you do that?'
> 'What helped?'
> 'What made it hard? Why?'
> 'Show us how you thought that through to find the right answer ... how did you know it was right?'
> 'What did you do first?'
> 'How did you decide what to do next?'
> 'What do you think might happen if ...?'

Reasoning skills are closely linked to the types of thinking that the CASE project engenders and this logical scientific thinking informs a problem-solving and investigative approach to science. Through this area of thinking, pupils come to make decisions about the control and manipulation of variables to set up increasingly more complex fair test investigations. By Year 9 pupils are expected to use the language of independent and dependent variables to design, analyse and reflect on investigations. They will discuss decision-making processes in selecting appropriate variables and a suitable range of value for those variables. Red Book 3 has at least one opportunity for a full investigation in every chapter, supported by formative assessment activities so that learners can gauge their progress and future learning needs.

Enquiry skills

Enquiry skills enable pupils to ask pertinent questions and to pose and define problems to investigate or research. In this book learners are encouraged to pose and define problems and plan systematically what to do in investigations, as well as to predict outcomes and anticipate consequences. Through considering the results of other people's investigations as well as planning and carrying out full investigations themselves, they are asked to test conclusions and improve ideas. The teacher should regularly challenge both correct and incorrect responses to develop an ethos of enquiry. Learners improve their secondary research skills by searching for information in a variety of media – internet, CD-ROMs, library books, magazines, pictures, diagrams and video materials.

Creative-thinking skills

Creative-thinking skills allow the pupils to generate and extend their scientific ideas, suggest possible hypotheses, apply imagination and look for alternative innovative outcomes. Through this book pupils are encouraged to practise imaging (visualisation) and exploring scientific ideas through a variety of creative activities; for example designing an 'ideal' trainer, three-legged chair or snow shoe (Chapters 2, 8), making posters and leaflets to communicate knowledge (Chapters 2, 6, 7), imagining a world without electricity (Chapter 3), school/health surveys with photos and PowerPoint presentations (Chapters 2, 6), concept maps (Chapter 7), designing a logo (Chapter 7) and creating a sinking competition (Chapter 8). Some of the 'Word play' activities and the 'Ideas and evidence' sections also promote thinking creatively. The emphasis on group discussions throughout the book helps learners to expand and explore their own imaginative ideas. This book develops the pupil's ability to build mental models which the CASE programme defines as a high order, abstract or formal mode of thinking. As Albert Einstein is often quoted as saying:

> 'Imagination is more important than knowledge.'
> 'When I examine myself and my methods of thought, I come to the conclusion that the gift of fantasy has meant far more to more than my talent for absorbing positive knowledge...'

Evaluation skills

Evaluation skills are linked with enquiry skills when they are incorporated into discussing and making decisions about social, moral and ethical issues, such as those concerning health (Chapter 2), acid rain (Chapter 6) or genetics and gene manipulation (Chapter 7). There are evaluation activities in every chapter that encourage learners to evaluate information, to judge the value of what they read, hear and do, to develop criteria for judging the value of their own and others' work or ideas, and to have confidence in their judgements. (Source: www.standards.dfes.gov.uk/schemes2/secondary_science/ links)

➡ *Progression*

Progression and continuity are important aspects of a curriculum and we have built these aspects into the scheme and framework throughout *Thinking Through Science*. This has been made explicit in the Pupil's Books by cross-referencing parts of chapters to support learners in linking ideas between different areas of the curriculum.

Our approach to progression begins at the start of each chapter in the Pupil's Book, with one or more activities designed to elicit understanding gained in Year 7 or Year 8 Science, and to refresh pupils' minds with the terminology and ideas to enable them to make progress in their Key Stage 3 work. This helps you to pitch the work within the topic at an appropriate level and pace to ensure that knowledge and understanding are enhanced. This method is further developed throughout each topic by including activities that encourage pupils to reflect on their work as well as provide assessment for learning activities. These activities are labelled 'Time to think' and occur part-way through each topic and again towards the end of each topic.

The Key Stage 3 Programme of Study (pages vi–xiv) demonstrates how units and subunits of the curriculum link together and provide progression throughout Years 7, 8 and 9.

➡ *Assessment for learning*

This type of assessment, formerly called formative assessment, is the ongoing feedback that teachers give to pupils during the learning process. Its intention is not to measure, grade or determine level, but to inform, support and develop the learning. It also involves helping the learners develop self-assessment strategies, so that they become less reliant on their teacher and become self-regulated learners.

In 1998, Paul Black and Dylan Wiliam carried out an extensive review of the research literature in this area and wrote an article in *Assessment in Education*. They also produced a short synopsis of their findings entitled 'Inside the Black Box'. Their findings showed that introducing formative assessment strategies into classrooms could greatly increase achievement and, while all learners moved forward with this intervention, the achievement of lower-ability learners was particularly enhanced.

From this review, many teachers and researchers put into action its advice and ideas, the best known being the King's, Medway and Oxfordshire Formative Assessment Project (KMOFAP) led by Paul Black, Chris Harrison and Dylan Wiliam. In this project, 24 science and mathematics teachers in six secondary schools interpreted the findings of several of the research studies highlighted in the review into their classroom practice. Several articles have been published in *School Science Review* and other journals, and more are in the pipeline. Details of these can be found at www.kcl.ac.uk/education. 'Working Inside the Black Box', and 'Science Inside the Black Box' are available from nferNelson publishers.

Various agencies have taken an interest in the development of assessment for learning, and useful websites to search are QCA (www.qca.org.uk), DfES Standards Site (www.standards.dfes.gov.uk), AAIA (www.aaia.org.uk) and ARG (www.assessment-reform-group.org.uk). Some of the ideas have been taken on board by both the Science Strategy and the Key Stage 3 strategy.

When teachers work formatively, they focus the pupils' learning so that they help the pupils see which aspects of their work are good and which need improvement. They then advise the pupils on what they might do to improve, and create the opportunity for them to do so, in a supportive environment where the pupils can check on their work as they move forward. The teacher then needs to assist the pupils in judging the improved quality of their work so that a similar quality can be attempted in a new context. Eventually this leads to the pupils attempting similar work without the support networks in place.

In essence, it is finding out where pupils are in their learning, being clear about where they need to go with their next learning step and then supporting pupils as they close this gap. While schemes of work may provide a context, regular opportunities should be created within a teaching programme for pupils to reveal their ideas and conceptual understanding either orally or in written form, followed by a time space for pupils to move these ideas forward. Teachers are seeking and improving the depth of understanding of specific aspects of a topic for their pupils, rather than planning for coverage of a topic.

In the classroom, specific strategies to promote assessment for learning vary from context to context, but its common features are listed here.

- A supportive classroom environment where the emphasis is on improvement rather than right or wrong.
- A belief by the teacher and the learners that good performance is incremental and not purely dependent on IQ or some other trait.
- Questioning strategies whereby the teacher tries to find out what is inside learners' heads rather than pupils guessing what is inside the teacher's.
- Teachers asking challenging and sometimes open-ended questions and then giving enough time for learners to think (and sometimes practise what to say) before giving an answer.
- Collaborative group work, where learners support and challenge one another; peer assessment.
- Feedback that provides detail of what the learner needs to do to improve.
- Sometimes giving feedback without a grade or a mark so that learners focus on the comments for improvement, rather than comparing outcomes with their peers.
- Prime time being given to improve and redraft work.
- Opportunity for learners to see other pupils' work that has better or worse features than their own, so that they can begin to judge good performance and recognise the criteria in action.
- Opportunity for learners to feed back to their teacher on how confident they feel about their work and to identify their improvements and learning needs.

- Encouragement for self-assessment and rising to a challenge.
- Support in setting short- and medium-term targets with action plans to achieve these.

Various strategies to help you create a good culture of assessment for learning are included in the Pupil's Book. For example, 'traffic lighting', where pupils mark their work with a red, amber or green dot depending on their confidence in understanding a section or piece of work, will begin training your pupils in self- and peer-assessment practices and provide you with feedback on their perceptions of their learning. It will enable you to deal with problems as they arise in the learning, or to fast-forward the work if everyone has grasped a particular idea, so creating a classroom environment that responds to your learners' needs.

Summative assessment

Each chapter ends with a test, taking around 20 minutes, to provide an opportunity for checking knowledge in a continuous summative manner throughout the course. These quick tests supplement the wealth of assessment evidence that can be derived from the activities in each chapter. They are not intended as a means of allocating specific levels of attainment.

Scientific investigation at Key Stage 3

Scientific investigation is the link between the pupils' practical experiences and the key scientific ideas. It involves testing out ideas, developing practical skills, questioning whether evidence supports the scientific interpretation, and evaluating the whole process.

However, investigative work at Key Stage 3 has caused problems for teachers:

> *'Teachers feel under pressure to cover content and see investigative work as time-consuming and less relevant to measurable performance.*
>
> *'All too often at Key Stage 3 it [Sc1] is relegated to an assessment activity, bolted on to the rest of the curriculum, mainly in Year 9.'*
>
> OFSTED: Progress in Key Stage 3 Science (2000)

and for pupils:

> *'The AKSIS project found that pupils focused on superficial aspects of investigations and failed to understand what they were supposed to be learning from their investigative work. Their interpretation of what they had learnt was different from what their teachers expected.'*
>
> AKSIS: Investigations – Targeted Learning (2000)

→ *Teaching investigative skills*

Investigative skills can be successfully taught if:

- the skills are taught separately
- the objectives of an exercise are shared with the pupils
- the teacher has a clear picture of the progression in each skill
- the criteria for the progression in each skill are shared with the pupils
- feedback on completion of an exercise points out how the pupils can improve next time
- the development of the skills is written into the Scheme of Work.

Types of exercise

1 A very brief exercise within a 'normal' lesson, for example:

'Explain why this practical is a fair test.'
'Are the results of this practical reliable?'
'Can you think of a way of improving the experiment described by the alchemist?'

- It can be done before, during or after practical work depending on the investigative skill to be developed.
- It can also be done within a 'theory' section.

2 A longer exercise as part/all of a lesson.

Objectives

The objectives for investigative activities should be shared with pupils. For example, the Evaluation exercise in Chapter 5, Pupil's Book pages 137–138 is mainly about the concepts of validity, accuracy and reliability, though it may also help to reinforce ideas about the order of reactivity. It is essential that pupils are aware of the learning intentions of every lesson and are helped to understand what and how they are learning.

The attainment targets for the Sc1 skill areas from the National Curriculum for Science can be converted into 'pupil speak' and separated into ladders of progression. For example, **Evaluation** can be separated into:

- evaluating the method
- evaluating the evidence.

These two elements can be taught separately, and both teacher and pupil can see the route to improvement through a progression ladder of the learning. See the following tables.

Evaluating the method

Level	In my evaluation, I can...
3	suggest some improvements to my enquiry
4	suggest some improvements to my enquiry **and explain** why they will improve my work
5	suggest **practical ways** for making improvements to my enquiry
6	suggest practical ways of improving my plan **and explain** why they will work

Evaluating the evidence

Level	In my evaluation, I can...
5	give a simple explanation for any differences in my repeated 'reliability' results **or** say why I think that my results are all reliable
6	pick out **'odd' results** that do not fit in with the general pattern **or** say why I think that I have no 'odd' results
7	• give **explanations** of how any 'odd' results could have happened • comment on the **reliability** of my results using the **line of best fit** • examine my results and conclusions and **decide whether more experiments are needed** to make sure that my conclusions are valid

The ladders are intended for use in assessment for learning activities. Some possible activities are given below.

Example 1
A wall display is made, showing the outline of an investigation and samples of the Evaluations of the investigation written by three pupils (fictional or real). Alongside are displayed the Evaluation ladders and the questions 'Can you level these evaluations?' and 'What should each pupil do to reach the next level?'.

Example 2
Pupils are given three samples of other pupils' work on 'Evaluating' for a recent part investigation that they have done. Working in groups and using the Evaluating progression ladders they are asked to give a level to each piece of work with reasons and to write a helpful comment on what the pupil should do to reach the next level.

In Books 1 and 2, the main focus in science enquiry has been to explicitly teach the separate skills with occasional full investigations. In Red Book 3, higher level enquiry skills are still being taught separately but there are an increasing number of whole investigations covering the full range of the different types of scientific enquiry.

Worksheets A–E

'Pupil speak' ladders for enquiry skills can be found on Worksheets A–E. These statements should be used as non-statutory guidance since the original National Curriculum level statements have been simplified and pruned to produce 'pupil speak' versions that can be shared with the pupils. Additional criteria have been added which are an important part of the teaching of separate enquiry skills, for example, the use of trial experiments and the ability to decide when to use a bar chart and when to use a line graph. They are presented as separate strands for each of the separate elements of Enquiry skills because the large number of statements in each of the five elements often prove to be too confusing for pupils. Also, some activities may concentrate on just one or two strands within the separate element, for example, 'Controlling variables' and 'Choosing equipment' within the Planning element.

→ _Whole investigations_

There are many ways to tackle scientific questions, although many scientific enquiries done in schools are of the 'fair-testing' kind. Pupils should experience a good range of enquiries during the key stage (see Key Stage 3 Programme of Study, Sc1.2a, '_Pupils should be taught to use scientific knowledge and understanding to turn ideas into a form that can be investigated, and to decide on an appropriate approach_'). Different types of scientific enquiry require different strategies and pupils need to know about the different types so that they can suggest an appropriate approach.

The different types of enquiry are not always distinct and some questions can be tackled using more than one type of enquiry. Pupils also need to recognise that some questions cannot be addressed through scientific enquiry, for example, questions of opinion depend on aesthetic, religious, emotional or other criteria. The following types of enquiry are mentioned in the QCA Scheme of Work.

Surveys and correlations (pattern seeking)

Observing and recording natural phenomena, or carrying out surveys, where variables cannot readily be controlled, and then seeking patterns in the data.

Examples

Do people with longer legs jump higher?
Do dandelions in the shade have longer leaves than those in the light?
Which is the rainiest month of the year?

Objectives

- to use preliminary work to decide what to measure and observe, and whether the approach is practicable
- to consider what other factors, including those that cannot be controlled, might affect the results and how to deal with them
- to collect and record data appropriately
- to identify and describe trends in data
- to evaluate the limitations of the evidence by considering sample size and the possible effect of other factors
- to use scientific knowledge and understanding to interpret results

Using secondary sources

Examples

What factors affect the pH of rainwater?
What is the rainiest place on Earth?

Objectives

- to decide which factors may be relevant to an enquiry
- to decide when it is appropriate to use data from secondary sources
- to search efficiently for information
- to decide which sources of information are appropriate
- to select appropriate data from secondary sources

- to identify and describe patterns in data
- to present information appropriately
- to look critically at sources of secondary data
- to look critically at results to decide how strongly they show a trend
- to interpret results using scientific knowledge and understanding

Controlling variables (fair test)

Observing and exploring relationships between variables or factors. Changing one factor and observing or measuring the effect, while keeping other factors the same.

Examples

How does the temperature of water affect the rate at which sugar dissolves?
What is the order of reactivity of the common metals?
How do plants get water?

Objectives

- to explain why a test is fair
- to decide if a fair test is needed and describe how to make the test fair
- to say which are the key variables if a fair test is needed
- to identify the most important key variables that need to be controlled
- to pick out the key variables in a complex investigation and explain how to control them

Note: in addition, there are many other objectives for a full 'fair test' enquiry, relating to planning and to obtaining and considering evidence.

Identification and classification

Either arranging a range of objects or events into manageable sets, or recognising objects and events as members of particular sets and allocating names to them.

Examples

How can we group these invertebrates?
Which things conduct electricity well and which do not?
What kind of waterweed is this?

Objectives

- to search for information and decide which sources of information are appropriate
- to select appropriate information from secondary sources
- to use preliminary work to find out whether an approach is practicable
- to implement an approach, refining where necessary
- to use knowledge to explain results
- to evaluate the methods used in terms of the quality of the product

Using and evaluating a technique

Designing, testing and adapting an artefact or system.

Examples

Can you design a pressure-pad switch for a burglar alarm?
Can you develop a technique for finding how much of an apple is water?
Can you design a method for making pure crystals of copper sulphate from copper oxide and dilute sulphuric acid?

Objectives

- to search for information
- to use preliminary work to find out whether a possible approach is practical
- to find out what apparatus is available for particular techniques
- to recognise common hazards in working techniques
- to relate results to scientific knowledge and understanding
- to control risks from identified hazards

Using experimental models and analogies to explore an explanation or hypothesis

Trying out explanations to see whether they work or make sense.

Example

Does the oxidation or phlogiston model best explain how magnesium burns?
How do plants get water?
How is food absorbed following digestion (using visking tubing)?

Objectives

- to use preliminary work with a model to decide what to measure and to determine the number of measurements to be taken
- to record measurements
- to record data on a graph and draw an appropriate curve/line to fit data
- to identify and describe patterns in graphs
- to evaluate the conclusion by considering how good the data is

Some topics lend themselves to certain types of enquiry better than others. For example, Sc2 offers many opportunities for 'Surveys and correlations' and Sc3 for 'Using and evaluating a technique'.

Pupils should realise that although scientists try hard to look for evidence, it is not uncommon for evidence to be interpreted differently by different scientists and other interested people.

Whole investigations in Red Book 3

Chapter	Complete investigation	Type
1	• investigating a technique for preparing a sample of a salt	• use and evaluate a technique
2	• plan and carry out an investigation about lung capacity	• survey and correlation
3	• investigating solar energy	• fair test
4	• investigating the use of light gates to measure the speed of a toy car on a ramp	• use a technique/fair test
5	• investigating the relative reactivity of different metals controlling relevant variables	• fair test
6	• surveying examples of weathering in an area and giving explanations • investigating acid rain by controlling relevant variables and taking into account those which cannot be controlled • investigating environmental change using evidence from secondary sources	• survey and correlation • fair test/correlation • secondary sources
7	• investigating the effect of selective breeding on a plant variety taking account of variables that cannot be controlled	• survey and correlation
8	• investigating force, area and pressure	• experimental model
9	• investigating changes in mass when magnesium burns	• fair test

Worksheets A–E

The level of attainment for all these investigations can be assessed using Worksheets A–E, Pupil speak ladders for Enquiry skills. Whole investigations are very time consuming and it is not suggested that all of the above activities are used. Some of them could be adapted to focus on the separate skills of planning, observing, analysing and evaluating.

➡ *Ideas and evidence*

It is important that pupils begin to see how the ideas that we deal with in science today were established. It is also essential that pupils realise that ideas are sometimes challenged and new ways of looking at scientific concepts emerge. Consequently, science is not simply a body of facts, but a collection of ideas that are continually challenged and upgraded.

Red Book 3 provides a variety of ways of developing an understanding of ideas and evidence by exploring the following:

- the use of scientific method to test explanations, for example Pupil's Book pages 14–15
- the initial ideas used to create stimulus for further research and thought, for example Pupil's Book pages 178–179
- the development of technology that accompanies or allows the ideas to develop, for example Pupil's Book pages 235–237
- the historic development of an idea. Pupils comment on the different conclusions, giving evidence and reasons for the changing theories, for example Pupil's Book pages 189–191
- the historical perspective. Pupils consider the work of a particular scientist and a comprehension exercise is used to test understanding, for example Pupil's Book pages 108–109.

'Ideas and evidence' is also supported by some of the Research and ICT activities that ask pupils to investigate science from the past as well as that involved in our lives today, for example Pupil's Book page 147.

→ # *The key scientific ideas*

There are five key scientific ideas underpinning the Key Stage 3 Programme of Study:

- cells
- interdependence
- particles
- forces
- energy.

Some chapters focus on one or two of these explicitly; other chapters indicate how key scientific ideas are linked together. All five key ideas involve abstract concepts and there are many common misconceptions associated with them. The most common pupils' misconceptions are given at the beginning of each chapter in this Teacher's Book. The text includes ideas on eliciting misconceptions and how to deal with correcting them.

Progression

Pupils will have some understanding of some of the key ideas from Key Stages 1 and 2 but the main difference at Key Stage 3 is the progression from the concrete to the abstract thinking. Pupils need to recognise, describe, use and apply these ideas in increasingly complex and unfamiliar contexts from Year 7 through to Year 9. The development of each key idea in Year 9 is set out below.

Cells

Cells are not part of the National Curriculum at Key Stages 1 and 2. By the end of Year 6, pupils should be aware of micro-organisms and have a limited understanding of their size.

In *Thinking Through Science 1*, pupils are introduced to cells. In Chapter 7, they are shown the similarities and differences between plant and animal cells, introduced to the idea that different kinds of cell do different jobs, learn that new cells are made by cell division, and are told that the nuclei of all cells contain the information that is transferred from one generation to the next. This is reinforced in Chapter 8, where fertilisation is shown to be the joining of the nucleus of male and female sex cells.

In *Thinking Through Science 2*, cells are developed further in Chapter 6, where pupils are taught to understand how the cell obtains energy with and without oxygen.

In *Thinking Through Science 3*, Chapter 2 links the cellular process of respiration (energy transfer) to multi-cellular organ systems in the human body. Pupils learn what conditions are needed to keep specialised organ systems fit and healthy. They learn that the digestive, circulation, and breathing systems increase the efficiency and effectiveness of the whole organism to supply its cells with nutrients and to remove wastes. Throughout the chapter pupils are helped to appreciate that, in order to grow and develop, their bodies must have time, the right conditions (nourishment, rest) and that the health and fitness of the whole body (organism) depends on the successful working of all its parts. Pupils learn that a range of drugs can damage and kill cells so that organ systems cannot function effectively. Pupils develop their ideas about how the human body, a complex, multi-celled organism, fights infections, and how these are often caused by single-celled organisms and viruses.

Chapter 7 reinforces the understanding that specialised cells are produced in the reproductive system to ensure that offspring are similar to their parents, a concept first encountered in *Thinking Through Science Book 1*.

Interdependence

By the end of Year 6, most pupils have some understanding of the links between life processes in animals and plants and the environments in which they are found. They know that the wide variety of animals, plants and materials can be classified according to their similarities and differences, and have been taught that animals and plants are often adapted to their environment through differences in their structure.

In Year 7 pupils will have developed knowledge and understanding that humans depend on and affect living organisms and their physical environment. They will know that organisms that belong to the same species share many characteristics, and that variation is fundamental and inevitable. They also have some understanding of reproduction and how this is affected by the environment, thus influencing population levels. In Year 8 pupils will have looked at interdependence as a fundamental idea in ecology and be able to define interdependence as sets of systems interlinking.

In *Thinking Through Science Book 3*, Chapter 7 helps pupils continue to develop their ideas about interdependence in and between biological and physical environments. They learn how natural and artificial selection can affect an organism's success in living and growing in its environment, and how the human need to maximise food production affects other living organisms and influences the balance in the environment.

Particles

By the end of Year 6, pupils know that materials can be grouped into solids, liquids and gases, and have been introduced to some reversible changes such as evaporation and condensation.

At Key Stage 3, the particle theory is fundamental to the explanation of a whole range of phenomena in physical, biological and geological settings. It is also essential in explaining the chemical changes in physical and biological systems, and the heat transfer mechanisms of conduction and convection.

In *Thinking Through Science 1*, the particle model was described in terms of the size, arrangement, proximity and movement of the particles in a solid, liquid and gas. It was then used to explain some physical properties of matter. It was also used to explain dissolving, distillation and chromatography. Pupils started to use the particle model to explain how chemical reactions take place.

In *Thinking Through Science 2,* the particle model was developed further to model and explain:

- the movement of substances through cell membranes by assuming particles are of different sizes
- dissolving and evaporating in the formation of sedimentary rocks
- the processes of conduction, convection, evaporation and change of state
- atoms, elements, compounds and mixtures
- the transmission, production and reception of sound
- the movement of substances through cell membranes by assuming particles are of different sizes
- how chemical reactions take place
- how crystals form.

In *Thinking Through Science 3 Red,* the particle model is developed further in Chapters 1 and 5 to:

- translate word equations into symbol equations
- use the formulae of reactants and products to explain how atoms join in different ways as a result of a reaction
- explain why a given symbol equation is balanced or unbalanced.

Forces

By the end of Year 6, pupils have some understanding of different types of forces, including friction and weight.

At Key Stage 3, the abstract concepts of forces are developed and used to underpin explanations of the behaviour of moving objects. This includes planetary motion, antagonistic muscle pairs, separating particles in melting and evaporation, and the weathering of rocks by the expansion and contraction of water.

In *Thinking Through Science 1*, Chapter 6 identified different types of balanced and unbalanced forces, showed that forces have magnitude and direction, distinguished between mass and weight, and identified advantages and disadvantages of friction.

In *Thinking Through Science 2*, forces were developed further in Chapters 2 and 11, where pupils:

- investigate the forces resulting from the freeze–thaw effect
- investigate the forces of attraction and repulsion between magnets
- investigate the Earth's magnetic field
- investigate the strength of electromagnets.

In Chapter 4 of *Thinking Through Science Book 3*, pupils develop the idea that forces affect the way that objects move, and investigate gravity. Ideas about gravity are used to reinforce the differences between weight and mass and to explain the motion of satellites and planets in the Solar System. In Chapter 8, pupils investigate the quantitative relationship between force, area and pressure, and look at how pressure is used in a range of devices. They also look for correlation between mass and distance in the turning effect of forces.

Energy

Energy is not part of the National Curriculum at Key Stages 1 and 2, and pupils are likely to start Key Stage 3 with some of the misconceptions surrounding this key idea.

At Key Stage 3, the abstract concepts of energy transfer and energy conservation are needed to explain a range of physical, biological, chemical and geological processes.

In *Thinking Through Science 1*, Chapter 1 introduces the idea that energy transfer takes place in food chains; Chapter 3 provides a model of energy transfer in electric circuits; Chapter 11 explains how energy is released when fuels burn, and Chapter 12 looks at renewable and non-renewable energy resources, and shows that all living things need energy for every activity.

In *Thinking Through Science 2*, Chapter 1 teaches pupils how to find out the energy content of food; Chapter 3 explains thermal energy and forms of energy transfer; Chapter 5 explains that sound travels by vibrations of particles, and links this with the transmission, production and reception of sound; Chapter 6 explains that the cell can obtain energy both with and without oxygen, and Chapter 12 looks at the transfer of energy between organisms.

Chapter 2 of *Thinking Through Science 3* continues to emphasise the links between what is eaten and physical activity in terms of energy transfer. There are opportunities to make pupils aware of the differences between the meaning of the word energy in everyday use and its scientific meaning. They develop ideas about the human body storing energy and human activity transferring this stored energy to somewhere else, linked specifically to the energy values of food and the use of energy by muscles in different kinds of activities.

➡ *Models and analogies*

Models and analogies are powerful tools for representing and illustrating abstract ideas. By Year 9 pupils should be able to use scientific ideas and models to explain scientific phenomena and events, and to understand a range of familiar applications of science. Chapter 2 of *Thinking Through Science 3* explores how simple three-dimensional models can represent breathing and movement in the human body. In Chapter 7 pupils use three-dimensional, abstract models and analogies to explain genetic inheritance. This chapter also encourages pupils to consider critically the advantages and disadvantages of the different models and analogies.

→ *Effective science lessons*

Science lessons are effective when pupils are clear about what is expected of them. A well planned lesson is usually composed of three parts.

1 Whole class introduction

There should be a clear, whole class introduction which sets the scene and engages pupils.

Starting activities

A 'starting point' is useful at the beginning of a unit of work, to identify the range of prior learning and any misconceptions. This enables the teacher to decide on the strategies and content of the lessons. Each chapter in *Thinking Through Science* starts with a 'What do you know?' activity as the starting point.

Other lessons in a unit might have a 'starter' – a short, stimulating activity, either before or after the 'scene setter'. This helps to get the lesson off to a brisk start and prepares pupils for the main activity. For example:

- a mental warm-up using an introduction to new phenomena, a thought experiment, or a 'What if...?' question to find out what pupils think and elicit their ideas
- a focus on key words through a loop card game, a word web or word dominoes
- a presentation and discussion of some 'amazing facts'
- a look at different types of text, such as explanations or questions that require pupils to provide alternative answers to interesting phenomena
- a problem to tackle, a challenging statement to explore, or opposing views to debate
- short data-handling activities, possibly using an OHP to display a graph, chart or table, and questions such as: 'What event or "story" could the graph illustrate?', or 'What do the data in the table show you?'.

The length of the starter will vary, depending on the nature of the lesson. For example, with four 50 minute lessons each week, you might have a starter of 15 minutes on one day, with a brief 2 or 3 minutes on the remaining days. In the longer starter, pupils might enter the room and start to work on a challenging problem posed on the board, with oral and mental work based on their initial thoughts on the problem taking place after 5 or 10 minutes.

Scene setter

The 'scene setter' should enable pupils to tune in, to link back and to look forward. It could include:

- an explanation of the purpose of the lesson using clear *learning objectives*: 'We will be learning to...'
- expectations and clear *learning outcomes*, conveyed to pupils in simple language: 'What I am looking for are pupils who can...'

- time for a brief review of previous work (including homework)
- an explanation of how the lesson develops from the previous one when the main activity spans more than one lesson
- an outline of the sequence of the lesson so that pupils know what to expect, an explanation of why a certain experiment or investigation is to be done, and an indication of where the lesson fits in with other lessons.

The learning objectives and outcomes should be clearly displayed – e.g. on an OHT, as a printed sheet in the pupils' exercise books, or on a poster. One learning objective may have several learning outcomes (differentiation by outcome).

2 Main activity

The main activity builds on the starter. Characteristics of a good lesson are high levels of interaction and probing questioning to challenge thinking. This is regardless of whether pupils are working as a whole class, in groups or individually, or whether the lesson consists of practical work, an extended investigation or written work. *Thinking Through Science* has been written with this style of teaching in mind. Organisation enables teachers to interact with as many pupils as possible. Tasks are matched to pupils' prior attainment and may allow for choice, taking into account different learning styles where possible.

Teachers should clearly explain what is expected. They should refer back to the learning objective(s) and learning outcomes to ensure that the pupils focus on the main aim(s) of the lesson, rather than being distracted by peripheral details such as practical apparatus.

Examples of main activities include:

- purposeful practical work
- the use of scientific models and analogies to explain phenomena or apparent conflicting ideas and evidence
- teaching specific skills, such as interpretation of graphs and evaluation
- extended discussion so that pupils have opportunities to air views, articulate ideas and hear the views of others.

Effective science lessons can have several cycles of activity and plenary (see opposite); 'mini' plenary sessions during the main part of a lesson allow misconceptions to be identified, challenged and discussed.

Throughout the main part of the lesson, the teacher should make time to assess informally the extent to which pupils are developing their understanding of key scientific ideas, by looking for gains, gaps and misconceptions. For example, the teacher can encourage pupils to make predictions before any demonstrations, especially those that give unexpected outcomes. As a result, the teacher feeds back, clarifies, models and reviews.

The teacher should also refer to relevant contemporary science applications or issues, including topical local examples or those currently in the national media, and *Thinking Through Science* provides many such examples.

3 Plenary

Short plenary sessions may take place during the main activity, as suggested above, while the concluding plenary rounds off the lesson. It should be far more than setting homework and running through the learning objectives. The learning outcomes from the beginning of the lesson lead naturally to self-assessment in a concluding plenary. The concluding plenary session can also be used to:

- help pupils to reflect on the lesson, say what was important about it and consider the progress they have made
- draw out and highlight the key learning points, such as facts, ideas and vocabulary
- get pupils to think about how they might apply the new ideas, by showing how the ideas can be used and where they fit in (bridging)
- look ahead to the next stage of learning, making pupils think and anticipate what the next steps might be.

The homework set should help pupils to consolidate or apply what they have learned, or to prepare for the next lesson.

The length and nature of plenary sessions will vary. For example, at the start of a new unit of work more time might be needed for demonstration, explanation and discussion with the whole class, interspersed with very short exercises for pupils; the plenary may then be very short.

On the other hand, when general errors or misunderstandings have been identified during the main part of a lesson, several 'mini' plenary sessions may be needed during the lesson to sort them out, as well as a final summing-up.

At the end of a unit of work the plenary can be used to look back with the whole class over a number of lessons, to draw together what has been learned and to identify key points and methods that pupils need to remember and use in the future. For this kind of plenary session, a much longer time would be needed than in other lessons.

→ *Using ICT in science*

ICT facilities and equipment are becoming increasingly available within school science departments, and many science departments now have interactive whiteboards available in their laboratories. ICT can be used effectively to add value to pupils' learning in a variety of ways:

- datalogging and analysis
- research using CD-ROMs and the internet
- modelling and simulations
- presenting information.

The *Chapter plans* in this Teacher's Book list the activities involving ICT in the lessons of that chapter.

Datalogging is an area that is found almost exclusively in science. As multiple sets of datalogging equipment become available, and portable laptop computers are more widely used, pupils will become increasingly competent at gathering a range of data from their experiments. They can easily manipulate, analyse and present data graphically, using suitable software packages.

Information gathering and research tasks offer further opportunities to use ICT, by accessing the internet or using CD-ROMs. This can be done in specialist science rooms that are suitably equipped, or using laptops.

Scientific concepts can be effectively illustrated using high-quality multimedia resources, which enable pupils to interact with the software. Simulations allow pupils to investigate situations which would normally be too time-consuming, difficult, dangerous or costly to perform practically themselves. Modelling is an important process in science, and this is an important theme throughout the Key Stage 3 course. The use of suitable software designed to explore a specific concept, or using generic software such as Excel, allows pupils to interactively develop their understanding of science.

Pupils are able to word process (or use DTP) to produce attractive material, which can then be easily modified and redrafted. Pupils can continue work at home, and can e-mail their material to school and others for further development and discussion. PowerPoint is now quite often used within science lessons by both pupils and staff. Some pupils are able to produce their own web pages for display.

Red or Blue book?

In Books 1 and 2, differentiation has been addressed either by providing alternative, support or extension worksheets or by including extensions to some of the activities and questions in the main text. In Book 3, we have taken a different approach by providing two books. The Blue book is intended for pupils achieving Levels 3, 4 or early stages of Level 5 at the start of Year 9, and is intended to help these pupils eventually achieve in the National Curriculum Levels 4–6 at the end of Key Stage 3. The Red book is intended for pupils secure in Level 5 or working above this as they enter Year 9, and will offer opportunity to achieve from Level 5 to above Level 7 at the end of the Key Stage.

To provide support and development for these two groups of learners the approaches in each book differs as shown below.

Blue	Red
Reading levels checked to focus challenge on the science rather than literacy skills	Extended reading pieces with questions that encourage linking of ideas and concepts
Matching, gap-filling and puzzle activities to support acquisition of key terms and definitions	Activities that often require research, choice of communication and opportunity to summarise ideas

Introduction

➡ Rationale

This chapter provides an introduction to the Year 9 Pupil's Book, revisiting and developing some of the skills introduced in Years 7 and 8. It is likely to take between 3 and 4 hours to cover the work.

➡ Overview

The textbook sections, activities and worksheets have been arranged into 1 hour blocks to aid lesson planning. Clearly several of the activities and worksheets could form part of a homework session. The planning includes reading time for individual sections but some teachers may prefer to organise this as homework preparation for the following lesson. Worksheets are of six types – extension (E), support for an activity (S), practical (P), key skills (K), developmental (D) and review (R) – to allow for differentiation and flexibility to accommodate teachers' preferred practice. The actual timing and emphasis on different sections will depend on the current knowledge base of the pupils, the ability of the teaching group and the preferences of the teacher.

Lesson	Worksheets
1 What do you know?	Worksheet 0.1R: Investigations skills check (D)
2 Asking questions	Worksheet 0.2R: Why? Why? Why? (K)
3 Answering questions	
4 Analysing data	

1 What do you know?

Science audit sheet

➡ *Pupil's Book page 1*

An audit sheet is a checklist that provides pupils with prompts to record and discuss the skills that they have acquired in science. In the example shown, there is space in the table to add other examples that they have used. The data in the table should provide a focus to talk about safe working in a science laboratory and also provide the impetus for pupils to familiarise themselves with the laboratory that they are working in. It also provides an inroad into discussion of the laboratory safety rules.

This session could be supplemented by demonstration or class practicals of some common tests, for example testing for oxygen and carbon dioxide, and testing pH. This could be followed up by the pupils writing 'A Guide to Key Stage 3 Science Skills' to enable them to summarise, check and revise their ideas and knowledge.

Activity

Enquiry: Investigations

→ *Worksheet 0.1R: Investigations skills check (D)*

This worksheet serves as a catalyst to get pupils talking about some of the science practicals that they have done and the measuring instruments that they have used. The main emphasis should be on getting pupils to articulate their ideas to one another and then to listen carefully to the answers as they are given in a whole class feedback. This should help them to find accurate and alternative ways of describing data, relationships and other process skills. By looking at three different practicals, pupils revisit ideas about variables and have the opportunity to plot graphical data. Some pupils may not be familiar with plotting both sets of data on the same axis and may need help in doing this.

Anomalous results are considered and the data are interpreted to look for a relationship between the input and outcome variables and then between the two experimental set-ups so that size of magnesium pieces and rate are thought about.

Depending on your class, this may be the time to introduce the terms dependent (input) and independent (outcome) variable. These two ways of referring to the variables will be used throughout the book, so use of both terms will become familiar.

Answers

2 In Experiment 1 the dependent (input) variable is potential difference (voltage) and the independent (outcome) variable is the current.

In Experiment 2 the dependent (input) variable is the weight in air and the independent (outcome) variable is the weight in water.

In Experiment 3 the dependent (input) variable is time and the independent (outcome) variable is the volume of gas. Alternatively, pupils may consider the size of the magnesium pieces as the input variable and the rate of gas production as an outcome variable.

3 a)

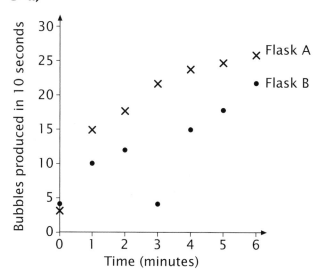

b) i) Anomalous means an outlying result which does not fit in with the pattern shown by the other plots in the data. It is probably a mis-read or a chance result.
ii) The reading for Flask B at 3 minutes.
iii) You plot it but do not take it into consideration when drawing the line of best fit. Some scientists circle or highlight the anomalous result so that they can point it out and refer to it in their evaluation of the experiment.

c) i) Time and volume of gas roughly show a directly proportional relationship, so as time increases the volume of gas increases.
ii) The results indicate that the smaller the pieces of magnesium, the faster the rate of reaction.

d) Hydrogen gas is produced, and the positive test for this is a lit spill put into the gas producing a small explosion (popping noise).

2 *Asking questions*

➡ *Pupil's Book page 1*

To find out what the pupils understand, rather than just what they know and can recite, you will need to challenge the pupils by activities that make them think and question what they do. This section immerses the pupils in a wide range of questions and contexts, and serves as continuing training for and emphasis on promoting discussion in the classroom.

How science works

Activity Reasoning: Sycamore

➡ *Pupil's Book page 3*

This section continues the questioning theme by encouraging pupils to ask questions from their observations of the sycamore tree and fruits at the top of page 3. Each group in the class should form a list of questions that they consider are good questions. They should decide how they might find answers to their questions; they need to consider what they already collectively know, and where they will look for answers that they don't know. This encourages focused research using books and websites.

Activity Reasoning: What happened next?

➡ *Pupil's Book page 3*

The second activity in this section highlights the difference between observations (strong evidence) and inferences (weak evidence) with the intention of helping pupils to theorise and self-check the data that they collect in their science lessons. The drawings of a thug pushing over a small boy and a tramp approaching an old lady will make most pupils suspect that the thug and the tramp are up to no good. Their preconceptions of the situation affect how they interpret the data. In fact, both the thug and the tramp are performing good deeds, which can be witnessed in the second pair of drawings, on page 4. Pupils should take away from this exercise that:

- they need to be wary of interpretations and should consider alternatives as well as what they might think is the obvious conclusion
- sometimes they need to collect more data to assess whether initial ideas from data inform on the whole story.

Activity Reasoning: Asking questions

Worksheet 0.2R

➡ *Worksheet 0.2R: Why? Why? Why? (K)*

This worksheet continues with the idea of reasoning. It introduces the pupils to two different contexts and starts them thinking about what questions to ask and how and where to start looking for answers. Depending on time, pupils could do one or other of the tasks or do one task in class and the other for homework. The latter approach provides them with a supported attempt in class and then an individual attempt for homework – this will provide useful feedback to the teacher and learner on the individual's competency in this area.

In the soil activity, pupils should observe and record the amount of water that has drained through the soil into the measuring cylinders. They could ask questions such as:

- If it is a fair test, then the same amount of water must have been poured through – so how much has passed through each soil?
- How much water has been retained?
- Why might some soils retain water more than others?
- What are these soils like in structure?

In the chemical tests activity, pupils need to use the data to reason out what each chemical is. They could ask questions such as:

- What does iodine solution test for?
- What reacts with acids to produce a gas?
- What gas is given off when you heat compounds?
- Why does powder C go blue in acid and in water, and when touching damp pH paper?

3 *Answering questions*

➡ *Pupil's Book page 4*

This will take up part of a lesson or a whole lesson, depending on pupils' capabilities and competency in this area. This section helps pupils to select information and build answers, so that they logically build an answer and link together ideas when necessary. Such skills are essential in science but also help prepare pupils for examinations. The basic idea is for pupils to look at a difficult question and break it down into a series of smaller questions. By doing this they can sift for the component parts to build a full answer to the original question.

Activity Reasoning: Good answers
→ *Pupil's Book page 5*

Answers
Answers will vary from pupil to pupil but should contain a range of similarities and differences.

Activity Reasoning: Is it always true?
→ *Pupil's Book page 6*

Answers
Answers will vary from pupil to pupil but should contain a series of steps that is summarised by a proof or disproof statement.

4 *Analysing data*

→ *Pupil's Book page 7*

This will form part of or a whole lesson depending on pupils' capabilities and competency in this area. Graphing skills have already been revisited at the start of this chapter.

This section returns to look at data analysis which was emphasised at Year 8 in Book 2. The example given here takes a historical perspective by looking at public health in the nineteenth century. The focus is on data selection and thinking carefully what questions the data allow us to answer. It initially looks straightforward but pupils may find difficulty as the data is about average ages – they have information on the midpoint of a range of data, but the questions sometimes demand that they answer for the range. Pupils also have to make inferences about the three groups of people, and they are encouraged to look closely at the title and row headings to do this.

This work also links with Unit 20 'Twentieth Century Medicine' in the History Scheme of Work.

Answers
→ *Pupil's Book page 7*

1 The ages of death are an 'average', therefore they are not raw data but have been analysed.
  The date, 1842, suggests that the data can be compared with today or other times.
  The title does not tell us anything about the people who died.
2 Same – people and their families.
  Different – jobs; living standards; place in the community; amount of money they had.
3 Both Wiltshire and Liverpool would have had a large population. Wiltshire is rural, whereas Liverpool is a large city.
4 The average age of death of gentry in Wiltshire and Liverpool is higher than that of labourers in the two cities.
5 a) It infers that on average people lived longer in the country than in towns.
  b) Row 1 and row 3.

6 A bar chart would help, as it would be easier to compare the town and country and the different types of people.

7 The summary should include both variables – type of people and place where living, and it should stress that this is based on averages.

Extension

8 Cannot tell the age of the oldest farmer, as the table provides the average age, and not the range.

If living in a town he could move to the country. Accept other references to improved diet, better sanitation, etc., but stress that we cannot tell this from the data.

We cannot tell if rich people in 1842 were more likely to reach 60, as we have no idea of the ranges nor sample size, only averages to compare.

From the table we cannot be certain that labourers' children died before adulthood. The averages are 37 (Wiltshire) and 32 (Liverpool), and if the range was wide then possibly this was so. If people died pre-37, it would need an equal number post-37 to balance out and reach an average of 37. What we cannot tell is how many of the pre-37 were children, and so we do not have the data to support this question.

Average age of death was lower in towns in 1842. We do not have data for present day. Also we do not know from this, but only by inference, that there was more illness in towns and therefore a need for more hospitals.

1 Salts of the Earth

→ Rationale

This chapter provides up to 7½ hours of teaching materials. In Book 1 pupils were introduced to simple chemical reactions: in Chapter 5 Acids and alkalis pupils studied neutralisation reactions, and in Chapter 11 Simple chemical reactions they identified the gases produced in the chemical reactions between acids and metals and their carbonates. In Book 2 the pupils developed their ideas in chemistry through atoms, elements, compounds and mixtures in Chapter 4 Atoms and elements, and Chapter 7 Compounds and mixtures.

The key idea of the particle theory is an integral part of this chapter. The overall approach to the particle theory across the three years of the course has been to develop models that are 'fit for purpose' to explain phenomena at each stage. If this intention is shared with the pupils they will understand that they have not been deliberately taught an incorrect model, but that the model was good enough for each stage. It is worth emphasising that the particle theory becomes more and more sophisticated throughout the science curriculum up to A level and beyond, as it is used to explain even wider ranges of phenomena.

In Book 2 the model that was developed included the ideas that the atom is the basic building block of all materials, and that these materials are made from a relatively small number of different atoms. Also, an element contains just one type of atom whereas a compound has two or more types of atom bonded together. This chapter develops a more sophisticated model that includes the concept of the combining powers of different atoms and the balancing of symbol equations.

This chapter is also about different ways of making metal salts. However, the main learning intentions are at a much higher level. After checking on prior learning and misconceptions, the reactions of acids with metals are used to develop the 'Ideas and evidence' concept of the scientific method. These reactions are also used to introduce the idea of the combining powers of different atoms to explain the stoichiometry of compounds, and to develop the skill of balancing equations. Subsequent sections on the reactions of acids with metal carbonates, oxides and hydroxides are used to reinforce the above concepts. These sections are also used to develop various scientific enquiry skills.

This chapter lays the foundation for Chapter 5 Patterns of reactivity.

→ Overview

The textbook sections, activities and worksheets have been arranged into 1 hour blocks (except for the half hour reviewing lesson at the end) to aid lesson planning. Clearly several of the activities and worksheets could form part of a homework session. The planning includes reading time for individual sections but some teachers may prefer to organise this as homework preparation for the following lesson. Worksheets are of six types – extension (E), support for an activity (S), practical (P), key skills (K), developmental (D) and review (R) – to allow for differentiation and flexibility to accommodate teachers' preferred practice. The actual timing and emphasis on different sections will depend on the current knowledge base of the pupils, the ability of the teaching group and the preferences of the teacher.

Lesson	Worksheets
1 What are salts?	Worksheet 1.1R: Do other acids react with magnesium to produce hydrogen? (P)
2 Formulae and symbol equations	Worksheet 1.2R: Using models to write formulae (information sheet) (E) Worksheet 1.3R: Using models to write formulae (answer sheet) (E) Worksheet 1.4R: Combining power cards (E) Worksheet 1.5R: Which one is the correctly balanced equation? (R)
3 Reacting metals with acids	Worksheet 1.6R: Do other metals react with acids to produce hydrogen? (P)
4 Reacting metal oxides with acids	Worksheet 1.7R: Making a pure metal salt by reacting a metal oxide with an acid (P)
5 Reacting metal carbonates with acids	Worksheet 1.8R: Do metal carbonates react with acids to form metal salts? (P)
6 Patterns in reactions	Worksheet 1.9R: Can you make a metal salt? (P) Worksheet 1.10R: Cards for 'Can you make a metal salt?' (P)
7 Reacting alkalis with acids	
Review	Worksheet 1.11R: Test on salts of the Earth (R)

→ *Chapter plan*

	Demonstration	Practical	ICT	Activity	Word play	Time to think	Ideas and evidence
Lesson 1	Reaction between magnesium and dilute hydrochloric acid	Reaction of magnesium with dilute acids				What do you know?	The scientific method
Lesson 2				Evaluation: Using models to write formulae	Use of the word 'balanced'		
Lesson 3	Formation of a metal salt	Reaction of other metals with acids		Information processing: Recognising patterns for metals			
Lesson 4		Making a pure metal salt by reacting a metal oxide with an acid		Enquiry: Using the scientific method

Enquiry: Obtaining evidence

Reasoning: Metal oxide equations | | | |
Lesson 5		Reaction of metal carbonates with acids		Information processing: Recognising patterns for metal carbonates			
Lesson 6		Can you make a metal salt?				Using word and symbol equations	
Lesson 7	Making sodium chloride by the titration method		Using CD-ROMs and the internet to find out about some salts	Reasoning: Metal hydroxide equations			
Review				Test on making salts		Designing questions	

→ *Expectations*

At the end of this chapter

in terms of scientific enquiry

most pupils will: make predictions based on a scientific hypothesis and design a test for the prediction; make observations and use these to identify similarities in chemical reactions; use preliminary work to decide on a method for preparing a salt and suggest ways in which their method could be improved

some pupils will have progressed further and will: use the evidence collected to evaluate a hypothesis; explain the steps they took to prepare a high-quality sample of a salt

in terms of materials and their properties

most pupils will: describe how metals react with acids and how acids react with metal carbonates, metal oxides and alkalis; identify evidence which indicates that a chemical reaction has taken place; represent reactions by word equations, identify patterns in these and produce general equations; name a variety of salts and describe the uses of some of them

some pupils will have progressed further and will: represent chemical compounds by formulae and combine these into symbol equations; use knowledge of reactions to make predictions about other reactions

→ *Links with CASE*

The use of formal models in terms of the particle theory is extended to include ideas of the combining power of elements, the rearrangement of particles in chemical reactions and balancing symbol equations.

The use of ratio and proportionality is continued in the formulae of compounds.

→ *Pupils' misconceptions*

Misconception	Scientific understanding
An element is part of an atom. Or an element is an everyday pure substance, such as salt.	An element is a substance that contains just one type of atom (same atomic number). An element cannot be split up into simpler substances.
Atoms are small bits of a substance. They have the same properties as the bulk substance.	Atoms are incredibly small particles which are the building blocks of the bulk substance. The properties of the bulk substance are related to the arrangement and bonding of the atoms.
A compound is a mixture of two or more elements.	A compound contains two or more elements chemically combined in a fixed ratio by mass.
'Strong' and 'concentrated' mean the same thing.	'Strong' and 'concentrated' are not synonymous. Strong/weak refer to the amount of ionisation, whereas concentrated/dilute refer to the concentration in solution. A strong acid or alkali is almost fully ionised in solution and is corrosive, even when it is quite dilute.
An acid is something that eats material away or that can burn you.	An example of a dilute, strong acid is dilute sulphuric acid which is corrosive. An example of a concentrated, weak acid is concentrated citric acid which is not corrosive.
A base is something which makes up an acid.	A base is a different, separate substance from an acid. An alkali is a soluble base.
A base is 'good' – it prevents an acid from 'burning'. It is not corrosive.	Strong alkalis are more corrosive than strong acids. They are particularly dangerous to the eyes.
Neutralisation is the breakdown of an acid or something changing from an acid.	When an acid reacts with a base in the correct proportions, neutral products are formed.
Reactions which produce gases result in a loss of mass.	Mass is conserved in a chemical reaction.
In chemical reactions, the atoms of the reactants are changed into new atoms of the products.	Atoms may change partners in a reaction but they are still atoms of the same elements, unchanged apart from electron transfers.

Pupils are much more aware of acids and their properties than they are of bases.

Pupils tend to use a non-particulate model for acids and bases, often attributing anthropomorphic qualities to acids such as 'eating' in a literal sense.

This chapter contains activities designed to:

- counter the above misconceptions
- emphasise the importance of the particle model in the reactions of acids and bases.

➡ # Literacy, numeracy and other cross-curricular links

There is scope in this chapter to develop pupils' speaking and writing skills. Discussion of evidence and articulating ideas will play an important part in accessing and working with this conceptually difficult topic. Pupils are also encouraged to look carefully at language in scientific and everyday usage.

Language for learning

By the end of this chapter pupils will be able to understand, use and spell correctly:

- words with a precise meaning in scientific contexts – for example, hypothesis, evidence, molecule, symbol, formula
- names of compounds, including salts – for example, magnesium sulphate, copper carbonate, copper nitrate, sodium chloride and potassium nitrate, recognising that the whole name is needed to specify a compound
- words that have different meanings in scientific and everyday contexts – for example, salt, reaction, product
- words and phrases relating to scientific enquiry – for example, evidence of reaction, hypothesis, prediction.

Through the activities pupils could:

- organise content into a whole piece of writing with the relationship between points and/or paragraphs clearly signalled
- structure paragraphs to develop points by using evidence and additional facts.

1 What are salts?

Learning outcomes

Check on prior learning that pupils can:

- identify the gas produced in the reaction between metals and acids and between metal carbonates and acids
- interpret the formulae for compounds in terms of the relative numbers of atoms of different elements
- list the typical properties of metals and non-metals
- name a variety of salts and give some uses
- identify evidence for a chemical reaction, for example, the test tube is getting hot
- identify simple particle pictures of solids, liquids, gases, elements and compounds

In new learning, pupils:

- use the idea of scientific method to hypothesise and predict

What do you know?

➡ *Pupil's Book page 8*

These starting point activities check pupils' prior learning of chemical reactions, symbols and formulae. Depending on the ability of the pupils, they may be short activities.

Answers

1 a) Hydrogen.
  b) Carbon dioxide.
2 a) i) Hydrogen.
    ii) Chlorine.
    iii) Sodium.
    iv) Oxygen.
  b) Sodium.
3 a) Sodium chloride.
  b) Hydrogen chloride (hydrochloric acid).
  c) Water.
4

Substance	Number of atoms of each type
NaOH	1 Na 1 O 1 H
NaCl	1 Na 1 Cl
H_2O	2 H 1 O

5 a) i) B
    ii) C
    iii) A
  b) D
6 Combustion = petrol + oxygen $\longrightarrow$ carbon dioxide + water
  Respiration = glucose + oxygen $\longrightarrow$ carbon dioxide + water
7 Heat energy is produced and new substances are formed.
8 Test tubes A and B. The bubbles of gas indicate the formation of a new substance.

Reacting acids with metals

➡ *Pupil's Book page 12*
There may be a range of answers for Question 1. The reactive metals rapidly tarnish and therefore do not appear to be shiny. Mercury is a liquid metal at room temperature. Some metals such as sodium do dissolve in water.

Answers

1 The main distinguishing property is that metals conduct electricity.
2 Yes.

Activity ## Demonstration: Reaction between magnesium and dilute hydrochloric acid

Pupil's Book page 13 shows a diagram from Book 1 to remind pupils of this reaction. Teachers may also wish to quickly demonstrate both the reaction and the test for hydrogen.

Procedure
Place 1 cm of magnesium ribbon in a test tube and add about 5 cm³ of 1 M hydrochloric acid. Retain the gas in the test tube by gentle thumb pressure. When the reaction is complete, remove thumb, count to five and ignite the hydrogen/air mixture with a burning spill. The 'pop' confirms the formation of hydrogen. Also point out that the magnesium has completely dissolved.

Equipment
- test tube
- magnesium ribbon (CARE: highly flammable)
- 1 M hydrochloric acid (CARE: irritant)
- wooden spill
- eye protection

Ideas and evidence: The scientific method

➡ *Pupil's Book page 14*

The reactions of acids with metals are used to develop the 'Ideas and evidence' concept of scientific method. The cartoon strip on page 15 gives the hypothesis that 'only hydrochloric acid reacts with magnesium to produce hydrogen because it is the only acid with '*hydro*' in its name'. This hypothesis can be tested (see below) and when it is proved to be wrong a new hypothesis can be suggested and tested.

Activity ## Enquiry: Do other acids react with metal to produce hydrogen?

➡ *Pupil's Book page 15*

Answers

If possible, pupils should write down their predictions and then do the practical activity.

Activity ## Practical: Do other acids react with magnesium to produce hydrogen?

Worksheet 1.1R

➡ *Worksheet 1.1R: Do other acids react with magnesium to produce hydrogen? (P)*

Equipment
- test tube
- 1 cm of magnesium ribbon (CARE: highly flammable)
- 0.5 M sulphuric acid (CARE: irritant)
- 1 M ethanoic acid (CARE: irritant)
- wooden spills
- eye protection

Answers

1 The magnesium dissolves; there is a gas produced; the test tube becomes warmer.
2 Incorrect.
3 H_2SO_4 (the formula for sulphuric acid is on Pupil's Book page 16). The formula contains hydrogen.
4 A hypothesis such as 'If an acid contains hydrogen, it will react with magnesium to produce hydrogen gas' may be suggested. Note that all acids contain hydrogen (or, more correctly, hydrogen ions in aqueous solution).
5 A chemical reaction occurs with ethanoic acid, and hydrogen is produced.
6 The evidence supports the above hypothesis.
7 This is an open question. The pupils may suggest using other acids and/or other metals. Phosphoric acid (present in cola drinks) could be demonstrated. Do not use nitric acid – oxides of nitrogen are produced, which is misleading as well as dangerous (toxic).

2 *Formulae and symbol equations*

Learning outcomes

Pupils:

- interpret the formulae for compounds in terms of the relative numbers of atoms of different elements
- construct word equations for reactions
- translate word equations into symbol equations
- use the formulae of the reactants and products to explain how atoms join in different ways as a result of the reaction
- explain why a given symbol equation is balanced or unbalanced

Chemical formulae

→ *Pupil's Book page 16*

The lesson has a brief starter activity with Question 3 checking on prior learning from Book 2 and the previous lesson.

Answers

→ *Pupil's Book page 16*

3 a) Magnesium and hydrogen.
   b) A compound.
   c) Hydrogen.

Some pupils may have noted that the ratio of atoms in similar compounds is different. For example, CuO, Na_2O, CO_2 and Al_2O_3. The first part of the lesson presents a teaching model that uses two-dimensional drawings to represent the combining power of elements and radicals. This model is good enough at this stage of development of the particle theory. It would be unsuitable for higher stages of development because:

- ionic compounds such as salts are represented as simple molecules, rather than giant ionic structures
- radicals such as sulphate are represented as a single particle, rather than showing the individual sulphur and oxygen atoms
- all particles are the same size
- all bonds are the same

The model is intended to help pupils to **interpret** complex formulae – not to write unknown formulae.

Answers

→ *Pupil's Book page 18*

4

Substance	Type and number of atoms		
HCl	1 H	1 Cl	
$MgCl_2$	1 Mg	2 Cl	
H_2SO_4	2 H	1 S	4 O
$Cu(NO_3)_2$	1 Cu	2 N	6 O
Na_2SO_4	2 Na	1 S	4 O

There are many other teaching models available to help pupils interpret chemical formulae and they all have advantages and disadvantages. Different models may be favoured by different learners. Pupils should be aware of different models and they should be encouraged to discuss the usefulness and limitations of some examples. The following extension activity allows pupils to compare three different models (combining power diagrams, Lego and combining power cards).

Activity

Worksheet 1.2R

Worksheet 1.3R

Worksheet 1.4R

Evaluation: Using models to write formulae

→ *Worksheet 1.2R: Using models to write formulae (information sheet) (E), Worksheet 1.3R: Using models to write formulae (answer sheet) (E), Worksheet 1.4R: Combining power cards (E)*

The main objectives of this extension activity are for pupils to:

• work out formulae using valency models
• understand that teaching models are used to help us visualise abstract ideas but they have their drawbacks
• evaluate different teaching models

The activity is intended for small group discussion work followed by a whole class plenary.

Equipment

• set of combining power cards cut out from Worksheet 1.4R
• set of Lego blocks. The worksheet indicates the following numbers, colours and sizes but you can modify to suit availability:

1 Ca brown 4-block   1 Na yellow 2-block   1 C   black 8-block
2 Al grey 6-block   3 O   red 4-block   3 Br blue 2-block
4 H   white 2-block

Answers

1

Pair of elements	calcium and bromine	carbon and hydrogen	calcium and oxygen	sodium and oxygen	aluminium and bromine	aluminium and oxygen
Name of compound	calcium bromide	carbon hydride (methane)	calcium oxide	sodium oxide	aluminium bromide	aluminium oxide
Formula	$CaBr_2$	CH_4	CaO	Na_2O	$AlBr_3$	Al_2O_3

2

Model	Combining power is represented by ...
1 'Combining power' diagrams	The number of 'arms'
2 'Combining power' cards	The number of 'notches'
3 Lego	One half of the number of connectors

3 Pupils may find a range of strengths and weaknesses, partly due to preferred learning styles.

Balancing equations

➡ *Pupil's Book page 19*
The combining power diagrams are used in chemical reactions to see how atoms join in different ways and to balance symbol equations, demonstrating conservation of mass.

Activity Reasoning: Explaining the formula

➡ *Pupil's Book page 21*
Pupils will have different ways of explaining the formula but they should show the idea of magnesium having a combining power of two and chlorine having a combining power of one.

Answers

➡ *Pupil's Book page 22*
5 The equation is balanced because on both sides there are:
1 Mg   2 H   1 S   4 O

Word play

➡ *Pupil's Book page 22*
1 Not scientific. A balanced viewpoint gives the arguments for and against – but not in exactly the same number of words or points.
2 Scientific. A balanced diet contains the appropriate amounts of necessary food chemicals, but not equal amounts.
3 Scientific. A balanced equation contains the same number of atoms of the same elements on both sides of the equation.
4 Scientific. A balanced see-saw has the same value for the clockwise and anti-clockwise moments.

Activity Discussion: Balancing an equation

Worksheet 1.5R

➡ *Worksheet 1.5R: Which one is the correctly balanced equation? (R)*
This activity is intended for small group discussion work followed by whole class feedback. It can be used as a plenary to review formulae and balancing equations.

Answers

Zoe: the formulae are correct but the equation does not balance.
Mark: the equation balances but some formulae are incorrect (ZnCl and H).
Nivendita: the formulae are correct and the equation balances.

Attainment targets

Work is the previous sections should provide evidence that pupils are working towards the following attainment levels.

Describe some metallic properties (for example, good electrical conductivity) and use these properties to distinguish metals from other solids	Level 5
Recognise that the atoms of elements can be represented by symbols	Level 6
Use word equations to summarise simple chemical reactions	Level 6
Interpret the formulae of compounds in terms of the number of atoms of each element present	Level 7

3 *Reacting metals with acids*

Learning outcomes

Pupils:

- write word equations for the reactions between metals and acids and explain the similarities between them
- use the formulae of the reactants and products to explain how atoms join in different ways as a result of the reaction
- predict that hydrogen and the appropriate salt will be made as a result of the reaction

This starter activity re-visits the scientific method introduced in lesson 1.

Activity ## Reasoning: Making predictions

➡ *Pupil's Book page 22*

Point out that the equation given in the book may help. Ask the pupils to work in small groups on Questions 1 and 2.

Answers

1 Possible hypothesis: 'The magnesium is changed into magnesium chloride' or 'The magnesium atoms have combined with the chlorine atoms to make magnesium chloride'.

2 Possible prediction: 'The magnesium chloride is dissolved in the acid/water'.
  Possible test: 'If we evaporate the solution, the solid magnesium chloride should be left behind'.
  The dissolving and the test can be demonstrated as described in the next activity.

3 The pupils may predict that other metals will react with acids and remember that copper does not react. This prediction can be tested by:
  - experiment (teacher demonstration or pupil practical), Worksheet 1.6R, see next page
  - and/or by the 'Information processing' activity, Pupil's Book page 23.

Activity Demonstration: What happens to the magnesium when it dissolves in dilute hydrochloric acid?

Quickly demonstrate that when a small piece of magnesium ribbon is added to dilute hydrochloric acid it dissolves. Do this by placing 1 cm of magnesium ribbon in a test tube and adding about 3 cm³ of 1 M hydrochloric acid.

Point out that it is dangerous to boil a solution that still contains some acid. This is because it can evaporate into the air (in this case, toxic fumes of hydrogen chloride). The acid can be removed by adding an excess of magnesium and then decanting the remaining solution into an evaporating dish, leaving the unreacted magnesium behind.

Set the pupils to work on the next section, while carefully evaporating the solution to produce the white solid, magnesium chloride.

Equipment
- test tube
- magnesium ribbon (CARE: highly flammable)
- 1 M hydrochloric acid (CARE: irritant)
- transparent evaporating dish
- eye protection

Activity Practical: Do other metals react with acids to produce hydrogen?

Worksheet 1.6R

→ *Worksheet 1.6R: Do other metals react with acids to produce hydrogen? (P)*
To save time each group could test the three metals with one of the acids, and the results then pooled.

Equipment
- test tubes and rack
- filings of coarse metal mesh of zinc, iron and copper; spatulas
- 1 M hydrochloric acid (CARE: irritant)
- 0.5 M sulphuric acid (CARE: irritant)
- wooden spills
- eye protection

Answers
1 a) iron + hydrochloric acid ⟶ iron chloride + hydrogen
  b) zinc + sulphuric acid ⟶ zinc sulphate + hydrogen
2 Copper is a less reactive metal than the other metals tested.

Activity Information processing: Recognising patterns for metals

→ *Pupil's Book page 23*

Answers
1 No.
2 Hydrogen.
3 The substance formed coats the metal, preventing further reaction (calcium sulphate is not very soluble, unlike the other salts produced in these reactions).

4 Aluminium appears to be less reactive than it really is because it is protected from corrosion by a thin layer of insoluble aluminium oxide. When the metal is placed in acid, this protective layer slowly dissolves away and the true reactivity of aluminium is then revealed.

5 **a)** calcium + sulphuric acid $\longrightarrow$ calcium sulphate + hydrogen

aluminium + hydrochloric acid $\longrightarrow$

aluminium chloride + hydrogen

b) metal + acid $\longrightarrow$ metal salt + hydrogen

6 $Ca + 2HCl \longrightarrow CaCl_2 + H_2$

7 $Ca + H_2SO_4 \longrightarrow CaSO_4 + H_2$

4 *Reacting metal oxides with acids*

Learning outcomes

Pupils:

- identify evidence for a chemical reaction – for example, a gas is produced, the test tube is getting hot
- represent reactions by word equations
- identify the patterns in word equations and produce a general equation

The starter activity asks pupils to think why some salts cannot be made by the metal + acid reaction. It then uses the scientific method to look for alternative methods.

Answers

➡ *Pupil's Book page 24*

6 **a)** Copper does not react with dilute sulphuric acid.

b) Sodium reacts explosively with nitric acid.

Activity ## Enquiry: Using the scientific method

➡ *Pupil's Book page 24*

A partially correct prediction is given. In addition to the metal salt, the second product is actually water (not hydrogen). This can be confirmed practically by experiment (Worksheet 1.7R) or by balancing the symbol equation.

Answers

1 For copper sulphate use copper oxide.
  For sodium nitrate use sodium oxide.

2 For copper sulphate use dilute sulphuric acid.
  For sodium nitrate use dilute nitric acid.

3 A list of appropriate safety precautions, such as 'wear eye protection' and 'carefully wipe up any spillages'.

4 Test tube (or beaker), spatula, stirring rod.

5 The metal oxide dissolves (if the hypothesis was fully correct, bubbles of hydrogen gas would also be expected).

6 Evaporate the water from the salt solution.

7 A metal oxide will react with a dilute acid to form a metal salt and water.

Activity

Worksheet 1.7R

Practical: Making a pure metal salt by reacting a metal oxide with an acid

Worksheet 1.7R: Making a pure metal salt by reacting a metal oxide with an acid (P)

Equipment
- copper oxide
- 0.5 M sulphuric acid (CARE: irritant)
- boiling tube, beaker (250 cm^3), tripod and gauze, filter funnel and paper, evaporating dish
- spatulas
- wooden spills
- eye protection

Answers
1 The boiling tube contained a mixture of a solution of the metal salt (copper sulphate) and unreacted copper oxide. The filtration step removed the copper oxide which would have contaminated the salt.
2 Copper sulphate.
3 The equation balances with 1 Cu, 5 O, 2 H and 1 S on each side of the equation.
4 copper oxide + sulphuric acid $\longrightarrow$ copper sulphate + water

Activity

Enquiry: Obtaining evidence

➡ *Pupil's Book page 25*

Answers
1 A 50 cm^3 beaker is too small to stir and heat 30 cm^3 of liquid – it may spill over.
   A 250 cm^3 beaker is too large to heat 30 cm^3 of liquid.
2 Acid fumes (vapour) may escape into the atmosphere.
3 The black copper oxide dissolved and a blue/green solution was formed.
4 All of the acid had been neutralised (used up).
5 Copper chloride.
6 The metal salt would get hot and may decompose (break down).
7 When a metal salt dissolves in water it is present as separate particles. These particles can fit through the small pores in the filter paper. Copper oxide does not dissolve and the particles remain packed together, forming grains which are too big to fit through the pores.
8 With slow cooling the particles have time to move into the right positions for a regular arrangement, and the crystal grows larger and larger.

Activity

Reasoning: Metal oxide equations

➡ *Pupil's Book page 26*

Answers
1 $CuO + 2HCl \longrightarrow CuCl_2 + H_2O$
2 **a)** zinc oxide + sulphuric acid $\longrightarrow$ zinc sulphate + water

b) calcium oxide + nitric acid $\longrightarrow$ calcium nitrate + water
c) magnesium oxide + hydrochloric acid $\longrightarrow$
magnesium chloride + water

3 a) $MgO + H_2SO_4 \longrightarrow MgSO_4 + H_2O$
b) $Na_2O + 2HCl \longrightarrow 2NaCl + H_2O$
c) $CuO + 2HNO_3 \longrightarrow Cu(NO_3)_2 + H_2O$

4 metal oxide + acid $\longrightarrow$ metal salt + water

5 a) $K_2O + H_2SO_4 \longrightarrow K_2SO_4 + H_2O$
b) $CaO + 2HNO_3 \longrightarrow Ca(NO_3)_2 + H_2O$

5 Reacting metal carbonates with acids

Learning outcomes

Pupils:

- identify evidence for a chemical reaction – for example, a gas is produced, the test tube is getting hot
- represent reactions by word equations
- identify the patterns in word equations and produce a general equation

Evidence for the formation of metal salts from the reaction of acids with metal carbonates can be obtained by experiment (Worksheet 1.8R) and/or from a data table (Pupil's Book page 27).

Activity ## Practical: Do metal carbonates react with acids to form metal salts?

Worksheet 1.8R

➡ *Worksheet 1.8R: Do metal carbonates react with acids to form metal salts? (P)*

Equipment

- test tubes
- sodium carbonate; copper carbonate (CARE: irritant)
- 1 M hydrochloric acid (CARE: irritant)
- 0 5 M sulphuric acid (CARE: irritant)
- wooden spills
- eye protection

Answers

1 a) Any three from: the copper carbonate dissolves; a gas is released; a temperature change; a colour change.
b) The final solution is coloured blue.

2 $CuCO_3 + H_2SO_4 \longrightarrow CuSO_4 + H_2O + CO_2$

3 copper carbonate + sulphuric acid $\longrightarrow$
copper sulphate + water + carbon dioxide

4 sodium carbonate + hydrochloric acid $\longrightarrow$
sodium chloride + water + carbon dioxide

5 a) The pattern suggests that metal carbonates do react with acids to form a metal salt and that additional products are water and carbon dioxide. However, this is based on just two results so the evidence is not very reliable.

b) Metal carbonates do react with acids to form metal salts. Evidence for this is the colour change in the copper carbonate reaction and the balanced symbol equation. Both copper sulphate and sodium chloride are metal salts.

c) Further reactions of metal carbonates with acids are needed to make the evidence more reliable.

Activity **Information processing: Recognising patterns for metal carbonates**

→ *Pupil's Book pages 27–28*

Answers

1

Metal carbonate	Acid	Observations	CO_2 formed?
iron carbonate	sulphuric	fizzing, green solid which dissolves	✓
magnesium carbonate	nitric	fizzing, white solid which dissolves	✓
potassium carbonate	hydrochloric	fizzing, white solid which dissolves	✓

2 Yes. All metal carbonates react with acid to produce carbon dioxide.

3 The gas produced when metals react with acids is hydrogen, whereas metal carbonates produce carbon dioxide. Some metals do not react with acids, whereas all metal carbonates react with acids. Metal oxides do not produce a gas but they all react with acids.

4 iron carbonate + nitric acid ⟶ iron nitrate + carbon dioxide + water

magnesium carbonate + hydrochloric acid ⟶ magnesium chloride + carbon dioxide + water

potassium carbonate + sulphuric acid ⟶ potassium sulphate + carbon dioxide + water

5 iron carbonate + hydrochloric acid ⟶ iron chloride + carbon dioxide + water

magnesium carbonate + sulphuric acid ⟶ magnesium sulphate + carbon dioxide + water

potassium carbonate + nitric acid ⟶ potassium nitrate + carbon dioxide + water

6 metal carbonate + acid ⟶ metal salt + carbon dioxide + water

7 Yes, there is the same number of atoms on both sides of the equation:

Element	Number of atoms
Fe	1
C	1
O	3
H	2
Cl	2

9 a) $MgCO_3 + 2HNO_3 \longrightarrow Mg(NO_3)_2 + H_2O + CO_2$
   b) $K_2CO_3 + 2HCl \longrightarrow 2KCl + H_2O + CO_2$
10 a) $ZnCO_3 + H_2SO_4 \longrightarrow ZnSO_4 + H_2O + CO_2$
   b) $Na_2CO_3 + 2HCl \longrightarrow 2NaCl + H_2O + CO_2$

Attainment targets

Work in the previous sections should provide evidence that pupils are working towards the following attainment levels.

Recognise that matter is made up of particles	Level 5
Use word equations to summarise simple reactions	Level 6
Recognise that the atoms of elements can be represented by symbols	Level 6
Recognise that compounds can be represented by formulae	Level 7

6 *Patterns in reactions*

Learning outcomes

Pupils:

- construct word equations for reactions
- translate word equations into symbol equations
- construct general equations for these reactions
- decide whether they need to modify planning within an investigation
- obtain a satisfactory sample of the salt
- identify where they found problems and the effect these had on their product
- produce an account of their work which identifies problems and corrects these, with clear explanations of how they were dealt with
- write, using evidence, in paragraphs that develop points

Time to think

→ *Pupil's Book page 29*

This 'checking progress' activity can be used as a starter to assess the pupils' understanding of the three general equations for making metal salts and the idea of balancing symbol equations.

1 The pupils choose one actual example for each of the following general reactions and write down the word equation and the balanced symbol equation:
   metal + acid ⟶ metal salt + hydrogen
   metal carbonate + acid ⟶
                         metal salt + carbon dioxide + water
   metal oxide + acid ⟶ metal salt + water
2 Pupils work in groups to produce cards for the symbol equations and swap them with another group for testing.

Activity

Worksheet 1.9R

Worksheet 1.10R

Practical: Can you make a metal salt?

➡ *Worksheet 1.9R: Can you make a metal salt? (P), Worksheet 1.10R: Cards for 'Can you make a metal salt?' (P)*

Equipment
- copper oxide
- copper carbonate
- sodium carbonate
- 0.5 M sulphuric acid (CARE: irritant)
- 1 M hydrochloric acid (CARE: irritant)
- eye protection
- beaker (250 cm³), tripod and gauze, filter funnel and paper, evaporating dish
- spatula
- wooden spills

Working in small groups with Worksheet 1.9R, pupils use the set of cards (Worksheet 1.10R) to decide which substances would react together to make the salts sodium chloride and copper sulphate.
  Likely answers are:
a) Sodium chloride from hydrochloric acid and sodium carbonate.
  Note that sodium cannot be used because it would react explosively with acid. Sodium sulphate cannot be used because it does not react (the reactions studied so far have been metal, metal oxide and metal carbonate).
b) Copper sulphate from sulphuric acid and either copper oxide or copper carbonate.
  Note that copper and copper chloride cannot be used because they do not react with dilute acids.

After the teacher has checked the chosen substances the pupils plan a method to make about 0.5 g of one of the salts. Worksheet 1.9R gives some useful information on safety and on the properties of the substances. There are also some prompting questions.

Note
The expected method for sodium chloride production is to add an excess of sodium carbonate to dilute hydrochloric acid, filter off the excess and partially evaporate the solution, leaving it to crystallise. However, the problem is that sodium carbonate dissolves in water, contaminating the salt. This can be confirmed by checking the pH of the final salt solution – sodium chloride is a neutral solution, but if it is contaminated with sodium carbonate it will be alkaline (test the pH of sodium carbonate solution) or acidic if the hydrochloric acid has not been fully neutralised. The solution to this problem is to use the titration method, which allows the acid to be exactly neutralised by a solution of sodium carbonate or sodium hydroxide. This is looked at in the next lesson.

7 *Reacting alkalis with acids*

Learning outcomes

Pupils:

- identify that a solution of pH 7 is neutral
- explain the safety precautions that need to be taken when using alkalis
- represent reactions by word equations
- identify the pattern in word equations and produce a general equation – for example, acid + alkali $\longrightarrow$ salt + water
- translate word equations into symbol equations
- make generalisations about reactions of acids with metals, using chemical names for products and reactants

Purity

→ *Pupil's Book page 30*

Alkalis, neutralisation and pH were introduced in Book 1. Remind pupils of the relevant details at the beginning of this section. The particle diagrams showing dissolving and filtering have reverted to a simple picture in which all particles are the same size. This allows pupils to focus on the explanation of why a soluble salt passes through a filter paper but an insoluble metal oxide does not. This idea may cause cognitive conflict and time should be allocated for pupils to voice their ideas and hear the explanations of others.

Answers

→ *Pupil's Book page 30–31*

7 The tap releases the solution. It can be carefully controlled to release one drop at a time. The volume of solution released can be measured using the scale.

8 A burette is much more accurate than a measuring cylinder. It measures to $0.1\ cm^3$.

9 Use an indicator to see if the solution is neutral.

Activity Demonstration: Making sodium chloride by the titration method

Equipment

- 0.4 M sodium hydroxide (CARE: irritant)
- 0.5 M hydrochloric acid (CARE: irritant)
- Universal Indicator solution
- burette ($50\ cm^3$) and stand
- pipette ($25\ cm^3$)
- pipette filler
- conical flask ($250\ cm^3$)
- white tile
- evaporating dish
- eye protection

Procedure
- Fill the burette with the sodium hydroxide solution.
- Using the pipette and filler measure out 25 cm^3 of hydrochloric acid into the conical flask.
- Add a few drops of Universal Indicator to the acid.
- Add the sodium hydroxide to the acid, continually swirling the conical flask. As the end-point approaches (indicator changes from red to orange), add the alkali drop-wise until the solution is neutral (green).
- Note down the volume of alkali added.

The final solution contains sodium chloride and Universal Indicator. To obtain pure sodium chloride crystals, repeat the experiment without the indicator and partially evaporate a portion of the solution.

To demonstrate an ICT technique, a pH probe connected to a computer could be used in place of or in addition to the indicator.

Activity Reasoning: Metal hydroxide equations
→ *Pupil's Book page 31*

Answers

1 Alkalis are particularly dangerous to eyes and eye protection is essential in this experiment. It is also important to carefully wipe up any spillages.

2 $2NaOH + H_2SO_4 \longrightarrow Na_2SO_4 + 2H_2O$

Time to think
→ *Pupil's Book page 31*

The pupils are asked to write five multiple-choice questions focusing on four given outcomes for the whole topic. This assessment for learning exercise is designed to encourage the pupils to reflect back on the unit. Deciding on a 'good' question requires pupils to check their own understanding of the topic, and the discussions that ensue from attempting one another's questions both challenge and consolidate their understanding.

Activity Review: Test on salts of the Earth
→ *Worksheet 1.11R: Test on salts of the Earth (R)*

| Worksheet 1.11R |

Answers

1 a) i) Blue.   (1 mark)
   ii) Black.   (1 mark)
  b) copper oxide + sulphuric acid $\longrightarrow$
                                      copper sulphate + water
                                                                          (1 mark)
  c) To separate/remove the copper oxide/black solid.   (1 mark)
2 a) i) magnesium + hydrochloric acid $\longrightarrow$
                                   magnesium chloride + hydrogen
                                                                          (2 marks)
      ii) Copper is less reactive than magnesium.   (1 mark)
  b) Sulphuric acid.   (1 mark)

c)

Formula	Name
CuSO$_4$	copper sulphate
MgCl$_2$	magnesium chloride

(2 marks)

3 a) It neutralises it. (1 mark)

  b) i) 3 (1 mark)

    ii) 9 (1 mark)

  c) potassium hydroxide + nitric acid $\longrightarrow$

potassium nitrate + water (2 marks)

4 a) Ammonium chloride and sodium sulphite. (1 mark)

  b) i) Bubbles/fizzing/gas/hydrogen. (1 mark)

    ii) Carbon dioxide. (1 mark)

  c) Potassium, carbon, oxygen. (1 mark)

2 Fit and healthy

→ Rationale

This chapter provides up to 8½ hours of teaching materials. When teaching this chapter, teachers should make reference to their school's sex education policy and PSHE scheme. Teachers will be aware of the need for sensitivity to the personal circumstances of individual pupils and their families. Links with this chapter can also be made with the PE department (health and fitness; sports injuries) and the Food Technology department (diet and nutrition).

The sections dealing with drugs need to be taught taking into consideration that, among 11- to 15-year-olds, drug use increases sharply with age. For example, in 2002 in England only 6% of 11-year-olds had used drugs in the last year, compared with two-fifths (36%) of 15-year-olds. Cannabis was the most frequently reported illicit drug used in the last year, used by 13% of 15-year-olds. 1% had used heroin, and 1% had used cocaine. In total 4% had used Class A drugs in the last year. For more information on young people and drug-related information see Department of Health (reference number 2003/0280) *Statistics on smoking, drinking and drug use among young people in 2002*, published 29th July 2003.

There are many professional health educators who would be happy to contribute materials and visit your school. Your local police force will have a youth liaison officer; you may have a community police officer who visits the school regularly; health visitors, nurses, youth workers and staff from detoxification units will be able to advise on the dangers of drugs.

Sections of this chapter relate to work covered in Year 7 and Year 8: Book 1 Chapter 7 Cells and Chapter 8 Reproduction; Book 2 Chapter 1 Food and digestion, Chapter 6 Respiration and Chapter 9 Microbes and disease.

In Year 8 pupils will have looked at interdependence as a fundamental idea in ecology and explored cell structure in depth when studying microbes and disease. This chapter explores interdependence through the interlinking of systems in the human body.

Energy is another key idea covered in this chapter, specifically the energy values of food and the use of energy by muscles in different kinds of activities.

This chapter lays particular emphasis on surveys and correlations (pattern seeking). Pupils can observe and record a range of phenomena linked to human exercise and physiology, or carry out surveys, where variables cannot readily be controlled, and seek correlation patterns in the data. There are several opportunities for full investigations – lesson 1 (Fitness test); lesson 3 (Worksheet 2.2R), lesson 7 (Worksheet 2.5R), lesson 8 (Fit and healthy questionnaire). When planning these investigation opportunities, check that the following objectives will be met.

- use preliminary work to decide what to measure and observe, and whether the approach is practicable
- consider what other factors, including those that cannot be controlled, might affect the results and how to deal with them
- collect and record data appropriately
- identify and describe trends in data
- evaluate the limitations of the evidence by considering sample size and the possible effect of other factors
- use scientific knowledge and understanding to interpret results.

There is an opportunity to look at controlling variables and fair tests in lesson 7 (DCPIP and vitamin C). Here pupils can observe and explore relationships between variables or factors and, while keeping other factors the same, change one factor and observe or measure the effect.

The following objectives need to be met:

- explain why a test is fair
- decide if a fair test is needed, and describe how to make the test fair
- say which are the key variables if a fair test is needed
- identify the most important key variables that need to be controlled
- pick out the key variables in a complex investigation and explain how to control them.

Throughout the chapter there are also opportunities for these different types of scientific enquiry:

- pattern seeking – in graphs, surveys and correlations about fitness and smoking
- using first-hand and secondary sources of information about fitness, health and drugs
- identification and classification of drugs; using and evaluating a technique or technological application such as taking pulse rates, using DCPIP as an indicator.

→ # *Overview*

The textbook sections, activities and worksheets have been arranged into 1 hour blocks to aid lesson planning. Clearly several of the activities and worksheets could form part of a homework session. The planning includes reading time for individual sections but some teachers may prefer to organise this as homework preparation for the following lesson. Worksheets are of six types – extension (E), support for an activity (S), practical (P), key skills (K), developmental (D) and review (R) – to allow for differentiation and flexibility to accommodate teachers' preferred practice. The actual timing and emphasis on different sections will depend on the current knowledge base of the pupils, the ability of the teaching group and the preferences of the teacher.

Lesson	Worksheets
1 Introduction to fitness	Worksheet 2.1R: Assessing what we know and what we don't know (R) Worksheet 2.2R: Key idea cards (S)
2 Muscles and bones	
3 Movement and respiration	Worksheet 2.3R: Plan and carry out an investigation about lung capacity (P)
4 The effect of smoking	Worksheet 2.4R: The cost of smoking (K)
5 Different drugs	Worksheet 2.5R: Drama: The dangers of drugs (S)
6 Other drugs	Worksheet 2.6R: A health survey (P)
7 Stress	Worksheet 2.7R: Stress (S)
8 Defence	
Review	Worksheet 2.8R: Test on fit and healthy (R)

→ *Chapter plan*

	Demonstration	Practical	ICT	Activity	Word play	Time to think	Ideas and evidence
Lesson 1			Internet search engines	Review: Assessing what we know and what we don't know Research: Kids' health Enquiry: Fitness test		What do you know?	
Lesson 2			Principle of individual differences	Creative thinking: Muscle types Reasoning: Muscles and sport Research: Sports-related injuries Information processing: Sports injuries Research: The Principle of Individual Differences Information processing: Training Creative thinking: Ideal footwear			
Lesson 3		Planning and carrying out an investigation about lung capacity		Reasoning: Lung capacity	Remembering tendons and ligaments	Microbes and the respiratory system	
Lesson 4			Cigarettes and health campaigns	Information processing: Diseases from smoking Research: Smoking Information processing: Respiratory infections Reasoning: Correlations Creative thinking: Stopping smoking Reasoning: Smoking Discussion: The cost of smoking			
Lesson 5				Reasoning: Addiction Drama: The dangers of drugs	Dictionary definitions	Checking meanings; social issues	
Lesson 6				Information processing: Alcopops Evaluation: What evidence? Evaluation: A health survey Enquiry: Effect of coffee and tea	Dictionary definitions	Effect of alcohol on the body	
Lesson 7	DCPIP test for vitamin C			Information processing: Energetic activities Evaluation: Diet Information processing: Vitamin C Reasoning: Diets Discussion: Stress Creative thinking: Pregnancy advice		Learning about minerals and vitamins	

	Demonstration	Practical	ICT	Activity	Word play	Time to think	Ideas and evidence
Lesson 8				Creative thinking: Immune system Information processing: Stress Evaluation: The effect of alcohol Research: Stress management Creative thinking: Fit and healthy Evaluation: Fit and healthy	'Lifestyles'	Chapter review	
Review				Test on fit and healthy			

➡ *Expectations*

At the end of this chapter

in terms of scientific enquiry

most pupils will: select and make use of secondary sources of information about health, indicating how strong evidence supports or does not support a conclusion; plan how to carry out an investigation using human subjects

some pupils will have progressed further and will: synthesise information about health and identify limitations in the data sample; explain some methods adopted to carry out an investigation on human subjects safely and appropriately; work collaboratively to collect sufficient valid and reliable data to form conclusions; evaluate conflicting evidence; investigate reaction time, considering how factors which cannot be controlled can be taken into account

in terms of life processes and living things

most pupils will: describe how the body uses energy in food, representing respiration by a word equation; describe some of the effects of diet, exercise, smoking, alcohol and other drugs on some organ systems; explain how different body systems work together in a healthy individual; know that some diseases are due to a lack of specific nutrients (vitamins and minerals)

some pupils will have progressed further and will: describe how cells in the respiratory system are adapted for their purpose and how they may be damaged by smoking and other forms of air pollution; represent respiration with a symbolic equation

➡ *Links with CASE*

An understanding of the interconnection between cellular respiration (at a microscopic level) and efficient blood supply in humans through the function of heart, lungs and blood circulation (at a macroscopic level) requires mental modelling, from realistic representations (a heart or a lung model or an anatomical picture) to the more abstract ability to 'picture' the movement of gases and sugars in and out of cells or oxygen from the lungs to and from the blood via the heart. This requires the ability to make a flow diagram of processes.

Probability and correlation reasoning patterns underlie all the work on sampling and surveying in this chapter but are not explicitly taught here. These are formal operational or high order thinking (HOT thinking) skills.

➡ *Pupils' misconceptions*

Misconception	Scientific understanding
All fats are bad for you.	There are two types of fats – saturated fats and unsaturated fats. Unsaturated fats can be thought of as healthy fats, and they are usually liquid at room temperature. Examples include fat in salmon, trout and halibut, and flax seed oil. Saturated fats are thought of as unhealthy fats. They may raise cholesterol levels.
The only way to burn off fat is to exercise vigorously. The more you exercise, the more protein you need for energy.	The way to burn off fat is to take in fewer calories than you use. Of the three major nutrients, protein, carbohydrate and fat, protein is the least efficient energy source. Carbohydrates provide the most energy.
As you get older you lose muscle and gain fat, no matter what you do.	Some research shows that with regular exercise, especially aerobic exercise such as weight training, and a low-fat diet, you can increase lean body mass and decrease fat mass at any age.
You should never drink water when you are over-heated.	You should drink water continuously before, during and after exercising to replace the fluid you've lost. Your muscles generate heat, causing your body temperature to rise. Heat from the muscles is carried away by water in the bloodstream and brought to the surface as perspiration.
If something is 'fat free' you can eat more of it.	Many 'fat free' foods replace fat with carbohydrates that may have just as many calories.
Most people who stop smoking put on weight. It's safe to smoke low tar cigarettes. Most lung cancer is caused by air pollution, petrol fumes etc. Most people smoke and many people who smoke all their lives live to a ripe old age, so smoking cannot be that bad for you.	All these statements are incorrect when statistical surveys are carried out. There will be a percentage of people that, just by chance alone, do not get cancer. The risks of smoking are only understood if you look for correlation patterns and consider these alongside probability (chance).
Physical activity and sport stretch the lungs and get the tar out of your system.	This has no basis in physiology.

➡ *Literacy, numeracy and other cross-curricular links*

Lessons 1, 2 and 4 encourage research on the internet. This could act as a basis for extended writing activities. The contribution to numeracy is not extensive in this chapter as mathematical calculations are routine and simple. This chapter has health-related links to PE, sport, nutrition and PSHE, and these links should be made explicit. Ask your PE department to provide information about GCSEs in sports- and PE-related subjects. You can also make useful links with careers advice about opportunities in sport and leisure for pupils who are interested in human biology.

Language for learning

By the end of this chapter pupils will be able to understand, use and spell correctly:

- words and phrases relating to health, fitness, addiction, minerals and vitamins
- words and phrases relating to investigating stratagems – for example, scientific method, developing technique, controlling variables, fair testing, carrying out a survey, sampling, probability, correlation using secondary sources
- words and phrases relating to evaluation – for example, reliability (trustworthiness) of data, validity of conclusions, most appropriate equipment.

1 *Introduction to fitness*

Learning outcomes

Pupils:

- identify aspects of fitness
- explain differences between fitness and health
- describe ways in which fitness differs in different individuals
- investigate how to test for fitness
- identify independent and dependent variables
- explain how to make results reliable
- define and measure heart rate
- describe the interdependence of systems in the human body

What do you know?

➡ *Pupil's Book pages 32–33*

Allow 10 minutes for this starter activity, which is concrete preparation (see CASE methodology) for the whole chapter. Evidence shows that unless pupils relate the scientific knowledge in this chapter to themselves, their behaviour and attitudes do not change as a result of what they learn. Pupils have a lot to say about what they think health and fitness are if you encourage them to talk.

After finding out what pupils already know and what misconceptions they may have, you can either develop their skills as researchers of secondary sources or get them to plan and carry out a full investigation. There is not time to do both activities in one lesson.

Answer

'Fitness' is different for different individuals. It means to be in good physical condition (being 'in shape'). 'Health' is a state of well-being; free from disease. You can be free from disease but be unfit. In some cases you can have an illness, such as diabetes, but still keep yourself fit. A useful website for looking up definitions is:

www.thefreedictionary.com

Activity

Review: Assessing what we know and what we don't know

Worksheet 2.1R

Worksheet 2.2R

➡ *Worksheet 2.1R: Assessing what we know and what we don't know (R), Worksheet 2.2R: Key idea cards (S)*

This is a formative assessment activity that will allow both you and your pupils to make an accurate assessment of what knowledge they have acquired by Year 9, and how well this information is linked together in integrated models explaining how the human body works.

It can be used here, after or to replace the 'What do you know?' activity (Pupil's Book page 33), or used at a later stage (lesson 2, 5 or 6) to assess progress through this chapter. The same set of cards can be used more than once so that pupils can monitor their own progress. To do this they will need to record what they know the first time the cards are used. You can use this technique at any time by making up your own word and phrase cards.

The cards that are handed back to you (the ones that pupils know nothing about) should determine how best to tailor this chapter to your pupils' needs.

Activity

Research: Internet search

➡ *Pupil's Book page 33*

If you have not yet shown pupils how to use the internet to investigate secondary sources of information, then this activity makes a good introduction. There are lots of high-quality websites relevant to health and fitness specifically designed for children. It is useful to bookmark a few suitable sites in advance of teaching this chapter, so that you can refer more able pupils or one group at a time to these to do some extension work. Useful sites include:

www.healthykids.org.uk

This is the site of the Healthy School Partnership.

www.wiredforhealth.gov.uk

'Wired for health' is series of websites managed by the Health Development Agency for the Department of Health and the Department of Education and Skills. It provides health-related information linking the National Curriculum and the National Health School Standard. There are four interactive health sites specifically tailored for young people of different ages. The sites relevant to Year 9 teaching are:

www.lifebytes.gov.uk for 11- to 14-year-olds
www.mindbodysoul.gov.uk for 14- to 16-year-olds.

Alternatively, this research section can provide homework at any stage in the chapter.

You can help pupils to become discerning browsers of the web by giving them criteria for assessing websites. An interactive exercise that checks pupils' ability to be good judges of websites can be found at www.quick.org.uk. This is the QUICK site (QUality Information ChecKlist). It outlines eight ways to check information on a website. These are as follows.

1 Is it clear who has written the information?
2 Are the aims of the site clear?
3 Does the site achieve its aims?
4 Is the site relevant to me?
5 Can the information be checked?
6 When was the site produced?
7 Is the information biased in any way?
8 Does the site tell you about choices open to you?

Activity   ## Enquiry: Fitness test

→ *Pupil's Book page 34*

This is an opportunity for pupils to design and carry out a full investigation to compare individual fitness, indicated by how quickly the heart rate returns to its normal resting rate after exercise. Remind pupils of the importance of planning techniques that ensure their results are reliable. Repeating the experiment should give similar results each time.

The Attainment targets table below will help you to assess this full investigation. If pupils are struggling with the concept of fair testing, use Worksheet 6.5 *Measuring pulse rates* from CD-ROM 2.

If you do not want to do a full investigation at this point, have a 10-minute group discussion and note-making session on one large piece of paper about the questions in the text, and summarise the answers as a whole class.

Attainment targets

The investigation should provide evidence that pupils are working towards the following attainment levels (table continues overleaf).

Level	Planning	Obtaining and presenting evidence	Considering evidence	Evaluating
5	Recognise the key factors in setting up a fair test, i.e, that the same person should have their pulse rate taken doing several types of exercise; or investigate a sample of people doing some activity	Make a series of observations, comparisons and measurements with precision appropriate to the task; record observations and measurements systematically	Draw conclusions consistent with the evidence, for example, the harder the exercise the faster the pulse rate, and the fitter a person is the quicker the pulse rate returns to normal; begin to relate these to scientific knowledge and understanding about rates of respiration based on knowledge and understanding of the differences between breathing and respiration	Know why repeat observations and measurements must be made; offer simple explanations for any differences encountered
6	Use scientific knowledge and understanding about the effect of exercise on the body to decide on appropriate approaches to an investigation; identify the input variables and how they will be controlled	Make enough measurements of pulse rate and time comparisons for the task; measure with precision, using instruments with fine-scale divisions; choose scales for graphs to show data effectively	Identify measurements and observations that do not fit the main pattern shown; draw conclusions that are consistent with the evidence and use scientific knowledge and understanding to explain them	Make reasoned suggestions about how working methods could be improved

Level	Planning	Obtaining and presenting evidence	Considering evidence	Evaluating
7	Use scientific knowledge and understanding to decide on an appropriate investigation, make predictions and decide on what evidence (outcome variables) to collect to test these predictions; identify the key factors in contexts in which variables cannot readily be controlled, and plan appropriate procedures	Make systematic observations and measurements with precision; identify when there is a need to repeat measurements, comparisons and observations in order to obtain reliable data; represent data graphically	Draw conclusions that are consistent with the evidence and explain these using scientific knowledge and understanding about respiration and breathing	Consider whether the data collected are sufficient for the conclusions drawn; communicate using scientific and technical language and conventions

The human body as a system

→ *Pupil's Book page 34*

This section can be given as homework if the lesson includes the full investigation. It pulls together work done in Years 7 and 8, so that pupils can build up their concept of interdependence. If you are doing it in class, start by engaging each group in a 2-minute discussion about what a system is, using the railway, education system and heating system analogies in Question 1. Now call the whole class together and make a list of what they think makes up each system on the board.

Answers

→ *Pupil's Book pages 34–35*

1 This question should help pupils to realise that systems are made up of interdependent components that interact to make the systems operate as whole – any part that is missing will cause the system to break down.
   a) Railway – train lines, engines, carriages, stations (you could also include the people).
   b) An education system – schools, playgrounds, teachers, pupils, education offices, etc.
   c) The heating system – boiler, radiators, water, air, fuel. Systems are complex interactive organisations that work together in intricate ways for specific outcomes. They need to be co-ordinated and controlled.

2 You can use this as a formative assessment exercise by putting up some answers and asking each group to come up with a score; for example, A for excellent, C for OK, E for awful. You can assess any major misconceptions or difficulties from previous work.

   A human system consists of organs, tissues and cells. Note that blood and nerves could occur in each system, as these are the main mechanisms for co-ordination and control.

a) The support and movement system is made up of the skeleton, which consists of bones, ligaments, tendons, cartilage and muscles. It also has blood vessels, blood cells and lymph. Joints are made up of synovial fluid as well as ligaments, tendons, bones and cartilage.

b) The respiratory system is made up of the mouth and nose, trachea (windpipe), lungs, blood vessels, blood cells and lymph.

c) The digestive system is made up of the mouth, oesophagus, duodenum, stomach, pancreas, liver, small and large intestine, rectum, anus.

d) The circulatory system is made up the heart, veins, arteries, capillaries, blood cells, and the lymph system, which links to the circulatory system.

3 The lungs.

4 The heart – without blood we could not get the necessary chemicals to each cell for cell respiration, to give energy.

5 We digest food in the digestive system (mouth, oesophagus, duodenum, stomach, pancreas, liver, small and large intestine, rectum, anus).

Attainment targets

Work in the previous sections should provide evidence that pupils are working towards the following attainment levels.

Demonstrate an increasing knowledge and understanding of life processes and living things; describe the main functions of organs of the human body and explain how these functions are essential to the organism	Level 5
Use knowledge and understanding of life processes and living things to make links between life processes in humans and the organ systems involved	Level 7
Construct mental models, for example, of interrelated body systems	Level 7

2 *Muscles and bones*

Learning outcomes

Pupils:

- identify the main parts of a human skeleton
- explain that muscle tissue requires energy from mitochondria
- describe how alternate contraction and relaxation of muscles moves limbs
- describe differences between bone, cartilage, connective tissue, ligament, tendon and muscle
- describe how a joint functions
- identify how injury impairs the function of a joint
- interpret graphical data

This lesson contains more material than is needed for 1 hour, so you can select what you want to cover, based on the assessment you made of pupils' needs in lesson 1. If recap is required, follow this sequence:

The human body as a system
The support and movement system
Information processing: Sports injuries
Knee joint
Creative thinking: Ideal footwear

If your pupils are ready for new information, start at 'The support and movement system' section, then go on to:

Slow- and fast-twitch muscle
Reasoning: Muscles and sport
Research: Sport-related injuries
Information processing: Training
Knee joint
Creative thinking: Ideal footwear

The skeleton
Answers
→ *Pupil's Book pages 36–37*

6 The basic parts of the skeleton need to be known by Year 9, and also that ligaments hold the bones together and tendons attach the muscles to the bone.

7 The skeleton is for support (spine, legs), movement (joints) and protection (skull, pelvis).

8 The flexor muscle (label 4) is getting shorter and the extensor muscle (label 3) is being stretched. The extensor muscle straightens the limb when it contracts, and the flexor muscle bends the limb when it contracts.

Slow- and fast-twitch muscle
→ *Pupil's Book page 37*

This paragraph can be used as a reading comprehension to check individual pupils' ability to read quickly and synthesise relevant information. There is no need for them to make notes, but you can check their understanding with some 'quick fire' questions that they can write down the answer to, and then mark themselves when you read out the right answers.

Suggested questions and answers include:

1 What do mitochondria do?
Convert glucose to energy.

2 Which have the most mitochondria – slow- or fast-twitch muscle? Why?
Slow-twitch muscles have the most mitochondria, as they need more energy over time.

3 What does 'genetically determined' mean?
It means 'inherited'.

4 What are the differences between aerobic and anaerobic respiration?
Aerobic respiration needs oxygen and produces water and carbon dioxide, as well as a large amount of energy;

anaerobic respiration does not need oxygen, and produces lactic acid and a smaller amount of energy compared to aerobic respiration. Use this opportunity to give the symbol equations for these reactions:

$$C_6H_{12}O_6 + 6O_2 \longrightarrow 6CO_2 + H_2O + 28880 \text{ kJ energy}$$

$$C_6H_{12}O_6 \longrightarrow 2C_2H_5OH + 2CO_2 + 210 \text{ kJ energy}$$

5 What does 'endurance' mean?
It means long lasting. A lot of energy is used over a long time, for example, in mountain climbing and marathon running.

Activity Creative thinking: Muscle types

➡ *Pupil's Book page 38*
Pupils can decide for themselves what information they want to show. Ask them to give their information sheet to another group who will check that it is factually correct.

Activity Reasoning: Muscles and sport

➡ *Pupil's Book page 38*
These are extension or homework questions, and could build on the previous 'quick fire' questions.

Answers

1 Different sports require energy expenditure over different lengths of time. High intensity, low endurance sports need a quick burst of energy, often from anaerobic respiration. This is because there is no time for the blood supply to carry oxygen and glucose to muscle cells in sufficient amounts, for example, in high jump, hurdles, javelin throwing, squash and tennis. Low intensity, high endurance sports need a long, slow 'burn', i.e. energy is needed over a longer time so there is less energy being required in each minute. This can be provided by aerobic respiration, for example, during long distance swimming, golf, marathon running.

2 Endurance athletes need slow-twitch muscle fibre; power athletes need fast-twitch muscle fibre.

3 Sprinters sometimes collapse in pain when they are running because of the build-up of lactic acid in their muscles, as a result of anaerobic respiration, causing cramp.

4 The muscles that control eye movement are made of fast-twitch fibres so that blinking and focusing the eyeball can be as rapid as possible.

5 The lower leg and intercostal muscles are mainly slow-twitch fibres because they need high endurance to keep moving all the time.

6 Slow-twitch muscles contain the most mitochondria. This is because they need large amounts of energy over a longer period of time, which they get from aerobic respiration.

Activity Research: Sports-related injuries
→ *Pupil's Book page 38*
This activity can be a brief class discussion.

Activity Information processing: Sports injuries
→ *Pupil's Book page 39*
This activity provides a check on pupils' ability to interpret graphical information.
1 The bar chart shows the areas of the body that suffer most from sports injuries, and the frequency of injury to that area.
2 The knees.
3 Both high intensity and low intensity sports tend to cause injury to the knee as it takes the most strain in walking, running and jumping.
4 Squash – knee, wrist, hand.
Football – knee, foot, groin.
Netball – knee, arm, leg.
5 Swimming causes fewer injuries compared with other sports because it puts less strain on joints since they do not have to bear weight.

Activity Research: The Principle of Individual Differences
→ *Pupil's Book page 40*
If you have people in your class who are athletes or interested in gym training, they will be able to contribute their own experiences to this section on 'The Principle of Individual Differences'. This can be combined with the next section, or made an extended piece of primary source research (personal experience/the PE department) and secondary source research (the internet).

Activity Information processing: Training
→ *Pupil's Book page 40*
The PE department may welcome the opportunity to link this activity with the work that they do. Meet with them to discuss this possibility, and borrow some of their display material for your classroom.

Knee joint
→ *Pupil's Book page 41*
This is based on SAT-type questions.

Answers
9 The knee joint needs to be a strong joint because it carries all the weight of the body.
10 The two pads of cartilage between the long leg bones act as cushions and shock absorbers.
11 The tendon could tear (this is extremely painful); either of the long bones meeting at the knee joint could fracture.
12 This gives the connective tissues time to re-grow new cells without being rubbed away by the friction of movement. This is a little similar to the function of the protective bubble formed by a blister.

Activity Creative thinking: Ideal footwear

→ *Pupil's Book page 41*

The diagrams highlight some of the injuries caused by wearing incorrect footwear during exercise. Take care that you do not put any pupils at a disadvantage because they do not have the latest fashion-based trainers (Questions 3 and 4). It is worth emphasising that the function of a good pair of trainers is far more important than their appearance. You may find that the design of footwear is a topic in the Technology department's design course, making this activity a useful cross-curricular link.

Answers

1 An 'ideal' running shoe should have a high back to the heel, thick soles with spongy shock-absorbing materials, no stitching across the toes, a tongue to protect the foot from the laces or a Velcro fastening to prevent chaffing.
2 The knees, back and hips could be injured by wearing incorrect footwear.

3 *Movement and respiration*

Learning outcomes

Pupils:

- describe how a joint functions
- explain the process by which the energy in food is utilised in muscle
- give the chemical reaction through which energy is utilised
- explain exhalation and inhalation in terms of chest volume increase and decrease
- describe how the respiratory system stays healthy
- define and measure lung capacity
- suggest questions for investigation
- plan and carry out an investigation

This lesson starts with an opportunity to test pupils' understanding of how joints move, recapping the previous lesson. It then introduces more detailed work, and recaps what pupils should already know about the respiration system in preparation for lesson 4 on smoking.

Arm bones

→ *Pupil's book page 42*

This is another set of questions based on SATs. If you spent some time on the 'Knee joint' questions on page 41, this can be used as an assessment activity.

Answers

13 The doctor told Shona that the bones in her forearm (radius and ulna) have fractured, snapped or broken near the wrist joint.

14

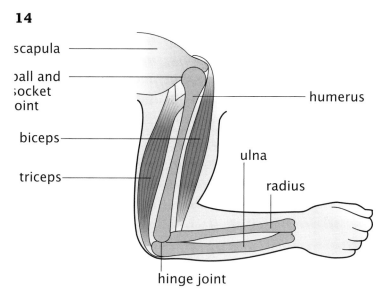

scapula

ball and
socket
joint

humerus

biceps

ulna

triceps

radius

hinge joint

15 A hinge joint makes an up and down movement (it only moves in one plane).

16 The different types of joints enable the arm to move in all directions working together.

17 The wrist joint is made up of many small bones and it has limited rotating movement as well as moving up and down.

18 The shoulder joint rotates around (ball and socket) giving 360° movement.

19 The biceps muscle (flexor) contracts.

20 Tendons connect muscle to bone.

21 Ligaments connect bone to bone (humerus to ulna).

The respiratory system

→ *Pupil's Book pages 43–44*

Answers

22 A – 1
B – 3
C – 2

23 glucose + oxygen ⟶ energy + water + carbon dioxide (aerobic respiration)
glucose ⟶ energy + lactic acid (animals) or ethanol (plants) (anaerobic respiration)

24 All living things respire but not all living things breathe. Mammals breathe to draw air into and out of the lungs. Plants do not breathe, they absorb air through holes in their tissues and through cell surfaces, and they rely on diffusion. Slugs and snails do not breathe; gases diffuse in and out of their moist skin. All micro-organisms rely on diffusion as they are so small, for example, amoeba and bacteria.

25 Running and blowing a trumpet would increase your breathing rate.

26 Swimming under water might cause less oxygen to be available to cells.

Activity

Worksheet 2.3R

Practical: Planning and carrying out an investigation

➡ *Worksheet 2.3R: Plan and carry out an investigation about lung capacity (P)*

This is an opportunity to assess pupils' ability to plan and carry out investigations. You can assess their ability to observe and explore relationships between variables or factors, their ability to plan how to change one factor, and how they measure the effect of these changes while keeping other factors the same. You can restrict which variables each group can investigate, according to their ability.

Make it clear that you will be assessing pupils' ability to explain why and how their investigation is fair, and that they need to make clear which are the key variables to control. Worksheet 6.4 *Planning and carrying out an investigation* from CD-ROM 2 provides clear guidance for pupils who need it.

Equipment

Each group will need:

- 2-litre milk bottle with lid
- rubber tube
- large bowl or trough
- measuring cup
- 2 straws (1 per student)
- funnel
- calculator

Answers

1 More accurate readings will depend on repeating the investigation to get an average for each person's lung capacity.

2 Straws are changed for hygiene.

5 Graphs: The type of graphs drawn will depend on the variable investigated. You can check if the pupils are clear about the differences between using line graphs for continuous variables, for example height and age, or discontinuous variables such as gender and participation in sports.

Attainment targets

Work in the previous sections should provide evidence that pupils are working towards the following attainment levels.

Describe and explain life processes and features of living things using appropriate terminology, such as respiration	Level 6
Use knowledge and understanding of life processes to explain respiration in terms of the main underlying chemical changes and energy transfer	Level 7
Demonstrate an extensive knowledge of life processes and living things by relating the structure of respiratory surfaces to the processes	Level 8

How we breathe

➡ *Pupil's Book pages 44–45*

Answer

27 Inhalation requires more effort, as we need to move the ribs up and out. The intercostal muscles contract and the diaphragm flattens. During exhalation the ribs fall back into place. The intercostal muscles relax and the diaphragm contracts back up into a dome shape.

Activity ## Reasoning: Lung capacity

➡ *Pupil's Book page 45*

Circulate around the groups and check that they know that lung capacity is the amount of air your lungs can hold. It can be measured using a spirometer, or more simply as shown in the diagram on Pupil's Book page 45.

Keeping the respiratory system healthy

➡ *Pupil's Book page 46*

This section can be read by pupils in about 5 minutes, as a quick revision of the work they did in Chapter 6 of Book 2. Ask Question 28 and get verbal answers only, as it is not necessary for pupils to learn this list.

Answer

28 Bronchitis, cancer, pneumonia, laryngitis, tracheitis, asthma, hay fever and emphysema are all respiratory system diseases.

Time to think

➡ *Pupil's Book page 47*

This section is a recap of Chapter 9 in Book 2. You could reintroduce the table from pages 98–99 of Book 2. Many students may misunderstand the way that mucus traps microbes and dirt and is removed by the beating cilia inside the respiratory tubes. It needs to be stressed that it is not the cilia that are stopping the microbes, but the mucus. The cilia simply remove the dirty mucus.

Answers

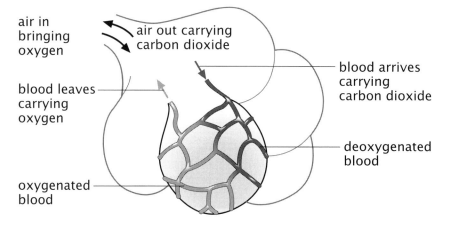

air in bringing oxygen

air out carrying carbon dioxide

blood arrives carrying carbon dioxide

blood leaves carrying oxygen

deoxygenated blood

oxygenated blood

1 Answers could include: common cold virus, influenza virus, tuberculosis bacteria, diphtheria bacteria, whooping cough bacteria.
2 Warm, damp conditions.
3 Warm and damp also describes the inside of lungs.
4 Burning fuels.
5 The masses of tiny blood-filled capillaries around the alveoli.
6 Because they are made of alveoli (little air-filled sacs).
7 It gets rid of microbes and dirt via the digestive system. The acid in the stomach kills most microbes, and others stay in the gut and are expelled in the faeces. This is why it is important to wash your hands after going to the toilet so that you do not transmit microbes that are still infectious, having passed through your digestive system.
8 This is part of your immune reaction to trap the microbes.
9 To get rid of the phlegm and mucus.
10 Gas exchange takes place at the interface between the blood supply and the surface of the alveoli. Carbon dioxide diffuses from the blood into the air sacs, and oxygen diffuses from the air sacs into the blood. See Chapter 6 of Book 2 for explanatory diagrams.

4 *The effect of smoking*

Learning outcomes
Pupils:

- listen actively, demonstrating understanding of the use of scientific terminology
- describe the effects of cigarette smoke on lung tissue and gas exchange
- explain how damage to alveoli reduces surface area for gas exchange
- explain the harmful effects of smoke components
- describe how ideas about smoking have changed as evidence has accumulated
- interpret data to look for correlations
- explain why smoking is addictive

Smoking, alcohol and drugs present huge risks to young people and their use is on the rise. This lesson and lessons 5 and 6 cover the dangers of smoking, drugs and alcohol. You need to spend some time gathering resources and arranging visits from professionals such as drug advisers, youth workers, and workers from Alcoholics Anonymous. Your local health centre is a good place to go to first.

Start the lesson by writing the word 'addiction' on the board and asking two or three pupils what they associate this with (you could give them 1 minute of talking time in pairs first, to break down any inhibitions). The danger of passive smoking (breathing in smoke-filled air from other people smoking in the same environment) may come as a surprise for some young people, and they may be anxious about their parents' smoking habits.

This lesson is a good opportunity to address personal and social aspects of science.

Activity Information processing: Diseases from smoking

→ *Pupil's Book page 48*
This activity should take approximately 5 minutes.

Answers

The diseases caused by smoking affect the respiratory system, for example, bronchitis, pneumonia, heart disease and lung cancer.

Activity Research: Smoking

→ *Pupil's Book page 48*

This research activity can be done over several weeks, and could provide material for a display somewhere visible in school.

Smoking and pregnancy

→ *Pupil's Book page 49*

Answer

29 Nicotine passes through the placenta to the baby – this causes the baby's heartbeat to speed up. Carbon monoxide also passes through the placenta, giving the baby less oxygen for respiration – this affects growth of the baby. Mothers who smoke run almost twice the risk of miscarriage or premature delivery. Premature babies are at greater risk of birth defects than those born full-term. Babies born to smokers are on average 200 g lighter. They are also usually weaker, so they are more likely to need special care.

Activity Information processing: Respiratory infections

→ *Pupil's Book page 49*
The information in the table is a real set of research data from the 1980s, when there was still some doubt about the links between smoking and a range of respiratory infections (not just lung cancer). Ask pupils to discuss the data in groups. The activity requires HOT strategy (formal operating), so is intellectually demanding. Collate their answers on the board so that, based on the class discussion, they can each write a summary in their notebooks. This will take about 20 minutes. This lesson is a good opportunity to develop the language and communication skills of science. Pupils may need some sentence stems such as 'These data suggest ...', 'While not conclusive, the evidence for ...', 'There is strong evidence for ...', 'When you consider ... you have to ...'.

Answers

1 The ratio of infection-reporting soldiers who smoked to those who did not smoke is 25.5 : 17. In other words, a soldier who smokes is approximately one and a half times more likely to have a respiratory infection.

2 Soldiers who smoke are at greater risk of infection because their immune system is lowered.

3 The high figures may indicate that these were less healthy individuals who started to find training very difficult and assumed that smoking was affecting their fitness, so they gave up smoking in an effort to improve their fitness.

4 There is no information about how representative these data are, for example, there is no age profile, no indication of general fitness levels, nor gender.

The soldiers who gave up smoking halfway through present contradictory evidence for the link between smoking and respiration infections.

The data are in percentages, so we do not know how many individuals were involved. The total number may be too small a sample to make general conclusions.

The data about respiratory infections come from soldiers' reports – this is subjective, not objective evidence.

Activity Reasoning: Correlations

→ *Pupil's Book pages 49–51*

This section requires advanced or high order thinking (HOT thinking), so it is an extension activity for the most able pupils. It takes about 20 minutes to complete. Check that pupils know what 'correlation' means from earlier work.

Answers

1 The investigation requires sampling. The sample of people selected needs to represent the population as a whole by having a balance of gender, ages, social and economic factors, and perhaps ethnic groups. The sample needs to be large enough to show significant correlation patterns.

2 The graph showing lung cancer and number of cigarettes indicates a strong correlation (shown by the nearly straight line) between the disease and smoking; the heart disease/number of cigarettes graph also shows the correlation from getting stronger as the number of cigarettes a day increases (the gradient gets steeper).

3 Breast cancer/number of cigarettes may show a very weak correlation; heart disease/number of cigarettes shows a growing correlation as more cigarettes are smoked.

4 Alcoholism/number of cigarettes does not appear to correlate.

5 By sampling.

6 a) 'Every time you smoke a cigarette you shorten your life by an a hour.'

This is probably the best statement for putting people off smoking as it is dramatic and personal, but some pupils may find the other statement better as it is more scientific.

b) 'In one year, more people are killed by diseases linked to smoking than die in all the road accidents in that year.'

This is the easiest statement to provide scientific evidence for as the data can be collected from official records and compared. The statement is directly linked to the statistics. The other statement begs the question 'how was that worked out?'.

7 Prescribed drugs, gas under pressure (in vehicles and canisters) and flammable materials all carry government health warnings.

Activity Creative thinking: Stopping smoking
➡ *Pupil's Book page 51*
Criteria for judging a good poster include that it is eye catching, the message is easy to absorb and it is accurate.

Activity Reasoning: Smoking
➡ *Pupil's Book page 51*

Answer
1 Both remarks are unscientific as they are based on single cases and not on probability and correlation.

Activity Discussion: The cost of smoking

Worksheet 2.4R

➡ *Worksheet 2.4R: The cost of smoking (K)*
This is a data processing activity, requiring no equipment or advanced preparation.

Answers
1 The approximate price of one cigarette is 20p (£4/20).
2 You need to check the current price of cigarettes – although some of you pupils will already know it!
3 As the number of cigarettes smoked per day goes up, so the risk of dying of lung cancer increases (or grows, or goes up).
4 The risk at 20 cigarettes per day is 15%; it goes up to 23% at 30 cigarettes/day, i.e. it increases by about 1½ times.
5 The correlation is positive because the more you do it the more likely you are to get lung cancer (both variables go up).
6 This could be a group discussion. Look for a good argument using facts or data.
7 It is illegal for under-16s to buy cigarettes because smoking causes greater damage in young developing and growing bodies. 16 is considered to be the age at which your body is fully developed, having gone through puberty.
8 We now know how damaging passive smoking is (see Pupil's Book page 48).
9 Check for rules on smoking in clubs and restaurants in advance.

It's not too late to quit
➡ *Pupil's Book page 51*
This is a good time to invite a health professional into the classroom or to show a video summarising the dangers of smoking. Government campaigns to stop smoking will be able to provide speakers and information.

Attainment targets
Work in the previous sections should provide evidence that pupils are working towards the following attainment levels.

Distinguish between related processes, for example, gas exchange and respiration	Level 6
Explain the processes of respiration in terms of the main underlying chemical change	Level 7
Describe and explain how biological systems function; relate the cellular structure of organs to the associated life processes, for example, gas exchange in the lungs; recognise, predict and explain the consequences of smoking for organ systems	Level 8

5 *Different drugs*

Learning outcomes
Pupils:

- categorise drugs
- recognise overlaps and inconsistencies in categorising drugs
- recognise that prescription drugs can be dangerous
- explain addiction and identify addictive drugs
- describe the effects of alcohol
- recognise that drugs change mental activity

Many teachers feel that this topic is beyond their expertise. There are however many professional support systems to draw on – your first port of call should be the school liaison officer who will be able to put you in touch with the community officer responsible for drug education.

Drugs
→ *Pupil's Book page 52*
The term 'drug' is not used consistently or scientifically in our society so it is worth starting this lesson with the dictionary definition.

This is another opportunity to have a drug expert talk to the pupils.

Answers
30 a) Aspirin; Ecstasy; penicillin; ibuprofen; nicotine; cannabis. A good argument, according to the definition given in the Pupil's Book, could be made to include caffeine and alcohol. There is also currently a debate about controlling the use and distribution of homeopathic 'drugs' from natural substances.
31 Aspirin, penicillin and ibuprofen are legal, and Ecstasy and cannabis are illegal to use.
32 Penicillin is restricted to groups of people who are ill with bacterial infections. It can only be prescribed by a doctor. It is illegal for alcohol to be sold to under-18s.
33 Recreational – beer, wine, alcopops (if alcohol is being classed as a drug), caffeine, nicotine, Ecstasy (illegal), cannabis (illegal).
Over-the counter – aspirin, ibuprofen.
Prescribed by a doctor – penicillin.

Time to think
→ *Pupil's Book page 53*

Answers
1 Co-ordination – here it refers to physical co-ordination, the way we link actions together.
Coma – unconsciousness.
Tranquilliser – calming drug or activity.
Depressant – suppresses feelings, makes people feel sad. Usually a drug.

The second part of this section gives pupils the opportunity to discuss their views and feelings about drugs. You may use the questions given on page 53 of the Pupil's Book to start a discussion, and then go on to the sections about addiction (Pupil's Book pages 54–55), which also ask for pupils to give their views and opinions.

Answers to the questions are a matter of opinion, but in general the more addictive drugs are, the more dangerous they are, although the level and type of drug that causes addiction seems to vary from person to person.

An alternative to using these questions is to give each group two pieces of coloured card and ask them to write their own questions on them. Sort them to exclude duplicate questions and to group similar questions, then use these as the basis for discussion.

Activity ## Reasoning: Addiction
→ *Pupil's Book page 55*
This activity can be done as homework or used for group discussion in class time. Improvements could include more detailed information, more visual appeal, and how to get help (contact names and telephone numbers).

Activity ## Drama: The dangers of drugs
| **Worksheet 2.5R** |

→ *Worksheet 2.5R: Drama: The dangers of drugs (S)*
This is a drama activity. You may want to use it in collaboration with the Drama department. You will need to find a suitable space for performances. Your class might be willing to perform for an assembly or for another, younger class. There are several good theatre-in-education companies that perform and run workshops about health-related activities. Ask your Drama department for information about those in your area.

6 *Other drugs*

Learning outcomes
Pupils:

- know the UK drinking laws
- interpret survey data
- evaluate evidence to draw conclusions
- identify caffeine as a stimulant
- describe the effects of overdosing on caffeine
- design and carry out an investigation

- recognise ethical issues involved in scientific research
- recognise that researchers must not influence results
- consider evidence and reasons, and reach conclusions

Alcohol

➡ *Pupil's Book page 56*

This section can be used in two ways, depending on your pupils' needs. If they need practice at reading for information and comprehension, start the lesson by giving individual pupils 10 minutes to read and complete the 'Time to think' section.

If you want to encourage more discussion, ask groups to read the passage and discuss the answers, then ask each group one of the questions and give the other groups a chance to add any other information.

Time to think

➡ *Pupil's Book page 56*

Answers

1 Alcohol is easily absorbed into the blood stream and is transported through the body.
2 The chemical processes that go on inside a living organism; the breakdown of molecules and the formation of new molecules.
3 It is a large organ with a big blood supply; its function is to 'clean' the blood flowing through it (it removes alcohol products from the blood).
4 By a process similar to the way it breaks down the products of anaerobic respiration – by oxidising it.
5 People under the influence of alcohol lack co-ordination and lose their sense of risk taking, putting themselves in danger of accidents and injury.

Alcohol and the law

➡ *Pupil's Book page 57*

Most pupils are unaware of the legal position about alcohol, so make sure that they read this section carefully.

Activity ## Information processing: Alcopops
Answers

➡ *Pupil's Book pages 57–58*

1 It can be inferred that in Scotland youths smoke, drink alcohol and take marijuana more as they grow older. It can also be inferred that more girls than boys smoke, and that more boys than girls admitted to taking marijuana.
2 Category or type of school (secondary modern/ comprehensive); gender intake (single sex/mixed).
3 In case the behaviour of pupils varies with these school variables.
  Girls are more at risk than boys of becoming a regular smoker, but the use is similar for the other drugs.
4 No, there are differences dependent on age of pupils and type of drug.
5 Alcohol looks to present the greatest risks because this is the most used drug at each age and for both sexes.

6 To stop pupils feeling inhibited about telling the truth, as these activities are mostly illegal.

7 No, because we do not know in what form the alcohol was consumed. But it is true to say that alcohol consumption increases rapidly with age of young people, so there may be indirect evidence. More research needs to be done.

8 This needs more research – find out what drugs besides marijuana are taken, and what proportion of the alcohol consumed is in the form of alcopops. It would be useful to be able to compare data on drug use before alcopops were available.

Activity Evaluation: What evidence?

➡ *Pupil's Book page 58*

This activity builds on the evaluation questions at the end of the previous section.

Answers

1 Yes, it is plausible from the information in the article, so this could be a hypothesis for future research.

2 Poor dental hygiene.

3 A survey to see if this effect was widespread; an experiment – putting teeth into solutions of alcohol and fruit juice in a controlled, fair test.

4 From dentists' records.

Activity Evaluation: A health survey

Worksheet 2.6R

➡ *Worksheet 2.6R: A health survey (K)*

This is an activity to develop pupils' critical thinking and their ability to evaluate data. It can be used here or in lesson 7. No equipment is required. It can also be used as an assessment activity for pupils to do individually for homework.

Answers

1 Agree with the first two points because the graphs show correlations:

Men are heavier smokers than women.

Most people knew that smoking causes heart diseases.

There is no evidence here to support:

Most people know that exercise is good for you.

Women and men both know how to stay healthy and look after their hearts. There is no data about heart care and the data about health indicates that women are better informed than men.

It is hard to tell if most people know what a healthy diet is as we are not told what the Year 9 pupils defined as a healthy diet. We can only see that most people were right according to the Year 9 pupils.

2 The Year 9 pupils need to give more information about the questions they asked their sample. They could also increase the sample size and check that they surveyed across the age ranges for both genders.

Extra questions might include:

What would you do to make sure you keep your heart healthy?

3 Disagree. Their data seem to indicate that men and women respond differently, so they do need to keep sampling both equally to keep the data representative.

Word play
➡ *Pupil's Book page 58*
Plausible – seeming reasonable or probable.
Assumption – taken as true, for the purpose of argument or action.

Caffeine
➡ *Pupil's Book page 59*
It comes as a surprise to most people that caffeine is a powerful drug.

Activity ## Enquiry: Effect of coffee and tea
➡ *Pupil's Book page 59*
1 This is a good opportunity to explore the concept of reliability. You can decide how much help to give each group of pupils.
2 Give pupils enough time to carry out their survey. This could be given as a homework activity, with each pupil asking five adults. This data can then be collated by putting it into a class spreadsheet as it is collected.

The digestive system
➡ *Pupil's Book page 60*
End the lesson with these three questions to set the scene for the next lesson. They take about 10 minutes. Provide large sheets of paper and coloured pens for each group to use.

7 *Healthy diet*

Learning outcomes
Pupils:

- describe how poor diet and lack of exercise worsen heart conditions
- describe a healthy diet, including the role of minerals and vitamins
- learn how to make very precise measurements of vitamin C content
- recognise that vitamin C declines with storage and processing
- interpret correlation data
- describe how pregnant women can stay healthy
- describe some eating disorders

Activity ## Information processing: Energetic activities
➡ *Pupil's Book page 60*
The table gives pupils practice at reading data and assessing how best to process it. A bar chart would show all the data easily (see the example on Pupil's Book page 57).

Activity Evaluation: Diet

→ *Pupil's Book page 61*

1 Set this review of diets over a week as homework. It recaps work done in Chapter 1 of Book 2.

2 This is an evaluation activity, as well as a formative assessment opportunity. Give pupils 10 minutes to do this once they have completed the diet homework (this may be at the start of lesson 8). Put pupils in pairs where they can provide support for each other; a more able pupil with a less able one gives both an opportunity to develop further understanding.

3 The bone structure of a 30-year-old woman is fully formed, whereas the skeleton of a 15-year-old girl is still growing.

4 Water is the basis for all metabolic activities; roughage (fibre) keeps the intestine's peristaltic action working, preventing constipation and discouraging bowel disorders.

Time to think

→ *Pupil's Book page 61*

This can be a formative assessment activity to assess the effectiveness of different strategies for learning the information in the table. Time should be planned for pupils to discuss how they set about this task, and to exchange ideas on alternative approaches.

Activity Information processing: Vitamin C

→ *Pupil's Book page 62*

This section is based on past SAT questions.

Answers

1 Citrus fruits (oranges, lemons), watercress, tomatoes, fresh uncooked vegetables such as carrots etc.

2 Bleeding gums and bleeding under the skin (symptoms of scurvy).

3 and 4 require pupils to check their understanding of the diagram of the vitamin C test procedure.

If pupils undertake the investigation the following equipment will be needed:

Equipment
- 1 boiling tube
- 1 pipette
- 1 juicer
- 1 pestle and mortar
- 1 syringe
- fruit
- DCPIP

Planning an investigation
5 This is another opportunity for a full investigation, or it can be given as homework to assess planning skills.

Activity Reasoning: Diets

→ *Pupil's Book page 63*

Pupils could use the data to plot a graph, either for homework or as a class-based test.

Answers

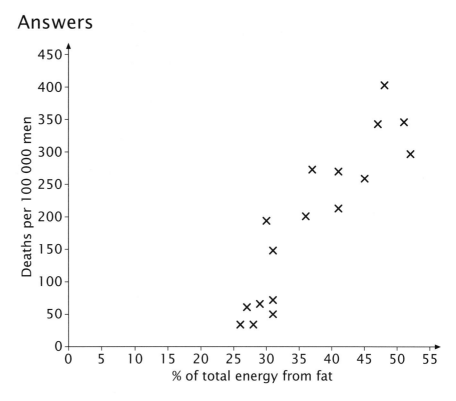

There is positive correlation between heart disease and fat percentage, but the graph shows variation around the line of best fit. The assumption that the more fat you eat the more likely you are to die of heart disease can be made, but this is extrapolating from the data and not direct evidence, as in Dr Jones' comment. You need other information about how the data were collected. Other variables that might be linked to heart disease include level of exercise, smoking etc.

Being 'out of balance'

➡ *Pupil's Book pages 63–64*

Eating disorders can be an area of great sensitivity. If you have pupils in your class that you suspect have issues about food, you may decide to let pupils read this section individually and make their own notes without a whole class discussion. A health visitor or dietician would be a good person to invite to give a short talk on this topic.

Activity

Worksheet 2.7R

Discussion: Stress

➡ *Worksheet 2.7R: Stress (S)*

This is an opportunity for pupils to discuss stress and their feelings about it in a safe and sensitive way. There is no need to ask each pair of pupils to report their discussion to the whole class. Give a time allocation of no more than 15 minutes.

Activity

Creative thinking: Pregnancy advice

➡ *Pupil's Book page 64*

This section is a recap of work done in Years 7 and 8, and also work done earlier in this chapter, so it could be used as a homework activity.

Attainment targets

Work in the previous sections should provide evidence that pupils are working towards the following attainment levels.

Planning – identify suitable approaches and key factors	Level 5
Use scientific knowledge to identify suitable approaches and make adequate measurements and comparisons	Level 6
Systematically organise the investigation with repeat measurements, observations and techniques to ensure precision and reliability	Level 7

8 *Defence*

Learning outcomes

Pupils:

- identify the body's defences against pathogens
- describe how the immune system is affected by unhealthy habits and behaviours
- identify healthy and unhealthy stress factors
- explain the role of adrenaline in stress physiology
- explain what cancer is and what might trigger it
- evaluate results from an investigation into acid levels in alcohol
- identify factors that affect fitness and health, and relate these to scientific knowledge and understanding

You could start this lesson with a card-based assessment activity so that you can recap or emphasise areas that you think pupils are weak in (see Worksheet 2.1R for method). You could use these words or phrases:

immune system
healthy diet
effects of caffeine
DCPIP
effects of smoking
carrying out a survey
depressant
tranquilliser
alcohol and the law

The body's defence against pathogens

→ *Pupil's Book page 65–66*

Answers

38 Pupils will have personal experience of drugs and disease; remind them that some useful drugs include penicillin for infections, and vaccines for TB, tetanus and polio.

39 Something that kills or stops the growth of disease-causing micro-organisms.

40 Wash it carefully with water or an antiseptic, and cover it with a dry dressing.

41 Aspirin is a pain reliever. It also thins the blood – some pupils may know people who take an aspirin a day to aid blood circulation. For a full description of aspirin, see page 149 of Book 2.

42 Salmonella and lysteria might cause food poisoning.

Activity Creative thinking: Immune system

➡ *Pupil's Book page 66*

This could be an opportunity for developing the skills to make a PowerPoint presentation.

The sections on cancer and stress are to address the health areas that pupils hear a lot about at home and in the media. The misconception that all stress is bad for you needs dispelling, as does the assumption that cancer is always fatal.

Cancer

➡ *Pupil's Book page 67*

Answer

43 A line graph sloping upward from left to right. See Pupil's Book page 50 for an example.

Stress

➡ *Pupil's Book page 67*

44 All of these situations cause stress, although some are nice and some are nasty.

Activity Information processing: Stress

➡ *Pupil's Book page 68*

2 Physical problems include allergic reactions such as a runny nose, blisters, hives/rash; immune reactions such as cold sores and itchiness; increased heart rate, sweating, going pale, blushing – most people show a range of physical stress reactions, and these vary from person to person.

3 The heart in particular, and the skin.

4 It seems that people find modern living more stressful, but it could also be that people recognise stress nowadays and did not recognise the symptoms of stress in the past.

Adrenaline

➡ *Pupil's Book page 70*

There is no need for pupils to learn details about adrenaline, but they should know how it relates to stress.

Answers

45 The heart pumping the blood faster and the arteries to the muscles widening means that more blood reaches the muscles. The blood is carrying higher levels of sugar, which enable the muscles to respire faster and so work more effectively.

46 Adrenaline is made in the adrenal glands.
The hypothalamus is in the brain.
It causes the adrenal glands to secrete adrenaline.

Activity Evaluation: The effect of alcohol

➡ *Pupil's Book pages 70–71*

Answers

1 To give the same pH as the stomach, so that the investigation models stomach conditions.

2 This is the pH of the stomach.

3 As a control.

4 Also as a control.

5 They do not need D because one can assume that water is neutral and that it is only a change in pH that alters the Universal Indicator.

6 The assumption is that alcohol reduces the pH of hydrochloric acid, making it more acidic (see page 97 of Book 1), so it probably changes the pH of the stomach environment in a similar way.

7 Alcoholic drinks contain different amounts of alcohol, measured by percentage. From the table you can see that whisky is far stronger than lager or wine. It is also more acidic. More acidic alcohols damage the lining of the stomach, and cause ulcers.

8 A major improvement would be to add the same amount of alcohol and water to each tube, for example, 20 drops. Repeat investigation to ensure results are reliable; increase the range of alcohol used, for example, red wine, other spirits; find a way of assessing alcohol percentage, other than from the labels. All or any will improve the investigation.

9 Each test tube contains 6 drops of hydrochloric acid and 3 drops of Universal Indicator solution.

Test tube	A	B	C	D	E
Added content	15 drops lager	10 drops whisky	15 drops white wine	30 drops water	no addition
Percentage alcohol	5%	40%	12%	0%	0%
pH	3	2	2	3.5	3.5

Activity Research: Stress management

➡ *Pupil's Book page 71*

This is a project or homework activity to find out what activities, courses and services there are in the school and local community to help people manage stress. Encourage pupils to ask at home how people cope with stress.

Word play

➡ *Pupil's Book page 71*

Lots of magazine articles and television programmes refer to people's 'lifestyle', so this activity is quite fun.

Activity Creative thinking: Fit and healthy

➡ *Pupil's Book page 72*

If your pupils need more practice at this kind of investigation they can design a 'fit and healthy' questionnaire for a health magazine to help readers see if they have 'risky' lifestyles. Again, this might be a link activity with the PE department.

It is a good idea to get pupils to compare calorie and fat content, and amount of minerals and vitamins in each type of milk by reading the labels. An extension activity for pupils working ahead of the class is to use ICT to design a table to record the milk contents so that they can be easily compared.

Activity ## Evaluation: Fit and healthy
→ *Pupil's Book page 72*
This raises the issue of the difference between fitness and health. Steve Redgrave is fit but not naturally healthy, because as a diabetic he has to control his sugar intake by diet and medication.

Pupils need to consider the question and work out how we could find out if we are healthier than our great grandparents were. This requires primary source research (anecdotes from older relatives), and secondary research into mortality rates over the last few generations.

Time to think
→ *Pupil's Book page 72*
The chapter ends with an assessment activity, thinking back over the work done in the chapter. It provides a good opportunity for learners, with peer and teacher support, to identify those areas that they need to remediate, and time should be found for them to do this.

Activity ## Review: Test on fit and healthy
→ *Worksheet 2.8R: Test on fit and healthy (R)*

Worksheet 2.8R

Answers
1

Tissue or organ	Function
Heart	Pumps blood around the body.
Ligaments	Connect bones together.
Cartilage	Cushions the ends of bones, preventing friction.
Muscle	Contracts to move bones.
Lungs	Respiratory surface for the intake of oxygen and removal of carbon dioxide.

(1 mark each)

2 Aerobic respiration uses oxygen, anaerobic does not; aerobic respiration produces carbon dioxide and water; aerobic respiration produces more energy; anaerobic respiration produces lactic acid in animals and ethanol in plants. (Any three.) (1 mark each)

3 diaphragm; contracts; flattens/moves downwards; intercostal; upwards/outwards; volume/amount of space; trachea/windpipe. (1 mark each)

4 Bronchitis; pneumonia; heart disease; lung cancer/throat cancer; emphysema. (Any three.) (1 mark each)

5 Jaundice; hepatitis; cirrhosis; obesity. (Any two.) (1 mark each)

3 Energy and electricity

→ # *Rationale*

This chapter provides up to 9 hours of teaching materials. It develops ideas from Key Stage 3, Units 7I Energy resources and 8I Heating and cooling. It relates to work on the reactivity of metals in Unit 9F Patterns of reactivity, and to work on fuels in Unit 9G Environmental chemistry. One of the key ideas identified in the Key Stage 3 Science Strategy is energy. Some of the difficulties of teaching energy are referred to in *Thinking Through Science Teacher's Book 1*, Chapter 12 Energy resources. This chapter aims to build on the ideas introduced earlier and to further develop and clarify pupils' understanding of the terms. They should by now be familiar with the idea of energy being released from various fuels, with the idea of primary fuels, and the terms renewable and non-renewable energy resources.

The term 'energy transfer' was emphasised in Book 1, and in this chapter the alternative idea of forms of energy and energy transformation is introduced. Energy transfer diagrams (Sankey diagrams) are used to represent a range of situations, and the ideas of energy dissipation and energy conservation are developed through them. The chapter distinguishes between energy and power, and the units in which they are measured. The idea of efficiency is introduced. Pupils are also encouraged to consider the ideas of energy at a particle level, and to use analogies to explain energy conservation. The importance of electricity as a means of energy transfer is considered in more detail. The chapter also looks at the use of electrical appliances in the home and their different power ratings and running costs.

Many pupils find difficulty in understanding the relationship between the volt and energy, and also the distinction between current and voltage. This chapter aims to introduce the volt through simple exercises measuring the voltage (either in imaginary circuits or practically) across different parts of a circuit. Again the dangers of high voltages are reinforced and this leads on to looking at the generation of electricity.

The final section of this chapter considers the energy policy for the twenty-first century and so provides an opportunity to deal with social, economic and ethical issues.

→ *Overview*

The textbook sections, activities and worksheets have been arranged into 1 hour blocks to aid lesson planning. Clearly several of the activities and worksheets could form part of a homework session. The planning includes reading time for individual sections but some teachers may prefer to organise this as homework preparation for the following lesson. Worksheets are of six types – extension (E), support for an activity (S), practical (P), key skills (K), developmental (D) and review (R) – to allow for differentiation and flexibility to accommodate teachers' preferred practice. There is sufficient material for up to 9 hours of teaching, although there are only 8 lesson blocks. The actual timing and emphasis on different sections will depend on the current knowledge base of the pupils, the ability of the teaching group and the preferences of the teacher.

Lesson	Worksheets
1 Revision of fuels, renewable and non-renewable energy resources	
2 Energy transfer and transformation	Worksheet 3.1R: Problems on energy (S)
3 Conservation of energy, power	Worksheet 3.2R: Numerical problems on power (S) Worksheet 3.3R: Comparing electrical appliances (K)
4 Electrical energy, power consumption, efficiency	Worksheet 3.4R: Electricity bills (S)
5 Measuring voltage, the volt	Worksheet 3.5R: Electricity crossword (R)
6 Electrical hazards	
7 Generating electricity	
8 Our energy future	Worksheet 3.6R: Electricity generation (R)
Review	Worksheet 3.7R: Test on energy and electricity (R)

➡ *Chapter plan*

	Demonstration	Practical	ICT	Activity	Word play	Time to think	Ideas and evidence
Lesson 1					Prefixes and suffixes	What do you know?	Clockwork radio
Lesson 2	Energy transformations			Consolidation: Problems on energy			
Lesson 3			Use of spreadsheets	Consolidation: Numerical problems on power Information processing: Power ratings Information processing: Comparing electrical appliances		Energy conservation and dissipation	
Lesson 4	Use of joulemeter Use of household electricity meter		Use of spreadsheets	Information processing: Electricity bills		Review of key terms	
Lesson 5		Measuring voltage in electric circuits	Using software to simulate electric circuits	Evaluation: Using a voltmeter Review: Electricity word quiz		Review of units and formulae	
Lesson 6				Creative thinking: Electricity			
Lesson 7	Generating electricity			Reasoning: Transmitting electricity Information processing: Power station Creative thinking: A world with no electricity			Electro-magnetic induction
Lesson 8		Solar energy investigation	Internet search	Research: Alternative energy sources Review: Electricity generation Enquiry: Solar energy			
Review						Concept map Review: Test on energy and electricity	

➡ *Expectations*

At the end of this chapter

in terms of scientific enquiry

most pupils will: identify patterns in measurements of voltage and use these to draw conclusions about circuits; identify and control key factors in investigating simple cells and identify patterns in their results, including observations that do not fit the main trends

some pupils will have progressed further and will: relate energy transfer devices in the laboratory to everyday appliances; synthesise information from secondary sources about the development of the electricity supply industry and communicate it clearly; consider whether data is sufficient, and account for anomalies

in terms of physical processes

most pupils will: describe some energy transfers and transformations in familiar situations, including dissipated energy, and devices; recognise that the voltage change across a circuit component is a measure of its energy transfer; describe how voltage originates from a chemical cell; give examples of the hazards of high-voltage circuits; compare the energy consumption of common electrical appliances; describe how electricity is generated by energy from fuels, and recognise possible environmental effects of this

some pupils will have progressed further and will: apply a model of voltage and energy changes to a circuit; recognise that although the total energy in a system is conserved, energy can be dissipated; use power ratings in comparing the costs of using different electrical appliances; link the function of an electric generator to magnetic effects

→ *Links with CASE*

This chapter offers some further opportunities for the development of fair testing, identifying relationships between variables and multi-variable reasoning in the work on voltage. There is reference to the use of models in the explanation of energy conservation. The activity on measuring resistance requires the comparison of ratios.

→ *Pupils' misconceptions*

Misconception	Scientific understanding
Energy is used up.	Energy cannot be created or destroyed; it can be changed from one form to another.
Electricity is a substance kept in the battery.	The battery is the source of energy for the circuit. It transfers chemical energy into electricity.
Energy is a source of power.	Power is the rate at which energy is transferred.
Voltage flows around a circuit.	The greater the voltage of the battery, the greater the energy transferred to the circuit by the current flowing round the circuit.
The brightness of a bulb is due to the current flowing.	The rate at which energy is transferred determines the brightness of the bulb.
A p.d. cannot exist unless a current is flowing.	A p.d. must exist for a current to be able to flow.

➡ *Literacy, numeracy and other cross-curricular links*

Literacy skills developed through this chapter include understanding the structure of scientific words through consideration of a number of prefixes and suffixes. A number of scientific passages are provided which are quite demanding – there is one on the development of the clockwork radio, and another considers the physiological effects of electric shock.

Some of the activities in this chapter encourage small group discussion. For example, pupils are asked to consider a range of energy transfer processes and to develop their understanding of these changes.

Several sections support pupils' writing in science. One approach is to ask pupils to research a topic and then produce a leaflet to explain it, for example, they have to write a plan for an investigation into the use of a solar cell, and they are asked to write an article imagining a life without electricity.

There are opportunities to link with citizenship and PSHE through considering the environmental implications of various energy resources and policies. Work in this chapter relates to Unit 9D Using control for electronic monitoring in the Design and Technology Scheme of Work, and to Unit 18 Twentieth-century conflicts and Unit 20 Twentieth-century medicine in the History Scheme of Work.

Language for learning

By the end of this chapter pupils will be able to understand, use and spell correctly:

- words and phrases relating to scientific enquiry – for example, independent and dependent variable, control
- words and phrases describing energy transfers and transformations – for example, movement as kinetic energy, position as potential energy, chemical energy, electrical energy, sound, heat and light
- words and phrases relating to energy supply and waste – for example, conservation, dissipation, electric generator, dynamo, power station.

Health and safety

Health and safety rules must be followed throughout all practical activities. Particular emphasis is made in this chapter on the dangers of electricity.

1 *Revision of fuels, renewable and non-renewable energy resources*

Learning outcomes
Pupils:

- identify renewable and non-renewable energy resources
- give examples of ways in which energy can be stored
- recognise that energy is routinely converted from one form to another in order to be useful
- categorise devices on the basis of type of energy input or output

What do you know?
→ *Pupil's Book page 73*
This introductory activity is essentially revision of work covered in Year 7 by Chapter 12 Energy resources, Book 1.

Pupils should by now be familiar with producing concept maps. However, for pupils who need help getting started teachers may wish to provide them with key words either on card or on the board. Pupils will produce a concept map again at the end of the topic, and comparison of the two will allow teachers and learners to evaluate the progress in their understanding of the topic.

Word play
→ *Pupil's Book page 74*
This activity is a useful reminder of the earlier work on energy, as well as reinforcing the usefulness of using word roots in science.

How is energy stored?
→ *Pupil's Book page 75*
In this section teachers can remind pupils of the energy transfers and transformations that they are familiar with from earlier work, either by pictures or by providing practical examples. (Possible examples could include the exploding can and icing sugar demonstrations from Chapter 6 Book 2, or a model steam engine lifting a load.)

Answers
→ *Pupil's Book pages 75–76*
1 Answers will vary from pupil to pupil. For example, chemical energy – batteries; kinetic energy – pushing a pram; thermal energy – hot-water bottle; potential energy – catapult, spring in a clockwork toy.
2 Our food.
3 It would change to kinetic energy.
4 Clockwork toys, kitchen minute timer, an old type of clock, etc.

Ideas and evidence: Clockwork radio

→ *Pupil's Book page 77*

This is a relatively short passage on the development of the clockwork radio, however it does allow for more wide-ranging issues to be introduced. This section provides an ideal opportunity to discuss environmental issues, such as decreased pollution when choosing clockwork machines, rather than conventionally-powered ones. The passage mentions pollution from batteries, but there is also the reduction in carbon dioxide output if less electricity is needed to be produced in power stations. Therefore, while clockwork energy is a necessity for remote areas of the world, it has a use in towns and cities too.

Answers

1 No batteries to be disposed of; does not cause pollution from electricity generation at coal or oil power stations.

2 Solar cells.

2 *Energy transfer and transformation*

Learning outcomes

Pupils:

- use energy transfer (Sankey) diagrams to represent how devices transfer/transform energy
- describe energy transfers in everyday changes
- describe the energy transfers and/or transformations in a range of toys and devices
- give examples of ways in which energy can be stored

This section looks in some detail at the energy transfers in a number of situations. Now is the time to consider how much emphasis you will place on using forms or types of energy that is stored, and how much emphasis you will place on discussing the process in terms of energy transfer. In this example the emphasis is towards the use of energy transfer processes: in a kettle the electricity transfers the energy to the heating element and then to the water, which gets hot. Alternatively you can consider energy transformations, as in this example of warming a beaker of water with a Bunsen: the chemical energy in the gas and oxygen changes to thermal energy, which heats the beaker and water.

Note that whilst the terms chemical energy, thermal energy, kinetic energy, gravitational potential energy and elastic potential energy can be useful as they indicate ways in which energy may be stored, electrical energy is a less useful term as it refers to the way in which energy is transferred rather than stored.

Energy transfer diagrams

➡ *Pupil's Book page 79*

Sankey diagrams are introduced as a useful way of representing energy transfers. Note that the width of the arrow gives a measure of the relative amounts of energy transferred.

Answers

➡ *Pupil's Book pages 79–80*

5 Candle burning:

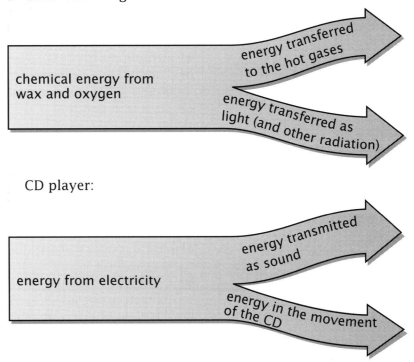

CD player:

There is energy in the movement of the CD, but note that after the initial transfer the only energy transfer is heat/friction in the bearings.

6 There are four suggestions in the Pupils' Book for energy transfer processes (page 80), and teachers will no doubt have their own activities to add to the list. You may prefer pupils to work in groups on a circus of some of these activities. Activities to beware of are those involving steady motion, such as a car moving at a steady speed (as the kinetic energy remains constant, any energy transfer is to the environment due to friction and air resistance).

  a) The balloon is pushed along the string.

  b) The force of air coming out of the small opening, because of greater air pressure in the balloon.

  c) Balloon:

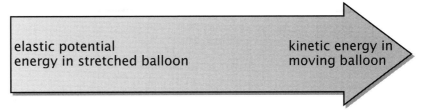

a) Clock is 'powered' by potatoes.

b) Potential difference created by ions in 'potato juice' connected to the leads causes current to flow and run the clock.

c) Potato clock:

a) Athlete pulls chest expander outwards.

b) Energy from respiration in arm muscle cells creates force which stretches chest expander.

c) Muscle expander:

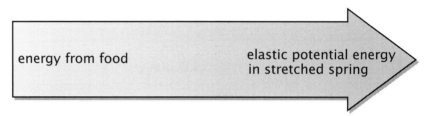

a) Bright, white light and large heat output from burning magnesium.

b) Chemical energy released as magnesium reacts with oxygen in the air.

c) Burning magnesium ribbon:

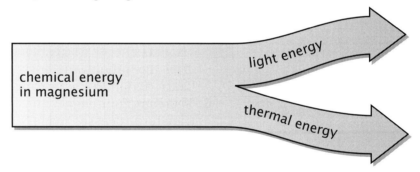

Activity

| Worksheet 3.1R |

Consolidation: Problems on energy

→ *Worksheet 3.1R: Problems on energy (S)*

Answers

1 Joule.

2

Input	Device	Output
energy from wax (candle)	candle	energy as light and heat
energy from petrol (chemical)	car	energy as movement, heat and sound
energy in chemicals	match	energy as light and heat
energy as electricity	hairdryer	energy as movement inside the hairdryer, heat and sound
energy stored in stretched rubber	catapult	energy as movement
energy as moving particles	hot air balloon	energy as movement and potential

Check pupils' Sankey diagrams.

3 *Conservation of energy, power*

Learning outcomes

Pupils:

- distinguish between useful energy and dissipated energy
- realise that when energy is transferred, the total amount of energy before and after remains the same
- recognise that the rate of transfer of energy is called power
- recognise that for a given state of matter, the increase in the temperature of the substance is associated with an increase in the kinetic energy of the particles

Conservation of energy

→ *Pupil's Book page 81*

Conservation of energy and energy dissipation are introduced through the use of a Sankey diagram representing the energy transfers in an electric kettle, and by the use of an analogy about money. This money analogy is further used to explain the difference between energy and power.

The 'Time to think' activity provides opportunity for pupils to discuss and consolidate their ideas here, and for teachers to listen out for any misconceptions that they may need to address at this point or later in the topic.

Energy and power
Answers
→ *Pupil's Book page 82*
7 50 hours.
8 10 hours.
9 a) Revlon, because it has the highest wattage.
   b) Pupils must be able to justify their reason.
   c) No. Vidal Sassoon and Babyliss are more expensive.
   d) Babyliss uses 1.2 kJ per second. So in 20 minutes it uses $1.2 \times 20 \times 20 = 1440$ kJ.

Activity Consolidation: Numerical problems on power
→ *Worksheet 3.2R: Numerical problems on power (S)*

Worksheet 3.2R

Answers
1 Watt.
2 Power = energy/time.
3 Electric toaster – Time = 120 seconds = 2 minutes.
Light bulb – Energy = 216 000 joules.
TV – Time = 7200 seconds = 120 minutes = 2 hours.
Kettle – Energy = 288 000 joules.
4 Kettle.
5 Portable TV.

Attainment targets
Work in the previous sections should provide evidence that pupils are working towards the following attainment levels.

Use abstract ideas in some descriptions and explanations, such as energy transfer in electric circuits	Level 6
Perform calculations to determine power, using correct units	Level 7
Relate dissipation of energy within ideas of conservation of energy	Level 8

Activity Information processing: Power ratings
→ *Pupil's Book page 83*
The list provided shows a wide range of power ratings, and this will require the pupils to give careful thought as to the best way of representing the data. They should identify the difficulty of using bar graphs and pie charts with such a wide range of values.

Activity Information processing: Comparing electrical appliances
→ *Worksheet 3.3R: Comparing electrical appliances (K)*

Worksheet 3.3R

This worksheet allows pupils to sort and rank data, and present it as a chart. Pupils can enter the data into a spreadsheet and use this to produce the chart.

Energy at a particle level
➡ *Pupil's Book page 83*

Answers
10 a) Heating the liquid causes the kinetic energy of the particles to increase, and the temperature rises until the liquid reaches its boiling point.

b) When ice melts, energy is required to rearrange the particles and overcome the forces of attraction. The kinetic energy of the particles does not change; the temperature remains constant but the potential energy of the particles increases.

c) The average speed of the particles is related to the temperature of the gas. However, individual particles may have more or less than the average speed.

d), e) An increase in the temperature of the air particles inside the tin can on heating results in them moving faster and so hitting the sides of the can more often, resulting in an increase in the pressure of the air inside the can.

Discussion of the pupils' statements will allow you to judge how accurately they can articulate the ideas of energy at a particle level, and it is an opportunity to reveal misconceptions.

4 *Electrical energy, power consumption, efficiency*

Learning outcomes
Pupils:

- recognise that electricity is a useful means of transforming energy
- give examples of some devices that use energy at a greater rate than others, for example, heating appliances transfer more energy than others
- give an example of their own use of an electrical appliance that has to be paid for
- contribute to planning and carrying out a survey of energy use of household devices
- relate use of electricity to energy supply in everyday situations/devices
- communicate data effectively through writing a coherent text

A useful interactive website with information on the different electrical devices in the home and how they affect your electricity bill can be found at:

www.article19.com/shockwave/ph.htm

Electricity
Answers
➡ *Pupil's Book pages 84–86*

11 a) Loudspeaker, radio etc.
   b) Electric fan.
   c) Electric hob, microwave oven.
12 Pupils are asked to produce their own table of different power ratings for a range of devices. Worksheet 3.3R suggests a range of devices. Alternatively, various items could be provided in the laboratory.
13 Taking this work a step further, pupils are asked to estimate the time for which various devices are used during a week. Pupils may have a range of appropriate answers here.

The kilowatt-hour is introduced as another unit for calculating energy used, and pupils calculate the cost of the devices they have selected. This is much easier to perform if a spreadsheet is used, and a possible template is provided for this activity on the CD-ROM.

14 3.5 kWh per day, so $7 \times 3.5 = 24.5$ units in a week.
15 1178 kWh – calculated by subtracting the previous reading from the present reading.
16 9 pence for the first 224 kWh and 5.410 pence for the rest.
17 The discount (deduction) when a household purchases electricity and gas from the same provider.
18 Pupils extend their tables or spreadsheets started in Question 13. There will be a range of answers to the previous question.

Power and efficiency
➡ *Pupil's Book page 86*
This section introduces calculations on efficiency.

Answers
➡ *Pupil's Book page 86*
19 390 000 J (2000 watts $\times$ 195 seconds).
20 Warms the kettle and the surroundings.
21 9.2% (36 000/390 000 $\times$ 100%).
22 Pupils should give a clear explanation. Filling the kettle completely means you are using energy to heat water that is not used; the limescale makes it more difficult for heat to reach the water so it takes more energy for the water to boil.

Activity

| Worksheet 3.4R |

Information processing: Electricity bills
➡ *Worksheet 3.4R: Electricity bills (S)*
This worksheet helps pupils interrogate a recent electricity bill and perform some calculations to work out costs for electricity. As well as familiarising them with bills, it also asks them to consider how electricity consumption can be reduced.

Time to think
Answers

→ *Pupil's Book page 87*

- The scientific unit of energy is the <u>joule</u>.
- The scientific unit of power is the <u>watt</u>.
- The kilowatt-hour is sometimes used to measure <u>energy</u>.
- The formula $\dfrac{\text{energy transferred}}{\text{time taken}}$ calculates <u>power</u>.
- In SI units, kilo means multiply the basic unit by <u>1000</u>.
- The formula $\dfrac{\text{useful energy}}{\text{total energy}} \times 100\%$ calculates <u>efficiency</u>.
- In SI units, mega means multiply the basic unit by a <u>million</u>.
- In household electricity bills, the consumption is measured in kilowatt-hours (kWh). This is often called a <u>unit</u>.
- When a 2 kW kettle is used for 2 hours, the number of units it will use is <u>4</u>.

There are a number of websites which compare the cost of electricity from different suppliers, for example:

www.uswitch.com/energy/index.asp?ref=timesmoney

Data could be provided for the pupils or they could enter their own information.

5 *Measuring voltage, the volt*

Learning outcomes
Pupils:

- describe current as not being used up in a circuit and as dividing along the different branches in a parallel circuit
- identify that an ammeter measures the flow of current
- use a voltmeter correctly
- draw conclusions from trends in numerical data about the way voltage varies around a circuit
- use a simple model to describe the link between voltage and energy in a circuit
- describe energy transformation from a cell/battery to a circuit

Revision of current and voltage

→ *Pupil's Book page 87*

This first section revises and checks the pupils' understanding of series and parallel circuits, and the use of a voltmeter.

You may want pupils to set up similar circuits themselves. Alternatively teachers may wish to demonstrate some of the circuits using appropriate software such as 'Crocodile Clips'.

Please note that the circuit diagram in Question 29 (page 90) is wrong in the first printing of the Pupil's Book. See the following answer.

Answers

→ *Pupil's Book pages 87–89*

23 A = series circuit, B = parallel circuit.

24 In series.

25 In parallel.

26 a) 0.2 A
   b) 3.0 V (assuming all cells are identical)
   c) 4.5 V
   d) 1.5 V (assuming all lamps are identical)
   e) 1.5 V

27 Pupils will come up with different rules, but they must be able to justify them. There is the opportunity here to listen for misconceptions that need to be dealt with.

28 a) 1, 2 = voltmeters, 3 = ammeter
   b) Off.
   c) Meter 1 = 3.0 V; meter 2 = 0 V; meter 3 = 0 A.
   d) On.
   e) Meter 1 = 3.0 V; meter 2 = 3.0 V; the reading on meter 3 is now non-zero.

PLEASE NOTE

29 a) If your pupils are using the first printing of the Pupils Book, the diagram for Question 29 on page 90 has a lower branch to the circuit containing only a meter, 5. Please ask your pupils to:
   • delete the lower branch of the circuit with meter 5
   • change the position of meter 4 so that it is connected across the lamp (as meter 2 and 3)
   • change part f) of the question to ask for the readings on meters 2, 3, and 4 (see diagram to the left)
   • delete the question about meter 5 in part g).

The publishers apologise for these errors which will be corrected in subsequent printings of the Pupil's Book. The answers are then as follows.
   b) 1 = ammeter; 2, 3, 4 = voltmeters.
   c) All lamps are off.
   d) The two lamps in series are on; the lamp below in parallel is off.
   e) All meters read zero.
   f) Meter 2 = 1.5 V; meter 3 = 1.5 V; meter 4 reads zero.
   g) Meter 2 = 1.5 V; meter 4 = 3.0 V.

Activity Evaluation: Using a voltmeter

→ *Pupil's Book page 91*

This activity provides three alternative sets of readings from an experiment to determine the value of an unknown resistor. Pupils are able to use the relevant data to draw conclusions and describe the relationships obtained. They can consider the relative merits of the approaches, and suggest improvements on the methods used.

Answers

1 The resistance of the unknown resistor X.

2 Any sensible and relevant title.

3 The value of the resistor.

4 The reading on the voltmeter.

5 For each circuit the ratio of the resistors is the same as the ratio of the voltages.

6 In the circuit with resistor X, X/100 = 1.8/1.2, so X = 150 ohm.

Activity

Worksheet 3.5R

Review: Electricity word quiz

➡ *Worksheet 3.5R: Electricity crossword (R)*

Pupils are asked to come up with clues for the answers on the crossword. This allows you to check their understanding and use of electricity terms and units.

Attainment targets

Work in the previous sections should provide evidence that pupils are working towards the following attainment levels.

Recognise which lamps are on or off in circuits with one or more switches	Level 4
Use quantitative reasoning to decide on pd and work out current in a circuit	Level 7

6 *Electrical hazards*

Learning outcomes

Pupils:

- relate the energy transfer in a circuit to both current and voltage
- give a reasoned report associating the use/hazards of high voltage with energy transfer

This would be a useful point to include work on reactivity. The worksheet 'Fruit and vegetable batteries' from Chapter 9 could be used here.

Voltage and energy

Answers

➡ *Pupil's Book page 93*

30 Lamps = building sites; current = lorries; wire = roads.

31 Pupils use and evaluate their own models.

Usefulness and hazards of high voltage

➡ *Pupil's Book pages 93–96*

In this section it is important to emphasise the hazards associated with high voltages.

Teachers may wish to demonstrate the activity on page 93 by connecting increasing numbers of batteries to the simple series circuit containing a bulb and a voltmeter. Similarly they may demonstrate the activity illustrated on page 95 – using the multimeter to measure resistance. This could be made into a quick class experiment if sufficient digital multimeters are available. Most pupils should be able to relate the experiment to the use of a lie detector (Question 33).

Teachers could explain the 'μ' symbol in the diagram on page 94.

Safety
• Warning! Pupils must **not** experiment with mains electricity.

This passage goes into some detail about the effects on the body of currents of different magnitude. Pupils are asked to choose one of a number of alternative approaches to demonstrate their understanding of the material.

Answers
→ *Pupil's Book pages 94–95*
32 The lamp would probably blow.
33 a) You may feel hot and sweat; face may go red as you blush.
  b) Sweat could change the resistance of your skin.
  c) It could be used to set up a lie detector.

Activity ## Creative thinking: Electricity
→ *Pupil's Book page 96*
The pupils' cartoon strips can be used to indicate how well they have understood issues of electrical safety.

7 *Generating electricity*

Learning outcomes
Pupils:

• identify a range of energy resources used to generate electricity
• describe a simple electrical generator
• understand the transmission of mains electricity

Transmitting electricity
→ *Pupil's Book page 97*
This is a good opportunity to reinforce the dangers associated with the very high voltages of the National Grid and transformers in electricity sub-stations.

The reason for generating electricity at high voltages can be demonstrated by using a model with step-up and step-down transformers, but the voltages involved must be low: of the order of 1.5 V, stepped up to 24 V.

Activity ## Reasoning: Transmitting electricity
→ *Pupil's Book page 97*
Pupils' questions can be used to test their understanding of electricity transmission. Examples of good questions are:

What voltage is mains electricity produced at?
What is the mains electricity voltage in our homes?
How is the mains voltage reduced to 230 volts?
What type of transformer reduces the voltage?
Why is it cheaper to transfer electricity at very high voltages?

Electricity generation

→ *Pupil's Book page 98*

The generation of electricity can be demonstrated if schools have suitable equipment, for example a bicycle-type generator or one like that pictured in the 'Ideas and evidence' passage on page 98. Other possibilities include using a water wheel or windmill to turn an electric motor acting as a generator; using a model steam engine to drive the generator; or demonstrating the action of a solar cell in producing electricity directly from the Sun.

Activity ## Information processing: Power station

→ *Pupil's Book page 99*

The activity described in the Pupils' Book requires pupils to draw a block diagram and explain the action of a coal-fired power station. This could be done as a poster, a PowerPoint presentation or a drawing in their exercise books.

A useful research activity would be to ask pupils to do a similar activity for a pumped storage hydroelectric power station.

Activity ## Creative thinking: A world with no electricity

→ *Pupil's Book page 99*

This activity allows pupils to produce some imaginative writing at the same time as demonstrating their scientific understanding. As a whole class, pupils could discuss and decide on the criteria for a good answer. Using these criteria, allow pupils to peer assess.

8 *Our energy future*

Learning outcomes

Pupils:

* present a considered viewpoint based on information from secondary sources, for example, identify the problems of pollution associated with electricity generation by fossil fuels, and the environmental impact of renewable and nuclear energy sources

Activity ## Research: Alternative energy sources

→ *Pupil's Book page 100*

There is an opportunity here for a 'jigsaw' type activity with groups of pupils researching different ways of generating electricity and then sharing their findings.

There are many websites that cover this topic. As websites often change, it is recommended that they are checked prior to the lesson. One useful website is:

www.knowledgehound.com/topics/altenerg.htm

'Electricity for the Future' is part of Channel 4's science resources, and information is available at:

www.channel4.com/learning/main/netnotes/ sectionid100663644.htm

A spreadsheet activity linked to the production of CO_2 can be found on the CD-ROM (Carbon dioxide and global warming).

Activity

Worksheet 3.6R

Review: Electricity generation

➡ *Worksheet 3.6R: Electricity generation (R)*
This worksheet can be used to find out how much pupils remember from work they have done on renewable and non-renewable sources of electricity.

Activity

Enquiry: Solar energy

➡ *Pupil's Book page 101*
Model solar panels can either be constructed or purchased. Solar cells are readily available in school science catalogues and electronics catalogues. This activity could be done as a full investigation or as a planning activity.

Attainment targets
The planning and the full investigation should provide evidence that pupils are working towards the following attainment levels.

Select suitable equipment and be able to recognise the main variables; vary one factor while keeping the rest the same	Level 4
Select equipment from a range and decide on measurements to be taken, including repeat measurements; record measurements systematically in a table; plot graphs and describe the relationship; suggest improvements to methods	Level 5
Use scientific knowledge and understanding to identify the appropriate approach; plan sufficient measurements and repeats for the task; use fine scale on a thermometer accurately; select appropriate scales to plot graphs and describe the relationship; give reasoned suggestions and alternatives to method	Level 6
Identify where repeat measurements need to be made; draw appropriate line graphs with lines of best fit; begin to question the reliability of data and conclusions	Level 7
Identify and explain anomalous readings and allow for these in line graphs; critically reflect on graphs and look at strength of conclusion	Level 8

Time to think

➡ *Pupil's Book page 101*
The concept map may be drawn again so that pupils can compare their knowledge and understanding at the end of the topic with that at the start. The worksheets for this chapter, if not already completed, provide a number of questions that will help pupils with revision and reinforcement, and further questions can be found on the CD-ROM.

Activity

Worksheet 3.7R

Review: Test on energy and electricity

→ *Worksheet 3.7R: Test on energy and electricity (R)*

Answers

1 a) Radio – sound and heat.
Car – chemical energy.
Candle – chemical energy → heat and light. (4 marks)

   b) Sankey diagrams show the proportion of energy input
and output. (1 mark)

2 a) Energy. (1 mark)

   b) Power. (1 mark)

   c) Electricity power consumption. (1 mark)

3 a) Energy transferred. (1 mark)

   b) Power. (1 mark)

   c) $1.5 \times 4 \times 60 = 360$ kilojoules (2 marks)

4 $2 \times 1.5 = 3$ units (2 marks)

5 In series, using crocodile clips/leads. (2 marks)

6 a) Reduce the current. (1 mark)

   b) Ohm. (1 mark)

7 Reduce high voltage to lower voltage. (2 marks)

4 Forces and space

→ Rationale

This chapter provides approximately 9 hours of teaching materials, and it covers the work in two of the units in the QCA Scheme of Work. These are Unit 9J Gravity and space, and Unit 9K Speeding up. It builds on Unit 7K Forces and their effects, and Unit 7L The Solar System and beyond. There is further work on forces in Chapter 8 Pressure and moments. It lays the foundation for work in Key Stage 4 on theories about the nature and evolution of the Universe. The historical impact of discoveries in astronomy is covered in Unit 21 Scientific discoveries, in the History Scheme of Work.

There are five key ideas underpinning the Key Stage 3 Science Programme of Study and one of these is forces. Some of the difficulties of teaching forces are referred to in *Thinking Through Science Teacher's Book 1*, Chapter 6 Forces and their effects. This chapter aims to further build on the ideas introduced in Year 7, and to develop and clarify pupils' understanding of the terms. Pupils should by now be familiar with the idea of balanced forces in static situations. They should also be able to label forces on a diagram to show their direction and magnitude. They should begin to draw free body diagrams, such as the example of a sky diver, to emphasise the forces acting on the body. They will be familiar with measuring forces and know the units used.

This chapter links the ideas of forces as seen on the Earth with the application of these concepts to the motion of celestial bodies, satellites and rockets. Towards the end of the chapter we look at measurement of speed and acceleration. Finally we look at terminal velocity and air resistance and link back to space exploration, with specific reference to the recent space shuttle Columbia disaster.

In this chapter there is a section that considers the conflicting theories and ideas associated with the motion of the Earth and other planets. We also look at modern theories about how the Universe began.

→ Overview

The textbook sections, activities and worksheets have been arranged into 1 hour blocks to aid lesson planning. Clearly several of the activities and worksheets could form part of a homework session. The planning includes reading time for individual sections but some teachers may prefer to organise this as homework preparation for the following lesson. Six types of worksheet – extension (E), support for an activity (S), practical (P), key skills (K), developmental (D) and review (R) – allow for differentiation and flexibility to accommodate teachers' preferred practice. There is sufficient material for at least 9 hours of teaching. The actual timing and emphasis on different sections will depend on the current knowledge base of the pupils, the ability of the teaching group and the preferences of the teacher. For example, the contents of lessons 3, 4 and 5 may be changed depending on the availability of, and ease of access to, the internet. This topic, more than most, has many opportunities for effective use of the internet. There are many sites for children, such as:

http://amazing-space.stsci.edu/

http://sciencemonster.com/gravity_inertia.html

This is a game to land a craft on the Moon or Mars.

www.scienceyear.com/wired/index.html?page=/planet10/

This website provides 3D animations of the Solar System, with the ability to zoom in and out.

www.hq.nasa.gov/office/pao/History/alsj/a15/
a15v.1672206.mov

Lesson	Worksheets
1 What do you know?	Worksheet 4.1R: Planets and gravity (R) Worksheet 4.2R: Losing and gaining weight (R)
2 More gravity	
3 Space exploration	Worksheet 4.3R: The Apollo 11 journey to the Moon (S)
4 How ideas change over time	
5 Introduction to satellites and rockets	
6 Artificial satellites	Worksheet 4.4R: Satellite motion (S)
7 Measuring speed and interpreting graphs	Worksheet 4.5R: Speedy questions (S)
8 Investigating air resistance	Worksheet 4.6R: Investigation of air resistance (P)
Review	Worksheet 4.7R: Test on forces and space (R)

→ *Chapter plan*

	Demonstration	Practical	ICT	Activity	Word play	Time to think	Ideas and evidence
Lesson 1			Internet research	Reasoning: Definitions Enquiry: Mars experiment Review: Planets and gravity Consolidation: Losing and gaining weight		What do you know?	
Lesson 2			Use of a spreadsheet	Evaluation: Gravity Reasoning: A conundrum Reasoning: Living in space		Review of work so far	Falling under gravity
Lesson 3			Internet research	Reasoning: Counting the cost Research: Space exploration Information processing: The Apollo II journey to the Moon			
Lesson 4			Internet research	Creative thinking: Starburst Research: Biography			
Lesson 5 and 6	Circular motion Weightlessness Rockets		Use of a spreadsheet	Evaluation: GPS Information processing: Artificial satellites Reasoning: Motion of satellites Evaluation: Model movement	Rhyming lyrics		
Lesson 7	Air-cushioned and air friction	Measuring speed using light gates	Use of a spreadsheet Use of light gates with computer interface	Consolidation: Speed Information processing: Looking for patterns Enquiry: Measuring the speed of a trolley down a slope			
Lesson 8		Investigation: Air resistance	Internet research	Research: Concorde			
Review				Test on forces and space		Review of chapter	

→ *Expectations*

At the end of this chapter

in terms of scientific enquiry (Gravity and space)

most pupils will: use a model of gravitational attraction to explain orbiting; describe how ideas of the nature of the Solar System have changed over time and relate these to available evidence; make effective use of secondary sources to find information from recent space exploration about the nature of the Solar System

some pupils will have progressed further and will:
explain how experimental evidence has led to changes over time in models of the Solar System; evaluate recent information and ideas about the origin of the Moon

in terms of scientific enquiry (Speeding up)

most pupils will: measure the speed of moving objects in the laboratory using a datalogger; describe patterns in data and use these to make predictions and check them; recognise that different degrees of precision are required for measuring speed in different contexts; interpret distance–time graphs of falling objects and relate these to the forces acting on objects; present a report, based on secondary sources, on an aspect of the development of faster vehicles

some pupils will have progressed further and will:
describe non-linear relationships between speed and distance travelled; justify appropriate levels of precision in measuring speed; interpret speed–time graphs of falling objects; explain how technological development contributed to faster travel

in terms of physical processes (Gravity and space)

most pupils will: recognise that gravity is a universal force of attraction between objects and that this force depends on their masses and distance apart; describe how weight is different on different planets; give examples of the use of artificial satellites

some pupils will have progressed further and will: use data to compare gravity on different planets; describe how forces on rockets or satellites vary as they travel away from the Earth

in terms of physical processes (Speeding up)

most pupils will: manipulate and apply the relationship between speed, distance and time; relate forces acting on an object to its movement; describe how streamlining reduces resistance to air and water and how this resistance increases with the speed of the object, and relate this to the particle model; apply ideas of unbalanced and balanced forces to falling objects

some pupils will have progressed further and will: use the definition of speed in calculations and conversions from different units; relate change in movement of an object to its mass and the forces acting upon it; explain increased air resistance with the speed of an object, using the particle theory

→ # *Links with CASE*

Data on the planets of the Solar System allow pupils to revisit ideas of proportionality and of classification.

Pupils are asked to look at relationships between variables that include inverse (square) relationships. They also look at the use of different models to explain how the Universe began.

→ *Pupils' misconceptions*

Misconception	Scientific understanding
The Earth is stationary.	The Earth moves around the Sun once a year.
The Earth is flat.	The Earth is spherical and we live on its surface.
The Sun moves around the Earth once a day.	The Earth rotates on its axis (spins) once every 24 hours.
The Sun and Moon move around the Earth.	The Moon orbits the Earth. The Earth (and Moon) orbit the Sun.
The Earth is the biggest astronomical object. The Moon and the Sun are about the same size. Stars are very small.	The stars (including our star, the Sun) are much larger than the planets, including Earth, which is larger than the Moon.
The Moon has no gravity, planets with thin atmospheres have little gravity, planets distant from the Sun have less gravity. Gravity is stronger between the most distant objects.	Two factors determine the magnitude of the gravitational force between two objects: their mass and the distance between them.
When a moving object stops, it runs out of force.	There is a clear distinction between force and energy.
Pupils often only consider one of a pair of forces.	Action and reaction act at the same time on different objects.
When something is moving at a steady speed there is a steady force acting on it.	No resultant force is needed to keep an object moving at a steady speed.
Friction acts all the time.	If an object is at rest, the forces acting on it must be balanced.
The words weight and mass can be interchanged.	Weight is the force of gravity on an object and is measured in newtons.
Space shuttle astronauts are weightless because there is no gravity above Earth.	Astronauts in a space shuttle only appear weightless because they are in free fall around the Earth.

→ *Literacy, numeracy and other cross-curricular links*

There are many opportunities in this chapter to encourage pupils to read and to extract information from a variety of sources. This includes an extract from the magazine *Wireless World* printed in 1945, as well as other articles and information from the internet. Pupils develop their speaking skills through small group discussion, and there is an opportunity to write in a range of styles including writing a biography, a newspaper article and translating information from an article into a table.

Numeracy is developed through a range of calculations, and through plotting and interpreting graphs.

Language for learning
By the end of this chapter pupils will be able to understand, use and spell correctly:

- words with similar but distinct meanings – for example, mass, weight, gravitational attraction, orbit, revolve
- words relating to planetary motion – for example, satellite

- words relating to measurement – for example, accuracy, precision
- words for describing the relationship between variables – for example, proportional
- words and phrases relating to movement – for example, constant speed, acceleration

Through the activities pupils will develop their skills in:

- understanding the effect of different aspects of formality (passive verbs, third person, abstract nouns)
- solving problems, considering alternatives, structuring plans and organising group activity.

1 *What do you know?*

Learning outcomes

Pupils:

- state that a ball dropped anywhere on the Earth will fall towards the centre of the planet
- state that the Earth exerts a force which pulls on everything, and that this pull is called the force of gravity or weight
- know that the force of gravity is greater on objects with a bigger mass
- understand that the gravitational force between two masses gets less with distance

What do you know?

➡ *Pupil's Book page 102*

This initial activity provides an opportunity for pupils to discuss and refresh their knowledge on space and gravity. It will help teachers to discover pupils' prior ideas, such as whether pupils have an awareness of an Earth-referenced 'down' or still consider 'down' as absolute (as in a flat Earth situation). Some children associate gravity only with the Earth, and think that without atmosphere pressing down there is no gravity. Many pupils may still hold the Earth-centred model of the Solar System, and many will think that heavy objects fall faster than light objects.

Gravity

➡ *Pupil's Book page 104*

Answer

1 Mass; force; weight; matter; force; gravity; weightless; force/upthrust.

Did you know?

➡ *Pupil's Book page 105*

This is an opportunity for teachers to reinforce the SI units used in science, and in particular to deal with the correct use of the term 'mass' and the kilogram as the SI unit of mass.

Activity Reasoning: Definitions
→ *Pupil's Book page 105*

Answer
Mass – 2; Weight – 3; Force – 1; Load – 4.

A key scientific idea
→ *Pupil's Book page 106*

Answers
2, 3 The force is great over a small distance but then quickly drops to very low over a large distance. In discussing the shape of the force–distance graph pupils should be clear that this is an inverse relationship (compensation for CASE teachers). Teachers would probably want to explain that it is an inverse square relationship only with the most able groups.
4 60 N (i.e. mass × force per kg).
5 Their mass is still 6 kg, but their weight is one-sixth that on earth, so 10 N.

Activity Enquiry: Mars experiment
→ *Pupil's Book page 107*
Again the relationship between mass and weight can be discussed so that pupils become more familiar with using the correct scientific terminology appropriately. Similarly, both analysing by graphing and looking for relationships can be checked from the extent and accuracy of answers.

Answers
1

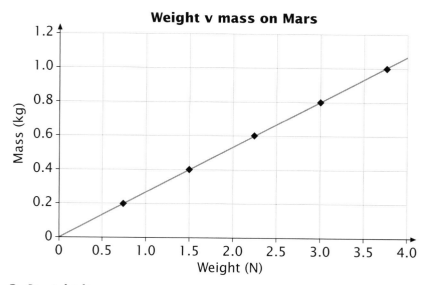

2 Straight line.
3 3.73 N if read from the graph; 3.7 N if read from the table.
4 1.87 N
5 1.6 kg
6 On Mars the gravitational pull is about one-third of that on Earth. The planets have different diameters and different masses.
7 135 N

Activity

Worksheet 4.1R

Review: Planets and gravity

➡ *Worksheet 4.1R: Planets and gravity (R)*

This activity helps pupils to articulate their ideas and misconceptions about gravity and planets. By considering data on a variety of ideas their paragraph should state that gravitational pull depends on the mass of the two objects involved and the distance between them. Useful websites to consult are:

www.exploratorium.edu/ronh/weight/index.html

to calculate your weight on different planets, and

http://kids.nineplanets.org

which provides further information to prove or disprove the hypotheses on the worksheet.

You will also need access to the internet to view the following video clips, in this lesson or later:

www.nasm.si.edu/collections/imagery/apollo/AS17/a17av.htm

www.hq.nasa.gov/office/pao/History/40thann/videos.htm

Activity

Worksheet 4.2R

Consolidation: Losing and gaining weight

➡ *Worksheet 4.2R: Losing and gaining weight (S)*

This follow-up activity will help to reinforce ideas developed and challenged by Worksheet 4.1R. It would provide a good reflective homework activity.

2 *More gravity*

Learning outcomes

Pupils:

- explain that falling objects get faster as they fall
- explain that the rate at which objects fall (at a given place) is the same for all objects, irrespective of their mass
- describe why objects have different weights on different planets compared to on the Earth

The following video clip could be viewed now:

www.hq.nasa.gov/office/pao/History/40thann/videos.htm

This website was set up with a selection of audio and video clips to celebrate NASA's 40th anniversary. Teachers may wish to select the clips and download them prior to the lesson. They are about 2–4 MB in size, depending on their length.

Gravity on different planets

➡ *Pupil's Book page 107*

Answer

6 An example of a possible simple Excel spreadsheet is provided on the CD-ROM.
The following websites allow pupils to find their weight on different planets.

http://btc.montana.edu/ceres/html/Weight/weight1.htm

www.schoolsobservatory.org.uk/study/math/weight/sswgt_rm.htm

http://starchild.gsfc.nasa.gov/docs/StarChild/solar_system_level2/planet_hop.html

Ideas and evidence: Falling under gravity

➥ *Pupil's Book pages 108–109*

This passage may prove demanding for some pupils, but is nevertheless important as it shows the changing ideas of the scientific method. Discussion groups will help pupils make sense of this section and provide valuable evidence for teachers to listen into and decide on the amount of support needed for the next few activites.

David Scott repeated the famous guinea and feather experiment on the Moon, and a video clip of this is available at:

http://nssdc.gsfc.nasa.gov/planetary/lunar/apollo_15_feather_drop.html

Activity Evaluation: Gravity

➥ *Pupil's Book page 110*

The discussion within the group should help to establish whether pupils have understood the concept of a scientific explanation.

Activity Reasoning: A conundrum

➥ *Pupil's Book page 110*

The discussion and any additions to the cartoon should help to establish how clearly pupils have understood Galileo's ideas.

Time to think

➥ *Pupil's Book page 111*

This is a review of the work in the chapter so far.

Answers

1 Aristotle, 384BC–322BC
Copernicus, 1473–1543
Galileo, 1564–1642
Newton, 1642–1727

3 Telescope, which he used for astronomy.

4 Galileo wanted scientists to be able to given an explanation of the reason why something happened, not just give it a name. He also used maths to describe natural phenomena.

5 The effect of gravity was 'diluted'.

6 He tried to reduce the effects of other variables.

Activity Reasoning: Living in space

➥ *Pupil's Book page 114*

Pupils can work in groups to discuss these questions.

3 *Space exploration*

Learning outcomes
Pupils:

- present an argument for continuing space research
- extract relevant information from the internet
- describe some of the landmarks of exploration of space, for example, Yuri Gagarin, Valentina Tereshkova, Neil Armstrong, Helen Sharman, Hubble space telescope, Galileo probe

Note that both this lesson and the next use the internet for research purposes. The two lessons need to be planned together, so that the facilities available are utilised most effectively.

Experimenting in space
➡ *Pupil's Book page 114*

Answers
➡ *Pupil's Book page 115*

7 At high speed, the shuttle encounters more air particles as it descends into our atmosphere. The shuttle collides with these air particles and they begin to slow it down and also heat it.

8 At entry the space shuttle is moving at 27000 km/h. Much of the kinetic and potential energy possessed by the shuttle is converted into heat on re-entry.

Activity ## Reasoning: Counting the cost
➡ *Pupil's Book page 115*

Pupils should present a well-reasoned argument with evidence to back up their ideas. They should be encouraged to look at advances that have resulted from space exploration (for example, Teflon coating on pans) and those as a result of space research (for example, satellite communication) rather than emotive arguments.

Activity ## Research: Space exploration
➡ *Pupil's Book page 114*

This research activity directs pupils to particular events in the history of space exploration, and pupils should be encouraged to give clear justifications for their answers. Pupils could be given one or more questions to research and then share these in a larger group. This activity could provide opportunities for pupils to develop ideas about what constitutes a 'quality' answer and a 'quality' poster, using either peer assessment and/or deciding on criteria for successfully completing the task.

This work requires access to the internet. Pupils should be encouraged to add additional dates and events to the ones suggested. There are many sites on this topic, including:

www.connected-earth.com/Journeys/Telecommunicationsage/Satelliteandmicrowave/Intospace/intospace.htm

www.solarviews.com/eng/history.htm

www.geocities.com/CapeCanaveral/Launchpad/4515/HISTORY.html#BG

Answers

1 Charles Conrad, 1969.
2 She was the first British person in space. She spent eight days on the Mir Space Station in May 1991.
3 Escape velocity is the speed needed to escape the Earth's gravitational pull, assuming that the object has no thrust of its own.
4 It is a comet. It is sometimes written as Shoemaker-Levy 9. It was discovered in 1993 and subsequently broke into fragments, which collided with Jupiter.
5 The Galileo spacecraft to Jupiter was launched on 18th October, 1989 by the space shuttle Atlantis. It reached Jupiter at the end of 1995 and its 14-year journey came to an end on 21st September 2003 when it disintegrated in Jupiter's atmosphere.

Activity

Worksheet 4.3R

Information processing: The Apollo 11 journey to the Moon

→ *Worksheet 4.3R: The Apollo 11 journey to the Moon (S)*
This sequencing activity helps pupils put events relating to space exploration in order.

Attainment targets
Work in the previous sections should provide evidence that pupils are working towards the following attainment levels.

Use simple models to explain day length and seasons	Level 5
Give explanations of factors affecting gravitational force and use data to support or refute ideas	Level 6
Apply abstract ideas in explaining why weight differs on different planets	Level 7
Explain and use patterns in data to argue ideas in explaining the role of gravitational attraction in determining the motion of bodies in the Solar System	Level 8

4 *How ideas change over time*

Learning outcomes
Pupils:

- describe an early model of the Solar System and how it differs from our present model
- argue a point of view in defence of a model of the Solar System, providing evidence for their position
- use more formal language in their summary, for example passive verbs, third person

The earlier references to the work of Galileo have already given examples of the changing models of the Solar System. This section extends this and considers more recent ideas about how the Universe began.

This website is useful for teachers:

www.damtp.cam.ac.uk/user/gr/public/bb_pillars.html

To get a feel for the immense size of the Universe, the 'Powers of Ten' video which was mentioned in Book 1 is worth another look, or the internet version which can be found at:

http://micro.magnet.fsu.edu/primer/java/scienceopticsu/powersof10/index.html

The following website is also useful:

www.kidsastronomy.com/space_size.htm

Activity ## Creative thinking: Starburst
➡ *Pupil's Book Page 117*

Pupils can use their imagination for this activity, but they should show some understanding of the energy we receive from the Sun. Peer assessment would be useful here to identify scientific accuracy as well as amount of interest in the final product.

Modelling the Big Bang
➡ *Pupil's Book page 118*

Answers

 9 Cake mixture – space between the stars; fruit – stars.
 10 Continue to expand forever, or begin to contract back.
 11 It could reach a steady state and stop expanding.

Activity ## Research: Biography
➡ *Pupil's Book page 118*

A starter website for famous names in astronomy is:

www.geocities.com/CapeCanaveral/Launchpad/4515/HISTORY.html#BG

The following website contains an alphabetical list of astronomers:

www.allaboutspace.com/subjects/astronomy/glossary/Astronomers.shtml

Extension

Here pupils have an opportunity to write for a different audience. A magazine article is suggested, but other approaches could be adopted such as a producing a web page or a PowerPoint presentation.

At the end of this session, there may be time to give a taster of the next lesson by performing one of the demonstrations.

5 *and* 6 *Satellites*

Learning outcomes
Pupils:

- state that the Moon is a natural satellite of the Earth, kept in orbit by the Earth's gravitational pull
- describe some uses of artificial satellites, for example to assist weather forecasting, TV transmissions

- explain why some satellites need to be in geostationary orbits
- describe how satellite probes provide information about the Solar System and how this information is used

This lesson has been scheduled as a double session because it requires pupils to research, discuss ideas and witness some observations, which will lead to further discussion. The order in which these are attempted will be driven by both the equipment available and the evidence of pupils' understanding that teachers have gleaned in lessons 1–4. It is important that these ideas receive full discussion as they are conceptually difficult.

This section adopts a historical approach and introduces the idea of satellites as first put forward by the science-fiction writer Arthur C. Clarke in *Wireless World* in 1945.

Answer

→ *Pupil's Book page 119*

12 The answers will depend on pupils' knowledge of science-fiction stories. Opportunity should be given for pupils to explain stories and judge scientific accuracy, possibly using criteria developed in the 'Starburst' activity on page 117 of the Pupil's Book.

Activity ## Evaluation: GPS

→ *Pupil's Book page 120*

Answers

Pupils should be able to justify why they consider each to be an advantage or a disadvantage; for example, 'GPS locates your position to within a few metres'. This is useful for checking on the progress of buses along bus routes, but it could also be used to check on individuals, which might be an invasion of privacy.

There are a number of CD-ROMs available with satellite images. Some pupils will have misconceptions about how the images are obtained, and will not be aware that they use remote sensing instruments to collect the data which is then transmitted back to the Earth as microwave signals. They should also understand that the raw data must be converted into images using computer software.

Activity ## Information processing: Artificial satellites

→ *Pupil's Book page 121*

Pupils summarise the information from the textbook in a table, then if time allows find out more facts to add to the table.

Activity ## Demonstration: Circular motion

Safety

- This should be performed outdoors.

The 'satellite' can be a rubber bung on the end of some thread, which is whirled around your head. Things to discuss are the tension force in the string, which keeps the bung moving in a circle, and the direction in which the bung would move if the thread was released or if it broke. Pupils should appreciate that there is unbalanced force acting on the bung, which produces the motion in a circle (otherwise it would be travelling in a straight line). This force is what we would call the centripetal force. This is entirely consistent with Newton's laws. As the bung is changing its direction, although it moves with a constant speed, its velocity is changing. It is therefore accelerating towards the centre of the circle.

Equipment
• rubber bung
• strong thread

Activity Reasoning: Motion of satellites

➡ *Pupil's Book page 121*

It is worth spending some time explaining Newton's 'thought' experiment as described in the Pupil's Book. It makes an easy transition to the idea of how a satellite orbits. The satellite is fired into orbit by a rocket, and at the correct speed it will follow a circular path around the Earth. It is high enough to be above the atmosphere so there is no drag to affect the speed. It has not escaped from the Earth's gravity. It is falling towards the Earth, but the Earth curves away by the same amount.

Answers

1 In a straight line because the forces holding it in the circular motion have been removed.
2 The varying gravitational pull over the Earth's surface. The Earth is not perfectly spherical.

Worksheet 4.4R

➡ *Worksheet 4.4R: Satellite motion (S)*
This worksheet provides ideas to be discussed and then checked by calculation, using the spreadsheet on the CD-ROM.

Activity Demonstration: Weightlessness

There is often confusion about the 'weightlessness' experienced by astronauts orbiting the Earth. Pupils will have just learnt that a satellite orbits the Earth because of gravity. In this situation the astronauts experience the sensation of weightlessness because inside the orbiting space station both the occupants and the spacecraft are falling at the same rate towards the Earth. Because of the curvature of the Earth they keep falling and follow a circular path around the Earth. The analogy on the Earth would be the sensation if you were in a lift and the cable snapped. As you fall down the lift shaft you are falling at the same rate as the lift and you would feel the sensation of weightlessness (but not for long!). This can be demonstrated in the lab by attaching a mass to a spring balance (newton meter) and then dropping it. The spring balance reads zero as it falls.

Activity Evaluation: Model movement
→ *Pupil's Book page 122*

Answers

1 The force of gravity on the ball in the upper part of its swing is being used to keep the ball in circular motion at a particular speed. (If the speed of swing is too low, the ball will fall.)
2 Pupils should try to identify what the different parts of the model represent and say how good they are at representing reality.

Activity Demonstration: Rockets
The water rocket is well worth demonstrating if you have plenty of space outside.

Safety
- Never use a breakable container as the rocket – DO NOT USE GLASS.
- Never aim the rocket at anyone.

Equipment
Ready-made kits can be purchased for about £9. One manufacturer's website is:

www.rokit.com/home.asp

Information on constructing your own rocket can be found at:

http://materials.npl.co.uk/waterrockets/rockets.php

http://ourworld.compuserve.com/homepages/pagrosse/h2oRocketIndex.htm

Through discussion teachers should make sure that pupils understand that a rocket can only take off if the upward force created by the rocket propulsion is great enough to overcome the force of gravity acting down. Most commercial rockets use liquid fuels. The fuels need oxygen to burn and the simplest fuel is hydrogen, which burns with oxygen to produce water vapour. This exhaust gas is blasted out at a high speed. Solid fuel engines are used in fireworks and model rockets, and also for the Space Shuttle launch booster. About 500 tonnes of solid propellant are used in a mixture containing aluminium (fuel) and ammonium perchlorate (the oxidiser) and a binder to hold it all together. Europe's first intended space probe to the Moon, SMART-1, uses an ion engine. SMART-1's revolutionary propulsion system was first successfully fired on 30th September 2003, taking it initially into orbit around the Earth.

Rockets
→ *Pupil's Book page 123*

Answers

13 As air is forced backwards out of the inflated balloon tube this pushes the balloon forwards (reaction force).
14 It needs to limit the weight and volume of gas carried. Oxygen is required for combustion and so only oxygen is carried.

Attainment targets
Work in the previous sections should provide evidence that pupils are working towards the following attainment levels.

Give explanations of factors affecting gravitational force and use data to support or refute ideas	Level 6
Apply abstract ideas in explaining why weight differs on different planets	Level 7
Explain and use patterns in data to argue ideas in explaining the role of gravitational attraction in determining the motion of bodies in the Solar System	Level 8

7 Measuring speed and interpreting graphs

Learning outcomes
Pupils:

* recognise that in some contexts, for example, a race of a given length, comparisons of speed can be made from measurements of time alone
* compare speeds from data of distance and time
* make measurements of distance and time and use these to calculate speeds
* use the quantitative relationship between distance, time and speed in a variety of contexts
* identify the difference between average speed and speed at a point
* collect readings of speed at a point using datalogging equipment
* describe the pattern in results, for example: the higher the ramp, the faster the car at the bottom; the car accelerates down the slope
* suggest reasons, for example reaction time, why hand-held timers may be less accurate than electronically triggered timers
* give reasons why some specific measurements need to be more precise than others

Some aspects of the work on speed were covered in Book 1. Teachers will find it useful to check pupils' recall of this earlier work. They should have looked at the units of speed, learnt how speed is calculated, interpreted simple distance–time graphs, and perhaps seen the use of a motion sensor connected to a computer.

Activity

Worksheet 4.5R

Consolidation: Speed
→ *Worksheet 4.5R: Speedy questions (S)*
This worksheet gives pupils the opportunity to practise using the equation speed = distance/time. It also allows them to use reasoning (proportionality) to short cut or check on answers.

Answers

1 a) 10:2 = 5:1

b) 400:10 = 40:1

c) Sprinter = 100 seconds; cheetah = 33.3 seconds; racing car = 2.5 seconds.

d) $340 \times 3 = 1020$ metres.

e) Using speed = distance/time, the park is 2400 metres across. A walker would take 1200 seconds = 20 minutes. This can also be worked out using proportional thinking, i.e. sprinter : walker = 5:1. So if the sprinter takes 4 minutes, the walker would take $5 \times 4 = 20$ minutes.

2 a) The skateboarder travels away from the start at 200/40 = 5 m/s.

b) The skateboarder is stationary.

c) The skateboarder is moving further away, at a speed of 150/20 = 7.5 m/s.

d) The skateboarder travels back to the start, at a speed of 350/40 = 8.75 m/s.

3

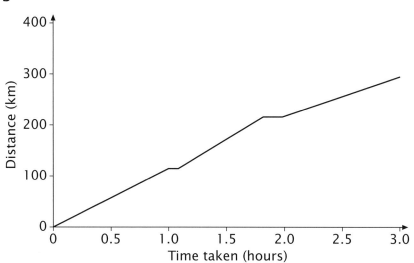

a) From 1 hour 10 minutes to 2 hours.

b) 120 km/hour.

c) 300/3 = 100 km/hour.

Activity Information processing: Looking for patterns

➡ *Pupil's Book page 124*

Answers

1 The last lap is faster than the average speed in the longer races, but slower in the 800m (2-lap) races.

2 Flat races over shorter distances.

3 It depends on the distance and the type of race.

4 Data should be presented as a bar chart.

5 No. The fastest is the Corvette, while the Alfa Romeo has the greatest acceleration.

6 There is no relationship.

Activity Enquiry: Measuring the speed of a trolley down a slope

→ *Pupil's Book page 125*

It is possible that the pupils will have seen the apparatus for measuring the speed of a trolley using light gates in Year 7. Worksheet 6.5 on CD-ROM 1 provides one approach using light gates. The activity described here is slightly different. The slope is fixed, and the speed is measured at different distances down the ramp. If the equipment is available, pupils should have an opportunity to use it or see it at this stage.

The final question allows pupils to predict and use their understanding of these ideas in a different situation. Listening in to conversations will provide valuable evidence for formative action.

Equipment
- trolley
- long runway
- pile of books
- light gates
- computer interface

Answers

1 Key variables – distance from light gate; speed at light gate; slope of runway.
Independent variable – distance.
Dependent variable – speed.
Constant – slope.

2

How speed changes with distance

3 15 cm/s from the graph.

4 The graph starts off as a constant slope up, and then begins to level off towards the end. After a large distance the trolley is accelerating less and eventually it will move at a constant speed (reaching a terminal velocity) when the friction forces balance the force of gravity providing the accelerating force. The relationship is linear and proportional up to almost 60 cm. It then increases at a lower rate for each 10 km distance from the light gate.

5 Pupils should write clear instructions and be able to justify their predictions. Pupils should be given the opportunity to test their predictions and evaluate their investigations.

Interpreting graphs
➡ *Pupil's Book page 126*
Some pupils may have seen this activity already in Year 7.

Answers
➡ *Pupil's Book page 127*
15 300 cm   **16** 50 cm   **17** 10 cm/s

Activity ## Demonstration: Air-cushioned and air friction
Page 127 of the Pupil's Book refers to a model hovercraft. It is worth showing a 'balloon' hovercraft. This is constructed from a flat disk of hardboard, 10 cm in diameter, with a hole in the centre fed by the air from a balloon. More ideas can be found at:

www.genuineideas.com/Toy_Ideas/balloon_hovercraft.html

www.wackyuses.com/experiments/balloncar.htm

A good demonstration of air friction is described in *The resourceful physics teacher* by Keith Gibbs, published by the Institute of Physics, whereby a polystyrene ball with a diameter slightly smaller than a vertical tube is dropped down the tube.

8 *Investigating air resistance*

Learning outcomes
Pupils:

- undertake an investigation into air resistance

Activity ## Investigation: Air resistance

Worksheet 4.6R

➡ *Worksheet 4.6R: Investigation of air resistance (P)*

Equipment
Each group will need:
- different thicknesses of card
- scissors
- knitting needle
- glass tubing
- plasticine
- thread
- stop clock
- metre rule or tape measure

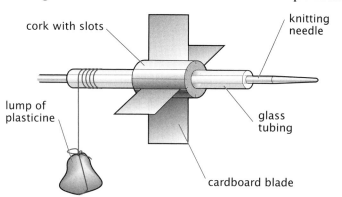

cork with slots · knitting needle · lump of plasticine · glass tubing · cardboard blade

Pupils build an 'air resistance test machine' and plan an investigation into the factors affecting its speed.

Attainment targets
This investigation should provide evidence that pupils are working towards the following attainment levels.

Level	Planning	Observing	Analysing	Evaluating
5	Plan an investigation based on fair test and change only one variable at a time	Make a series of measurements, such as time, for lump of plasticine to drop	Present data as a bar chart comparing different blades	Begin to relate to scientific knowledge and make suggestion for improvement
6	Use fair test ideas and plan for repeat readings	Fix apparatus so that plasticine falls a set distance (e.g. 1 metre) and take a set of measurements	Work out speeds of different blade types and present comparative data on a bar chart	Select and use appropriate qualitative and quantitative data to reason conclusion
7	Alter blades systematically to seek data patterns	Identify where they need repeat readings		Begin to decide whether sufficient data has been collected
8	Identify and explain anomalous results		Consider data critically	Communicate conclusions with regard to confidence in results and reliability awareness

Air-cushioned vehicles – hovercraft

Answers

➡ *Pupil's Book page 128*

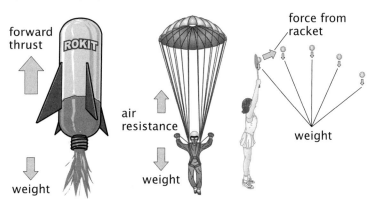

Activity Research: Concorde

➡ *Pupil's Book page 128*

Pupils use the internet to find out about Concorde's last days.

Time to think

➡ *Pupil's Book page 128*

Pupils are asked to produce explanations of some of the concepts covered in the chapter.

Activity Review: Test on forces and space

➡ *Worksheet 4.7R: Test on forces and space (R)*

Worksheet 4.7R

Answers

1 C, D (1 mark); **2** B; **3** B; **4** C (1 mark each);

5 A (1 mark); **6** C, F (1 mark);

7 The force of the Earth is gravity. It is acting downwards. The force of the shelf is upthrust. It is acting upwards. (1 mark)

8 1 – e; 2 – d; 3 – b; 4 – f, 5 – a, 6 – c. (6 marks);

9 C (1 mark); **10** A (1 mark)

Thinking Through Science Teacher's Book 3 Red

5 Patterns of reactivity

→ Rationale

This chapter provides up to 7½ hours of teaching materials. It builds on concepts that were first introduced in Book 1 (the key idea of particle theory and the application of this model to new phenomena). These ideas were developed further in Book 2 with a more sophisticated idea of particles in terms of atoms. This emphasised that the particles of all substances are different and that atoms of elements combine together to form particles called compounds. In Chapter 1 of this book the particle theory was extended even further to include the concept of the combining power of different elements, and symbol equations. These ideas are revisited in this chapter through a range of different types of reaction.

As a key idea, the particle theory impacts on many other areas of Key Stage 3 Science, including Chapters 6 and 9 in this Year 9 book. The development of all of the threads of the particle theory in *Thinking Through Science* is described in 'The key scientific ideas' on page xxi of the Preface.

The other main theme of this chapter is the activity series of the metals. Evidence gathered from different types of reaction is used to build up an order of reactivity. Once established, the order is used to make predictions.

The chapter also lays the foundation for work in Key Stage 4 on metals and their compounds.

→ Overview

The textbook sections, activities and worksheets have been arranged into 1 hour blocks to aid lesson planning. (The review lesson at the end will probably take only half an hour.) Clearly several of the activities and worksheets could form part of a homework session. The planning includes reading time for individual sections but some teachers may prefer to organise this as homework preparation for the following lesson. Worksheets are of six types – extension (E), support for an activity (S), practical (P), key skills (K), developmental (D), and review (R) – to allow for differentiation and flexibility to accommodate teachers' preferred practice. The actual timing and emphasis on different sections will depend on the current knowledge base of the pupils, the ability of the teaching group and the preferences of the teacher.

Lesson	Worksheets
1 How do metals react with water?	
2 Using the periodic table	
3 The reactivity of metals with acids	Worksheet 5.1R: The reactivity of some metals with acids (P)
4 Predicting the reactions of metals with oxygen	
5 Can metals displace each other?	Worksheet 5.2R: Can the activity series predict which displacement reactions will happen? (P) Worksheet 5.3R: Results table for displacement reactions (P)
6 Using the activity series	Worksheet 5.4R: Planning an investigation into the reactivity of some metals with acids (P)
7 Extraction and uses of metals	Worksheet 5.5R: Aluminium is an unusual metal (S) Worksheet 5.6R: Modern alloys (S)
Review	Worksheet 5.7R: Test on patterns of reactivity (R)

➡ *Chapter plan*

	Demonstration	Practical	ICT	Activity	Word play	Time to think	Ideas and evidence
Lesson 1	Tarnishing of potassium, sodium and lithium Reaction of some metals with water		Using a CD-ROM: reactive metals			What do you know?	
Lesson 2				Enquiry: Planning		Explaining the activity series	
Lesson 3		Comparing the reactivity of metals with acids (quick method)		Enquiry: Quality of evidence Evaluation: Order of reactivity			
Lesson 4	Burning metals in oxygen		Using a CD-ROM: Burning metals in oxygen	Enquiry: Predicting			
Lesson 5		Displacement reactions	Sorting a results table	Enquiry: Planning			
Lesson 6	The Thermit reaction			Planning: To compare the reactivity of metals with acids		Review of chapter so far	
Lesson 7		Comparing the reactivity of metals with acids (full investigation)	Internet/ CD-ROM research	Discussion: Aluminium is an unusual metal Research: Modern alloys	Word puzzle		The metals of antiquity
Review				Test on patterns of reactivity		Sorting and listing	

➡ *Expectations*

At the end of this chapter

in terms of scientific enquiry

most pupils will: select and make effective use of secondary sources about the origins and uses of metals; identify relevant observations and describe patterns in these; suggest a workable approach to investigating the reaction of metals with acids, identifying variables to be controlled; explain results using scientific knowledge and understanding

some pupils will have progressed further and will: synthesise information from secondary sources; point out where reactions do not fit the pattern expected

in terms of materials and their properties

most pupils will: identify and describe similarities in chemical reactions; identify differences in the reactivity of different metals and use these to explain some everyday uses and occurrences of metals; represent chemical reactions by word equations

some pupils will have progressed further and will: use the reactivity series to make predictions about the reactions of metals; relate the reactivity of a metal to its uses, how it occurs and when it was first extracted and used; represent some reactions by symbol equations

➡ *Links with CASE*

The use of formal models in terms of particle theory is reinforced through the idea of rearranging particles in chemical reactions. The use of ratio and proportionality is reinforced in the writing of formulae of compounds.

➡ *Pupils' misconceptions*

Misconception	Scientific understanding
Some physical changes are thought to be chemical changes.	A physical change can be easily reversed but a chemical change cannot.
Products of a chemical reaction are stored inside the reactants and are released when the mixture is stirred or heated.	The products are different from the reactants because the atoms are bonded together in different combinations.
There is an overall loss in mass after a chemical reaction.	Mass is always conserved in a chemical reaction. Some reactions result in a gas as one of the products and this can escape the reaction vessel.
In chemical reactions, the atoms of the reactants are transmuted into new atoms of the products.	Atoms may change partners in a reaction but they are still atoms of the same elements (although there may be electron transfers).
Chemical changes only take place in an experiment and usually require heat input.	Many reactions (e.g. rusting) take place in the environment and do not require heat to start the reaction.

➡ # Literacy, numeracy and other cross-curricular links

Literacy skills are developed in this chapter by asking pupils to interpret data from a range of sources.

Oracy skills are developed through discussion of evidence and articulating ideas, particularly through small group discussion. This plays an important role in accessing and working with the high level concepts in this topic.

Language for learning

By the end of this chapter pupils will be able to understand, use and spell correctly:

- words with different meanings in scientific and everyday contexts – for example, displacement, nature
- words with a precise scientific meaning – for example, compound, reactivity, react, salt, equation, reactant, product
- names of chemical compounds – for example, copper sulphate, magnesium nitrate, zinc chloride
- words and phrases relating to scientific enquiry – for example, order of reactivity, qualitative observations.

Through the activities pupils will also develop their skills in:

- identifying information needed and using different texts as sources
- structuring paragraphs to develop points, using evidence and additional facts.

1   How do metals react with water?

Learning outcomes

Pupils:

- describe how metals change due to exposure to the air – for example, iron rusts, silver becomes dull
- identify some metals that corrode readily and some that do not
- give a reason why sodium, potassium and lithium seem to be metals – for example they are shiny (when cut), and a reason why they seem not to be – for example, they are not hard, they can't be left in the air without tarnishing
- identify evidence for a chemical reaction – for example, bubbles of gas, heat produced
- describe some similarities and differences in the reactions of the group 1 metals with water – for example, hydrogen produced, pH shows alkali produced, flame produced with potassium but not with sodium or lithium
- describe and explain some of the safety precautions to be taken when dealing with reactive metals

What do you know?

→ *Pupil's Book page 129*

The aims of this starting exercise are to establish prior knowledge in:

- the characteristics of metals and their position in the periodic table
- the component parts of air

and understanding of:

- the nature of evidence
- the use of word equations to represent reactions
- the use of symbols and formulae to represent elements and compounds
- the use of symbol equations to represent reactions.

This activity can be used in different ways:

- with individual pupils as a semi-formal test to establish the knowledge base of all pupils. In this case, it is best done as a homework or at the end of the previous lesson to allow the teacher time to identify individual problems;
- in small discussion groups to enable pupils to piece together the knowledge and ideas they developed in Years 7 and 8. Listening to the discussions and getting groups to feed back their ideas and comment on the ideas of others will provide valuable evidence to help planning for this topic.

In either case, before pupils do the questions introduce the table and show the tarnishing of lithium, sodium and potassium. This can be done by demonstration, by showing video footage or by using relevant CD-ROMs.

Activity Demonstration: Tarnishing of potassium, sodium and lithium

Ask pupils to explain why the freshly cut surfaces of the metals become dull. Challenge pupils to say whether these are metals or not, asking them to produce reasons for and against. Refer back to work done previously on the periodic table. While pupils need to accurately record and compare the results of these demonstrations, there is no need for them to write up these experiments. One novel way of recording would be to split the page into four and record observations for each one of the three metals in a separate section and then use the fourth to write a conclusion.

This demonstration will allow you to discuss physical and chemical changes and to address misconceptions about these and the idea that reactions do not require heat input.

Equipment

- samples of potassium, sodium and lithium (CARE: corrosive and highly flammable)
- white tile
- scalpel
- forceps
- eye protection, safety screen

Remove the metal from the storage jar, wipe off the oil with a paper towel or filter paper and cut on a white tile. Compare the properties of the three metals in terms of storage, appearance, softness and time taken for a freshly cut surface to tarnish.

Safety
• These metals are corrosive and highly flammable. Use eye protection and safety screens.

ICT
The 'Group 1' programme in *Multimedia Science School* (PLATO Learning) has video clips of the tarnishing of lithium, sodium and potassium.

Answers
→ *Pupil's Book pages 130–132*
2 **a)** The freshly cut surface is shiny like silver.
  b) The solids have a dull appearance.
  c) i) Group 1.
     ii) Metals.
  d) sodium + oxygen $\longrightarrow$ sodium oxide
3 Oxygen, water and carbon dioxide.
4 Pupils discuss the concept cartoon in small groups.
  Water in a stream contains oxygen and carbon dioxide. All three substances are needed to form the green *verdigris* – basic copper carbonate $Cu(OH)_2.CuCO_3$.
  Pupil 1: could be correct. Further evidence – boil some pure water to remove any dissolved gases, and leave to cool in a sealed container. Place a piece of copper in the water, seal and leave for some time to see if it turns green.
  Pupil 2: could be correct. Further evidence – place a piece of copper in a sealed container with dry oxygen and leave for some time to see if it turns green (or use heated copper and a gas jar of oxygen to speed it up).
  Pupil 3: could be correct. Further evidence – boil some pure water to remove any dissolved gases, cool in a sealed container and then bubble oxygen through it. Place a piece of copper in the water, seal and leave for some time to see if it turns green.

An optional extension could be:
After the pupils have completed Questions 1–4, supply them with the following additional evidence:

• a labelled jar of 'copper oxide' (copper(II) oxide) – the oxide is black, not green
• a labelled jar of 'basic copper(II) carbonate' with the formula $Cu(OH)_2.CuCO_3$ on it – it must need at least carbon dioxide, water and oxygen from the formula
• a piece of 'used copper water pipe' which is not green inside – the water in the pipe contains less oxygen and carbon dioxide than is available to exposed copper.

5 Gold, silver and copper, lead, iron, sodium, potassium (the evidence for the first four metals is not particularly accurate or valid).

6 a) calcium + oxygen $\longrightarrow$ calcium oxide
  b) $2Ca + O_2 \longrightarrow 2CaO$

Reacting metals with water
Answers
→ *Pupil's Book page 132*
1 Sodium and lithium.
2 The metal dissolves; a gas is produced; (the solution becomes warmer).
3 To protect them from reacting with the oxygen and water vapour in the atmosphere.

The reactions of some metals with water can be shown either by demonstration, video footage or relevant CD-ROMs, before pupils do Question 4.

Activity ## Demonstration: Reaction of some metals with water

Add small pieces of some less reactive metals such as iron, zinc, magnesium or copper to water. Note that they do not react immediately, although the magnesium may produce a few bubbles of gas after a while.

Ask pupils to predict whether the rapidly-tarnishing metals seen in the previous activity would react with water, and to suggest an order of reactivity. Demonstrate the reactions of sodium, potassium and lithium to test their predictions. Ask pupils to identify similarities and differences in the reactions of sodium, potassium and lithium with water. Establish an order of reactivity of these metals and help pupils to write word equations.

Extend this by showing pupils a video clip or CD-ROM of the reactions of rubidium and caesium with water. Compare the reactions of the alkali metals with those of the other metals used earlier and agree a tentative order of reactivity.

Equipment
• small pieces of iron, zinc, magnesium, copper
• samples of lithium, sodium, potassium (CARE: corrosive and highly flammable.)
• Universal Indicator paper
• 5 test tubes
• glass trough
• eye protection
• safety screen

Cut small, rice-grain sized pieces of sodium and potassium. Remove the oil on a piece of filter paper and use tongs to add one piece to a trough of water. Note that the metal dissolves. Test the solution with Universal Indicator paper to show that an alkali is produced.

For the lithium demonstration, place a small piece of lithium in a beaker of water and collect the gas produced in a test tube. Test the gas (hydrogen – 'pop' test) and the solution (an alkali – Universal Indicator).

Safety
* Potassium, sodium and lithium are corrosive and highly flammable. Small pieces the size of rice grains should be used.
* Eye protection and safety screens should be used.
* A perspex sheet can be used to slide over the trough after the sodium and potassium have been added.

ICT
The 'Group 1' programme in *Multimedia Science School* (PLATO Learning) has video clips of lithium, sodium, potassium, rubidium and caesium reacting with water.

Answers
→ *Pupil's Book page 133*
4 **a)** The metal floats.
 b) Hydrogen.
 c) The lithium has reacted with the water to form a soluble compound.
 d) i) An alkali.
  ii) For example, sodium hydroxide.
 e) lithium + water ⟶ lithium hydroxide + hydrogen

2 *Using the periodic table*

Learning outcomes
Pupils:

* identify patterns in the periodic table and use them to make predictions

Uses of the periodic table
→ *Pupil's Book page 133*
This section revisits work from Year 7 and Year 8. Pupils should work in pairs and be given opportunities to check and discuss their answers with another pair. The ratio in Question 7b) and c) might be expressed as 1:2 rather than 2:1, and pupils should be encouraged to articulate the difference between these two ratios. The use of models may help pupils see the difference here.

Answers
→ *Pupil's Book pages 133–134*
 5 The reactivity of the metals increases on going down the group.
 6 Barium.
 7 **a)** 1:1
 b) 2:1
 c) 2:1
 8 **a)** NaCl
 b) Rb_2O
 c) Na_2SO_4
 9 **a)** potassium + water ⟶ potassium hydroxide + hydrogen
 b) caesium + water ⟶ caesium hydroxide + hydrogen

Thinking Through Science Teacher's Book 3 Red

10 a) $2K + 2H_2O \longrightarrow 2KOH + H_2$
   b) $2Cs + 2H_2O \longrightarrow 2CsOH + H_2$

Summary

→ *Pupil's Book page 135*
The summary points out that iron, copper and zinc cannot be placed in order in the reactivity 'league' from the evidence so far. This leads on to the need for more evidence, such as the reactions of metals with acids.

Reacting metals with acids

→ *Pupil's Book page 135*
This is revision of experiments done in Chapter 1, which will help pupils' understanding of reactions (so misconceptions in this area can be sought and addressed) as well as developing their ideas on the reactivity of metals.

Answers

11 a) Hydrogen.
   b) The magnesium reacts with the hydrochloric acid to form magnesium chloride and bubbles of hydrogen gas.
   c) magnesium + hydrochloric acid $\longrightarrow$
       magnesium chloride + hydrogen
   d) metal + acid $\longrightarrow$ metal salt + hydrogen
   e) $Mg + 2HCl \longrightarrow MgCl_2 + H_2$

Activity ## Enquiry: Planning

→ *Pupil's Book page 136*
This activity could be used for a homework to introduce the practical activity in the next lesson (Worksheet 5.1R). There is an option to use this problem for a whole investigation in lesson 7.

Time to think

→ *Pupil's Book page 136*
This is an assessment for learning activity, designed to encourage pupils to reflect on their learning about the activity series. It allows pupils to check their ideas and gives feedback to the teacher and pupils on which they can take action.

Attainment targets
Work in the previous sections should provide evidence that pupils are working towards the following attainment levels.

Explain what is meant by the 'activity series'	Level 5
Use word equations to summarise simple chemical reactions	Level 6
Explain how the periodic table can be used to predict formulae and equations	Level 7
Recognise that elements and compounds can be represented by symbols and formulae	Level 7

3 *The reactivity of metals with acids*

Learning outcomes

Pupils:

- identify relevant observations, for example, extent of bubbling, rise in temperature
- use observations to suggest an order of reactivity
- demonstrate an understanding of the terms accurate, reliable and valid
- identify an anomalous result and explain why it may have happened

Activity

Practical: Comparing the reactivity of metals with acids

Worksheet 5.1R

➡ *Worksheet 5.1R: The reactivity of some metals with acids (P)*
This activity is intended as a quick practical exercise to establish the relative reactivity of magnesium, zinc, iron and copper, which could not be clearly established from the reaction of these metals with water. Alternatively, the results could be reviewed in the summary table (Pupil's Book page 136). The method can be evaluated in terms of accuracy, validity and reliability through the follow-up questions. This theme is also developed on page 137 of the Pupil's Book.

Equipment
Each group will need:

- 4 test tubes
- test tube rack
- 0.4 M sulphuric acid or 0.8 M hydrochloric acid
- coarse-mesh filings of magnesium, iron, zinc and copper
- beaker (250 cm^3)
- tripod and gauze
- eye protection

Safety
- Eye protection must be worn.
- Coarse-mesh magnesium is highly flammable.
- Hydrogen sulphide (CARE: toxic) may be formed in the reaction with iron – ensure good ventilation.

Answers

1 The same order reactivity should be found for both acids.
2 **a)** Use a measuring cylinder (10 cm^3).
  b) Weigh the metal filings on a balance.
3 Measure the volume of gas released in a given time.
4 The changes would ensure that the volume of acid and the mass of metal are kept the same for each experiment.
5 Repeat each experiment and average the results for the rate of formation of gas.
6 This is a quick, simple method. With the improvements, it would take much longer to complete the investigation.

Activity Enquiry: Quality of evidence

→ *Pupil's Book pages 136–137*

This exercise is designed to develop the concepts of validity, accuracy and reliability. By comparing methods used, pupils will reveal their ideas and be encouraged to identify and articulate their understanding. To achieve this, it is important that pupils listen to peers giving their explanations/answers and be encouraged to comment on and compare the oral answers of their peers.

Answers

1 a) The timings for potassium, sodium and lithium.

   b) The descriptions of the reactions with water and with acid; the tarnishing times of the less reactive metals.

2 a) Accuracy at throwing darts (2 out of 6 bull's eyes) is valid evidence of a good darts player, although there are other skills involved as well.

   b) James.

   c) Kath.

   d) Susan.

   e) Kath.

   f) This is an open question. It may be argued that more tries are needed and that maybe the test should be repeated on other days.

Activity Evaluation: Order of reactivity

→ *Pupil's Book pages 137–139*

In this exercise it is intended that the pupils apply the concepts of validity, accuracy and reliability to a scientific enquiry. Again, discussion will provide formative feedback for pupils and for the teacher.

Answers

1 a) They should use repeat experiments and calculate the mean results.

   b) The dependent variable is the volume of gas produced in 1 minute. The independent variable is the metal.

   c) The following variables were kept the same: mass of metal; volume of acid; time before the volume of gas was measured; type and concentration of acid.

2 a) Measuring the volume of acid using the marks on the side of a conical flask.

   b) Use a measuring cylinder (20 cm^3 or 25 cm^3).

3 Zinc.

4 a) Experiment 2 for iron (17 cm^3 compared with 6 and 7 cm^3 for the other two readings represents a large percentage error).

   b) Any reasonable answer such as 'They forgot to empty the gas syringe after the previous experiment'.

   c) By including the anomalous result in the mean, it has led to the conclusion that iron is more reactive than zinc.

5 a) The conclusion is not accurate because zinc is more reactive than iron.

   b) The conclusion is valid from a fair test point of view.

4 *Predicting the reactions of metals with oxygen*

Learning outcomes

Pupils:

- use the activity series to make a sensible prediction – for example, sodium would be more reactive with oxygen than copper
- evaluate the evidence obtained – for example, magnesium reacted more violently than copper, but it was difficult to compare sodium and calcium
- state that all the metals tested produced oxides

Activity ## Enquiry: Predicting

➡ *Pupil's Book pages 139–140*

Pattern seeking is an essential skill that pupils need to develop in science. Remind pupils that metals also react with oxygen (or the oxygen in the air) to form oxides. This enquiry asks pupils to use the activity series to suggest how readily different metals would react, and then to write some word and symbol equations.

Answers

1 Potassium and sodium.
2 Gold and silver.
3 **a)** magnesium + oxygen $\longrightarrow$ magnesium oxide
  b) sodium + oxygen $\longrightarrow$ sodium oxide
  c) zinc + oxygen $\longrightarrow$ zinc oxide
4 **a)** $2Mg + O_2 \longrightarrow 2MgO$
  b) $2Ba + O_2 \longrightarrow 2BaO$
  c) $2Ca + O_2 \longrightarrow 2CaO$
5 **a)** All three equations have the ratio 2 metal : 1 oxygen : 2 metal oxide.

  b) All three metals are in group 2 of the periodic table.

A mixture of demonstration, video footage and relevant CD-ROMs can be used to test whether the predictions are correct.

Activity ## Demonstration: Burning metals in oxygen

Metals such as sodium, potassium, magnesium and copper are each heated and placed into a gas jar of oxygen. We are looking for evidence of the formation of a new substance (metal oxide), and for differences in the reactivities of the metals. If a sample of gold is available, it could be treated in the same way to show that there is no reaction.

  Point out that the evidence is only qualitative, so the established order of activity is not secure and in some cases it is not clear at all. However, the order of reactivity of metals with oxygen is generally similar to that with water and with acids.

Equipment

- gas jars of oxygen
- 3 combustion spoons
- tongs

- white tile
- scalpel
- samples of sodium and potassium (approximately 3 mm cube cut from the storage sample; remove the oil on a paper towel) (CARE: corrosive and highly flammable)
- magnesium ribbon (approximately 3 cm)
- small piece of copper foil
- eye protection
- safety screen

Safety
- Magnesium, sodium and potassium are highly flammable.
- Avoid looking directly at burning magnesium.
- Wear eye protection.
- Safety screens should be used.

ICT
The 'Group 1' programme in *Multimedia Science School* (PLATO Learning) has video clips of lithium, sodium and potassium burning in oxygen.

5 *Can metals displace each other?*

Learning outcomes
Pupils:

- identify where reactions occur and where they do not
- relate results to the position of the metal in the activity series
- describe the pattern – for example, a metal high in the activity series will displace one lower down, but a lower one won't displace a higher one
- use an analogy or model to explain the results – for example, the zinc has a stronger pull on the sulphate than the copper does
- present results clearly and appropriately

Displacement reactions of metals
→ *Pupil's Book page 140*
The cartoon uses the analogy of the metal 'pulling' on the sulphate. Although this analogy is not strictly correct, it may be helpful to pupils in establishing the principles of displacement reactions. Word equations can also be used to establish that whether there is a reaction or not depends on the metal and the metal in the salt, not on the acid from which the salt was derived.

Answer
12 magnesium + copper sulphate $\longrightarrow$

magnesium sulphate + copper

Activity Enquiry: Planning
→ *Pupil's Book page 141*

Answers
1 Tests 1 and 3.
2 A more reactive metal will displace a less reactive metal from a solution of its salt.
3 No. More evidence is needed to be really confident.
4 zinc + copper sulphate $\longrightarrow$ copper + zinc sulphate
   magnesium + iron sulphate $\longrightarrow$ iron + magnesium sulphate
5 $Zn + CuSO_4 \longrightarrow Cu + Zn SO_4$
   $Mg + FeSO_4 \longrightarrow Fe + MgSO_4$
6 **a)** Silver or gold.
   b) Aluminium, lead, lithium, etc.

Activity Practical: Displacement reactions

Worksheet 5.2R

Worksheet 5.3R

→ *Worksheet 5.2R: Can the activity series predict which displacement reactions will happen? (P), Worksheet 5.3R: Results table for displacement reactions (P)*
The purpose of this practical is to encourage pupils to make predictions using their scientific knowledge and then to test out the predictions.

This activity provides an opportunity to use ICT to reorder the results table to see the pattern more clearly (Worksheet 5.3R).

Extension
Pupils could be asked to write the symbols and formulae for reactants and products, and from these write symbol equations.

Equipment
Each group will need:

- spotting tile
- 4 small pieces of magnesium, iron, copper and zinc
- access to dropper bottles of 0.4 M solutions of magnesium sulphate, zinc sulphate, iron(II) sulphate, copper sulphate and silver nitrate
- eye protection

Safety
- 0.4 M copper sulphate solution. CARE: harmful if swallowed, irritant to eyes and skin.
- 0.4 M silver nitrate solution. CARE: irritant; harmful if swallowed; very dangerous to eyes; blackens the skin.
- Eye protection should be worn.

Answers
2 A metal high in the activity series will push out one lower down, but a lower one won't push out a higher one.
3 **a)** magnesium + copper sulphate $\longrightarrow$
                          copper + magnesium sulphate
   b) zinc + iron sulphate $\longrightarrow$ iron + zinc sulphate
   c) copper + silver nitrate $\longrightarrow$ silver + copper nitrate

6 *Using the activity series*

Learning outcomes

Pupils:

- explain that energy released by the reaction is sufficient to melt the iron
- describe how molten iron is used in welding – for example, on railway lines
- summarise reactions of metals, making use of patterns in the activity series
- use the activity series to make predictions about the reactions of metals
- identify where an element cannot be given a position or where a firm prediction cannot be made, giving reasons for the difficulty

Activity series

→ *Pupil's Book pages 142–143*

Additional metals are now introduced to the activity series. This offers further opportunities for pupils to make predictions related to the series.

Answers

13 a) Yes, a reaction will occur.
   b) Yes, a reaction will occur.
   c) No, a reaction won't occur.

14 lead + silver nitrate $\longrightarrow$ silver + lead nitrate
   zinc + iron oxide $\longrightarrow$ iron + zinc oxide

15 $Pb + 2AgNO_3 \longrightarrow 2Ag + Pb(NO_3)_2$
   $Zn + FeO \longrightarrow Fe + ZnO$

16 a) In between iron and lead.
   b) For example, tin should displace copper from copper sulphate, however it should not displace iron from iron sulphate. This is because a metal will displace a less reactive metal from its compounds.

17 a) aluminium + iron oxide $\longrightarrow$ iron + aluminium oxide
   b) Any metal that is above aluminium in the activity series, such as magnesium. Metals such as sodium and potassium may be too dangerous to use because they would release too much heat energy.

18 a) In order of voltage: silver–copper, copper–iron, copper–zinc, silver–zinc, zinc–magnesium.
   b) i) Generally, the further apart the two metals in the activity series, the greater the voltage.
      ii) The least reactive metal is always the positive pole of the cell.
   c) The activity series.
   d) For example, magnesium and silver.

Activity Demonstration: The Thermit reaction

This experiment should be tried out in advance with the guidance of a colleague if you have not done it before.

To ensure that the reaction is initiated, other substances are used in addition to the aluminium and iron oxide reactants. A piece of magnesium ribbon acts as a fuse, and a mixture of magnesium oxide and barium peroxide are present to help the reactants to ignite.

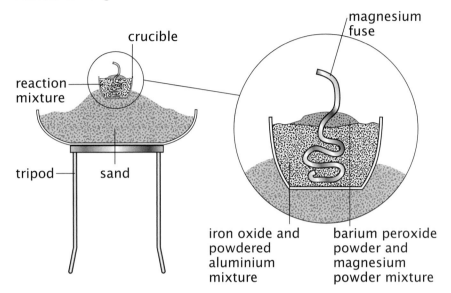

Equipment
- 10 cm of magnesium ribbon (CARE: flammable)
- 6 g dried iron(III) oxide powder
- 2 g dried aluminium powder
- 0.2 g magnesium powder (CARE: flammable)
- 1.7 g barium peroxide powder (oxidising agent)
- sand tray
- crucible
- bar magnet
- eye protection, safety screen, fume cupboard

6 g of powdered iron(III) oxide and 2 g of fine aluminium powder should be dried separately prior to the demonstration by gentle warming in an oven. Mix these reactants with a wooden spill in the reaction crucible. A 10 cm length of magnesium ribbon should be coiled at one end by wrapping it around a pencil, and then placed into the mixture as shown in the diagram above.

Sprinkle a mixture of barium peroxide and magnesium powder around the magnesium fuse as shown. Place the crucible in the sand tray and check safety procedures before igniting the magnesium with a Bunsen burner or a butane blow lamp. Move back to a safe distance, as sparks and fumes are produced. When the mixture has cooled down, remove the sample of iron and test it with the bar magnet.

Ask the pupils to explain where the energy to melt the iron has come from. It has not come from the burning magnesium as this simply acts as a fuse. Use the displacement model to describe what is taking place during the reaction.

Safety
- A risk assessment should be followed.
- Carry out in a fume cupboard.
- Safety screens and eye protection should be used.
- Pupils should stand no closer than 3 metres from the reaction.

Activity Planning: To compare the reactivity of metals with acids

Worksheet 5.4R

→ *Worksheet 5.4R: Planning an investigation into the reactivity of some metals with acids (P)*

A full investigation of the fair test type could be set at this point. The plan could be written for homework and the investigation carried out in the following lesson if time is available.

Remind pupils of the work they did in Chapter 1 on the reactions of acids with metals, and ask them what is formed.

Dependent variables that could be used for measuring the order of reactivity are changes in temperature, amount of gas produced and time for metal to dissolve. Control variables for a fair test are type of acid, concentration of acid, volume of acid, mass of metal and state of division of metal.

Time to think

→ *Pupil's Book page 143*

This provides an opportunity to review the work covered so far.

Attainment targets

Work in the previous sections should provide evidence that pupils are working towards the following attainment levels.

Summarise the reactions of metals, making use of patterns in the activity series	Level 5
Use word equations to summarise simple chemical reactions	Level 6
Use patterns of reactivity in the activity series to make predictions about the reactions of other metals	Level 7
Recognise that elements and compounds can be represented by symbols and formulae	Level 7

7 *Extraction and uses of metals*

Learning outcomes

Pupils:

* make connections between reactivity and aspects of use of metals – for example, aluminium is reactive, and therefore hard to extract (this is why it wasn't used as early as iron)
* make connections between reactivity and aspects of methods of extraction of metals from their ores
* identify a workable procedure and the variables that need to be controlled in an investigation – for example, to measure the temperature of the reacting mixture every minute for 10 minutes and control the quantity of metal and volume of acid
* recall key ideas about the relative reactivity of different metals
* use and apply these ideas in different contexts

Activity Practical: Comparing the reactivity of metals with acids

If sufficient time is available, the reactivity of metals with acids can be investigated through the pupils' plans from Worksheet 5.4R. In this case, the plans must be checked for health and safety before practical work begins. The pupils may have selected different methods to measure the relative reactivities – for example, volume of gas produced in 2 minutes; height of froth 2 minutes after adding a few drops of liquid detergent; time taken for the metal to dissolve; maximum temperature rise during the reaction.

It may be useful to compare the different methods that have been selected and provide a further opportunity for pupils to critique ideas. This will help pupils use the correct terminology and challenge their ideas on investigations.

Equipment
Each group will need:

- 4 test tubes
- test tube rack
- 0.4 M sulphuric acid or 0.8 M hydrochloric acid
- coarse-mesh filings (or other available forms requested) of magnesium, iron, zinc and copper
- beaker (250 cm^3) and tripod and gauze
- any other equipment requested
- eye protection

Safety
- Eye protection must be worn.
- Coarse mesh magnesium is highly flammable.
- Hydrogen sulphide (CARE: toxic) may be formed in the reaction with iron – ensure good ventilation.

Ideas and evidence: The metals of antiquity
➡ *Pupil's Book pages 143–145*

Answers
1 Silver tarnishes, forming a black coating which makes it difficult to find, whereas gold stays shiny yellow in appearance.
2 Silver sulphide.
3 Lead has a much lower melting point than the impurities so it can be poured off.
4 a) $2HgS + O_2 \longrightarrow 2Hg + SO_2$
  b) Sulphur dioxide.
5 a) Gold, silver or mercury.
  b) Copper, lead, tin, mercury.
  c) Iron.
  d) The more energy needed to extract it, the higher up the metal is in the activity series.
  e) Below copper.
  f) It is so unreactive that it does not easily form compounds.
  g) Bronze is an alloy of copper and tin. Both of these metals are easier to extract from their ores than iron from its ore.

Activity

Worksheet 5.5R

Discussion: Aluminium is an unusual metal

→ *Worksheet 5.5R: Aluminium is an unusual metal (S)*
This worksheet could be used as a group activity or a homework.

Answers

1 It has a protective layer of oxide that prevents it from taking part in any reactions.
2 Because aluminium is more reactive than iron, it holds on to the oxygen more strongly so it is more difficult to extract (more energy is needed).
3 The pylons would collapse under the weight of iron or copper cables. Some steel is used to improve the strength of the aluminium cable.
4 More energy is needed to extract aluminium so there is a greater saving made by recycling it.

Activity

Worksheet 5.6R

Research: Modern alloys

→ *Pupil's Book page 147*
→ *Worksheet 5.6R: Modern alloys (S)*
This worksheet can be used for the 'Research' activity suggested on page 147 of the Pupil's Book.

Word play

→ *Pupil's Book page 147*
1 smelt
2 alloy
3 anneal
4 aluminium

Time to think

→ *Pupil's Book page 148*
The pupils are set three group activities connected with sorting and listing in Key Stage 3 Science to encourage them to reflect on different areas connected with these two concepts. The periodic table combines both ideas by sorting similar elements into vertical groups and listing the elements in these groups in some sort of order. However, in this case the arrangement is dictated by the atomic number of each element, and in some groups the reactivity increases down the group whereas in others it increases up the group.

Activity

Worksheet 5.7R

Review: Test on patterns of reactivity

→ *Worksheet 5.7R: Test on patterns of reactivity (R)*
This worksheet provides a 20-minute test to check on the understanding in this chapter.

Answers

1 a) Hydrogen. (1 mark)
   b) i) Region 3. (1 mark)
     ii) Region 1. (1 mark)
     iii) Region 2. (1 mark)
   c) It is a compound; it is not an element; it is made up of more than one element. (Any one.) (1 mark)

   d) i) copper + iron sulphate   (1 mark)
       ii) The nail becomes brown **or** pink **or** copper
       coloured.   (1 mark)

2 a) Aluminium oxide.   (1 mark)
  b) Aluminium; iron; copper (from most to least
     reactive).   (1 mark)
  c) i) No reaction.   (1 mark)
     ii) Zinc; silver; magnesium. (Any one.)   (1 mark)
  d) zinc + oxygen $\longrightarrow$ zinc oxide   (2 marks)

3 a) E; D; C; A; B (from most to least reactive).   (1 mark)
  b) i) B   (1 mark)
     ii) E   (1 mark)
    iii) A   (1 mark)

Environment

→ Rationale

This chapter provides up to 10 hours of teaching materials. It builds on Unit 7E Acids and alkalis, Unit 7F Simple chemical reactions, Unit 8G Rocks and weathering and Unit 8H The rock cycle. It relates to work on the reactions of acids in Unit 9E Reactions of metals and metal compounds, and to work on using energy resources in Unit 9I Energy and electricity. The chapter provides opportunities to revisit and revise topics met in Years 7 and 8. With some pupils, teachers may wish to concentrate on some of the new topics, extending activities, and with others to spend more time on revision of previous work. The work in this chapter covers Levels 5–7 and the pupils use abstract models to explain and predict scientific phenomena.

This chapter covers the material in the Year 9 units:

- Environmental chemistry (9G)
- Plants and photosynthesis (9C)
- Plants for food (9D).

Environmental chemistry

Pupils will learn that rocks, soils and building materials have a variety of chemical characteristics and that chemical weathering alters rocks and building materials over time. They will consider how the atmosphere and water resources are affected by natural processes and the activity of humans. They will learn how environmental conditions are monitored and controlled, and to make a distinction between different environmental issues, for example, global warming and ozone depletion.

Plants and photosynthesis

Pupils will study photosynthesis as the key process in producing new plant biomass, and learn that the carbon dioxide for photosynthesis comes from the air and that the water is absorbed through the roots. Pupils need to appreciate that chlorophyll enables a plant to utilise light during photosynthesis, and they consider the role of the leaf in photosynthesis. They also learn about the importance of photosynthesis to humans and other animals.

Plants for food

Pupils learn about humans as part of a complex food web and consider how management of food production has many implications for other animal and plant populations in the environment. Pupils consider some of the key issues involved in sustainable development of the countryside and the factors affecting plant growth.

→ # *Overview*

The textbook sections, activities and worksheets have been arranged into 1 hour blocks to aid lesson planning. Clearly several of the activities and worksheets could form part of a homework session. Lesson planning must allow sufficient review time for the learning outcomes to be clearly assessed. This forms a key element of the process of formative assessment. The planning includes reading time for individual sections but some teachers may prefer to organise this as homework preparation for the following lesson. The worksheets to support the learning process have been written to consolidate recall of key facts and the continued development of key ideas. Worksheets are of six types – extension (E), support for an activity (S), practical (P), key skills (K), developmental (D) and review (R) – to allow for differentiation and flexibility to accommodate teachers' preferred practice. The actual timing and emphasis on different sections will depend on the current knowledge base of the pupils, the ability of the teaching group and the preferences of the teacher.

Lesson	Worksheets
1 How are soils different from each other?	Worksheet 6.1R: Acid rain quiz (R) Worksheet 6.2R: Measuring soil pH (P) Worksheet 6.3R: Neutralising soils (P) Worksheet 6.4R: Selecting soil for a sports field (P) Worksheet 6.5R: Soil analysis (D)
2 The causes and effects of acid rain	Worksheet 6.6R: Rock cycle definitions game (S) Worksheet 6.7R: Types of weathering (S) Worksheet 6.8R: Take a weathering walk (P) Worksheet 6.9R: Rock cycle sequence (E)
3 Reducing the effects of acid rain	Worksheet 6.10R: Treating polluted water (P) Worksheet 6.11R: Heating limestone (P)
4 What factors affect pH of rainwater?	Worksheet 6.12R: Testing water samples for pH levels (D)
5 Is pollution worse now?	Worksheet 6.13R: Effect of soil pH on bean plant growth (P, E) Worksheet 6.14R: Global warming – fact or fiction? (S) Worksheet 6.15R: Lichens as pollution indicators (S)
6 Green plants	Worksheet 6.16R: Testing leaves for starch (P)
7 Use of plants	
8 What are the best conditions for photosynthesis?	Worksheet 6.17R: Fertilisers (D)
9 The role of the leaf and the root in photosynthesis	
10 The importance of green plants to the environment	
Review	Worksheet 6.18R: Test on the environment (R)

→ *Chapter plan*

	Demonstration	Practical	ICT	Activity	Word play	Time to think	Ideas and evidence
Lesson 1		Measuring soil pH Neutralising soils Selecting soil for a sports field	Digital photography: Examples of weathering	Acid rain quiz Information processing: Soil analysis Creative thinking: School survey		What do you know?	
Lesson 2		Take a weathering walk		Reasoning: Carbon dioxide Evaluation: Which materials are most affected by acid rain? Reasoning: Rock cycle definition game Reasoning: Rock cycle sequence Information processing: Types of weathering			Acid rain
Lesson 3		Treating polluted water Heating limestone					
Lesson 4		Testing water samples for pH level		Enquiry: Acid rain investigation Enquiry: Analysing data			
Lesson 5		Effect of soil pH on bean plant growth		Information processing: Global warming – fact or fiction? Information processing: Lichens as pollution indicators		Review of chapter so far	
Lesson 6		Testing leaves for starch					
Lesson 7			Internet research	Research: Cotton Creative thinking: The importance of plants		Photo-synthesis	The story of wheat
Lesson 8				Evaluation: Mung bean experiment Information processing: Fertilisers			van Helmont
Lesson 9				Information processing: Underwater photosynthesis Reasoning: Mineral salts			The discovery of oxygen

	Demonstration	Practical	ICT	Activity	Word play	Time to think	Ideas and evidence
Lesson 10				Reasoning: Atmosphere model		Review of chapter	
Review				Test on the environment			

 # *Expectations*

At the end of this chapter

in terms of scientific enquiry

most pupils will: identify and explain the strengths and weaknesses of the evidence about environmental change obtained from secondary sources and decide which factors may be relevant to an enquiry; decide when it is appropriate to use data from secondary sources and how to search for information

some pupils will have progressed further and will: make effective use of secondary sources of information about the relationship of soil type to plant growth and have the opportunity to record their findings using ICT; identify and describe possible sources of information about the environment and select from these evidence about environmental change over time, identifying some strengths and weaknesses in the evidence; look critically at sources of secondary data and at the results to decide how strongly they show a trend

most pupils will: identify variables relevant to an investigation of photosynthesis and suggest how these might be controlled; make observastions and measurements using an appropriate technique, and use measurements to produce a graph; explain patterns in graphs using scientific knowledge and understanding

some pupils will have progressed further and will: relate findings about the production of oxygen in photosynthesis to wider environmental issues, for example, seasonal changes

most pupils will: decide on an appropriate approach to investigating a question about the effects of fertiliser, identifying relevant variables and choosing an appropriate sample size; present results in tables and graphs which show features effectively; draw conclusions that are consistent with the evidence, identifying shortcomings, where appropriate, and relate them to scientific knowledge and understanding

some pupils will have progressed further and will: consider critically tables of results and graphs and explain how additional data would enable them to have more confidence in their conclusions

in terms of materials and their properties

most pupils will: describe using their understanding of chemical reactions how acid rain occurs and how it affects rocks, building materials and living organisms; describe how air and water pollution are monitored and how they might be controlled

some pupils will have made more progress and will: describe a variety of environmental issues and be able to evaluate and explain the implications of these on our environment

in terms of life processes and living things

most pupils will: identify carbon dioxide from the air and water as the raw materials, and light as the energy source, for photosynthesis; explain photosynthesis as the source of biomass and represent photosynthesis by a word equation; describe how leaves are adapted for photosynthesis and how roots are adapted to take in water; distinguish between photosynthesis and respiration in plants

some pupils will have progressed further and will: describe how cells in the leaf and root are adapted for photosynthesis and for taking in the water; represent photosynthesis as a symbol equation; describe the relationship between photosynthesis and respiration in plants

in terms of life processes and living things

most pupils will: name the products of photosynthesis and some of the nutrients supplied by fertilisers; identify conditions in which crops will grow well; describe how the abundance and distribution of organisms may be affected by pesticides or weedkillers, relating this to knowledge of food webs; describe how other plants compete with food crops, and other animals compete with humans for the food crops, and that there are ways of achieving a balance between communities

some pupils will have progressed further and will: relate crop production to pyramids of numbers and explain some ways of achieving a balance between the demands of different communities within an environment; explain how toxic materials can accumulate in a food chain

→ # *Links with CASE*

Further work is done in this chapter to consolidate the pupils' ability to select and control key variables. In line with the nomenclature encountered in SATs examinations the input variable is also referred to as the independent variable, and the outcome variable as the dependent variable.

In lesson 4 pupils have the opportunity to investigate the 'Effect of soil pH on bean plant growth' (Worksheet 6.13R). This work relates to CASE 14 activities 13 and 14, which develop the idea of stochastic variables and reinforce the key words frequency, median and range. In lesson 8, consideration of an investigation on fertilisers allows pupils to consider comparative data and it touches on the use of correlation. This links with CASE 18, Treatment and effect.

➡ *Pupils' misconceptions*

Misconception	Scientific understanding
Pupils consider that the greenhouse effect and ozone depletion are indistinguishable in terms of cause and effect.	These are different problems: the former is linked to global warming, and the latter is linked to an increase in UV radiation levels.
Pupils think in terms of environmentally friendly and unfriendly effects.	There is a range of seriousness of pollution, from mildly irritating annoyances to lethal situations.
Chemicals cause pollution.	Pollution is caused not only by man-made substances and energy sources, but also by the imbalance of natural substances in the environment arising directly or indirectly from human activity.
Scientists pollute our planet.	While there have been serious pollution problems, such as the industrial revolution, many scientists now work to reduce pollution problems and improve conditions on Earth.
Plants respire using different gases.	Green plants release oxygen when they are photosynthesising. This is the way they feed and oxygen is a waste gas. They respire using oxygen and releasing carbon dioxide, like animals.
Plants photosynthesise in the day and respire at night.	Plants respire all the time (otherwise they would die), and photosynthesise when there is available light.
Plants feed by sucking up soil/nutrients.	Plants get their glucose and starch from photosynthesis by reacting together carbon dioxide and water. Nitrates are taken up through the roots in tiny quantities by comparison but help in protein production by combining with the carbohydrates.

➡ *Literacy, numeracy and other cross-curricular links*

There are opportunities in this chapter to understand, use and spell correctly key words and phrases related to environmental topics. Science and citizenship is addressed by considering the issues relating to global warming, air and water quality, and sustainable development. Pupils are asked to discuss, consider and evaluate the opinions of a wide range of interested parties as part of a role play in the 'Time to think' activity in lesson 5.

There are opportunities to calculate data from graphs and to analyse and interpret numerical data.

1 How are soils different from each other?

Learning outcomes

Pupils:

- identify a range of differences between soils and use the results from work with soil-testing kits to rank soils in terms of acidity
- identify and make a record of plants that are likely to grow well in a particular soil
- suggest the use of and evaluate the suitability of methods of reducing acidity or alkalinity of soils

What do you know?
Answers

→ Pupil's Book pages 150–152

1

Description	Type
it 'polishes', i.e. makes a shiny smooth coating on your fingers, and is greyish-brown in colour	clay
very gritty and a pale colour	sand
crumbly and dark, but not especially gritty, smooth or shiny	loam

2 b) A – clay.
  B – sandy.
  C – chalk.
  D – peat.
  E – loam.

c) Sandy soils have larger spaces between the grains, which allows nutrients to be leached out when it rains.

d) Mix in other soil types, for example some clay or loamy soil.

e) The favourable conditions would also result in the colonisation of unwanted plants (weeds).

3 a) The addition of acid would result in fizzing/bubbling.
  b) acid + carbonate $\longrightarrow$ salt + water + carbon dioxide
  c) Limestone; marble; calcite; coral.

4 All have an optimum soil pH in the range 5.0–6.5, indicating a preference for acidic soils.

5 Add some indicator powder to the measuring tube. Add a small sample of the soil to be tested. Add distilled water, shake and allow to settle. Match the colour of the solution with the pH chart provided.

6 Alkali (base); neutralisation.

7 It is a strong alkali with a pH of 14; it is very corrosive and would damage/kill plants.

8 Fruit juice is the better choice; lemonade consists of carbonic acid, which decomposes easily.

Activity

Worksheet 6.1R

Acid rain quiz

➡ *Worksheet 6.1R: Acid rain quiz (R)*
This activity is intended to establish the extent of pupils' knowledge about acid rain and its effects.

Answers

1 Neutral.
2 Natural processes; exhaust fumes from cars; burning fossil fuels.
3 Carbon dioxide; sulphur dioxide; nitrogen oxides.
4 Fish dying in Scandinavia; corrosion of buildings; deforestation.
5 Is still increasing.
6 Catalytic converters in cars; less private traffic and less air traffic; filters in chimneys of power plants and factories.
7 Has already damaged a quarter of the trees; affects some forest areas less than others.

What happens to building materials over time?
Answers

➡ *Pupil's Book pages 152–153*
1 **a)** The limestone cottage will be more prone to chemical weathering than the granite cottage, where weathering will still take place, but more slowly.
  b) Most likely to be physical weathering (freeze-thaw effect).
  c) Plants growing on the stones indicate physical biological weathering. The presence of lichens would indicate some chemical biological weathering.
  d) Spain: hotter temperatures would suggest that the stones are expanding during the day and contracting at night, resulting in physical weathering.
  UK: colder conditions suggest that the freeze-thaw effect would be more common, particularly with the higher rainfall. Greater rainfall combined with traffic pollution would result in more chemical weathering in London due to acid rain effects.

There is a wide choice of practical activities available with this lesson.

Activity

Worksheet 6.2R

Practical: Measuring soil pH

➡ *Worksheet 6.2R: Measuring soil pH (P)*
In this experiment pupils collect soil and measure its pH. Pupils are also asked to survey the plants and animals that live in the area where they collected the soil. Area surveys provide information about how well plants and animals can live under different conditions.

Equipment
• garden soil pH test kit
• distilled water
• soil from different locations (including different areas within the school grounds)
• spatulas

- digging tool
- self-sealing plastic bags

Answers to all the questions set on the worksheet will depend on the soil samples tested.

Activity

Worksheet 6.3R

Practical: Neutralising soils

→ *Worksheet 6.3R: Neutralising soils (P)*

Equipment
- pH paper and colour chart (pH range 2–10) or garden soil pH test kit
- soil from a garden, wooded area, lawn, or school grounds
- distilled water
- white vinegar (ethanoic acid)
- beakers
- stirring rods
- filter funnel
- filter papers

Answers

The missing steps in the method are:
  2 Put one filter paper into the funnel and fill it with soil from one location. Do not compact the soil down.
  3 Hold the filter paper over the measuring cylinder and slowly pour the vinegar/water mixture over the soil until some water collects in the measuring cylinder (the filter may clog quickly, but you need only a small amount of water).
  4 Check the pH of the collected water using either pH paper or a garden soil pH testing kit, and record the results.

2 Lime or powdered limestone.
3 Carbon dioxide (if calcium carbonate used).
4 Calcium ethanoate.
5 calcium carbonate + ethanoic acid $\longrightarrow$ calcium ethanoate + water + carbon dioxide
6 Powdered limestone (calcium carbonate), which is an antacid used by gardeners to neutralise acid soil and increase the pH.

Activity

Worksheet 6.4R

Practical: Selecting soil for a sports field

→ *Worksheet 6.4R: Selecting soil for a sports field (P)*

1. Water and humus content

Equipment
- eye protection
- balance
- tin lid
- tongs
- spatula

2. Dissolved chemical content

Equipment
- evaporating basin
- heating apparatus

Answers
1 Pure (distilled) water contains no dissolved contaminants.
2 No indicator reagent will mix with the sample.
3 Evaporation.
4 Soil through which water has been transported.

3. Air content

Equipment
• measuring cylinder

4. Soil density

Equipment
• measuring cylinder
• filter paper
• balance

Answers
1 Suitable consistency to support footwear; dense soils may have poor drainage which can result in waterlogging.
2 Humus will float on water; it is less dense than rock grains.

Answers to questions
1 Test 4. This would separate the humus from the rest of the soil.
2 Test 3, because it would indicate the extent of air spaces in the soil to allow effective drainage.
3 Different drainage; density of soil would affect the bounce of the ball.
4 Test 1, because the humus content would indicate the level of essential nutrients, and test 2, which would test for dissolved nutrients.
5 Tests 1, 2 and 3.
6 Better drainage; high air content.
7 Clay is more dense because the particles are very closely packed together; it can be waterlogged and heavy.
8 Toxic chemicals would wash out of the sandy soil because of its better drainage, and contaminate surrounding areas.

Activity

Worksheet 6.5R

Information processing: Soil analysis
→ *Worksheet 6.5R: Soil analysis (D)*
The tables contain data on different soils. Pupils can use the data and the diagrams of the different soil types to match the soil samples with the soil types.

Air content
1 To allow all the air to be released.

Water and humus content
2 Water.
3 Soil B.
4 Humus.
5 To ensure that all the humus has been removed.
6 Soil C. Powdered limestone (calcium carbonate) may have been added to the soil – this is an antacid used by gardeners to neutralise acid soil and increase the pH.

Filtrate analysis

7 Soil C.

8 Variation in the volume of filtrate suggests water retention by soil.

9 A mixture of B and C, giving good drainage but retention of nutrients.

10 A – clay: poor drainage, large water retention, least air content.

B – sand: highest filtrate volume, highest air content due to spaces between grains.

C – loam: dissolved nutrients, high humus content.

Activity Creative thinking: School survey

→ *Pupil's Book page 153*

Work on this could be given as homework.

2 The causes and effects of acid rain

Learning outcomes

Pupils:

- identify the causes and effects of acid rain
- identify burning of fossil fuels, for example, in vehicles, and volcanic activity as leading to acids in the environment
- identify which solutions are acidic and recognise that solutions with lower pH will be more corrosive
- represent, by drawing flow diagrams or equations, a sequence of reactions in which acid rain is formed

How pure is rainwater?

The use of state symbols is introduced at this point in the book.

(s) = solid, for example, magnesium, sugar

(l) = liquid, for example, water, ethanol

(g) = gas, for example, hydrogen, oxygen, carbon dioxide

(aq) = aqueous solution (solute disolved in water), for example, salt water.

Answers

→ *Pupil's Book page 154*

2 The energy that is released from respiration is used to carry out all the life functions (growth, reproduction etc.).

3 They are really opposites. Respiration is exothermic (releases energy), whereas photosynthesis is endothermic (absorbs light energy). Photosynthesis uses carbon dioxide and releases oxygen; respiration uses oxygen and releases carbon dioxide.

4 carbon dioxide + water $\longrightarrow$ carbonic acid

$$CO_2(g) \quad + H_2O(l) \longrightarrow \quad H_2CO_3(aq)$$

Activity Reasoning: Carbon dioxide
Answers
➡ *Pupil's Book page 155*
1 The release of carbon dioxide through plant and animal respiration, burning and bacterial decay is balanced by the removal of the gas from the air by the process of photosynthesis.
2 Burning of fossil fuels releases masses of carbon dioxide into the environment.
Deforestation and the removal of greenbelt land is reducing the photosynthesising capacity of green plants.

What causes acid rain?
Answers
➡ *Pupil's Book pages 156–158*
5 Fossil fuels contain varied amounts of the element sulphur or its compounds. When the sulphur combines with oxygen during combustion, sulphur dioxide is formed.
6 The flow chart would show sulphur combining with oxygen during combustion to produce sulphur dioxide. The sulphur dioxide then combines with water and oxygen in the air to produce sulphuric acid.
7 Natural gas, as it contains only a trace of sulphur.
8 Pupils' bar charts should show 1970, 1990 and 1999 emission levels.
9 a) The sequence will continue with the nitrogen oxides dissolving in water droplets and becoming oxidised within these airborne droplets to produce nitric acid.
b) nitrogen + oxygen ⟶ nitrogen dioxide
nitrogen dioxide + oxygen + water ⟶ nitric acid

Activity Evaluation: Which materials are most affected by acid rain?
Answers
➡ *Pupil's Book pages 158–159*
1 The more reactive metals, zinc and iron, have reacted. Stainless steel (an unreactive alloy) and copper (very low in the activity series) have not reacted. Aluminium reacts less than might be expected from its position in the activity series.
2 Make observations on a daily basis. Take digital photographs at regular intervals.
3 Stainless steel and copper are not affected by the acid, and aluminium showed little change. Three out of the five metals tested would therefore not support the conclusion.
4 Of limited use. Pupils may justify their answer in terms of the size of the sample of materials and may develop their ideas by considering their answer to Question 5.
5 A wider range of metals, for example, magnesium, tin and lead.
6 Ensure that the pieces are of equal size and surface area, so that it is a fair test.

7 There would be much less damage to building materials such as limestone and marble. Metals would be less at risk from the corrosive effects of sulphuric acid, for example iron railings and railway lines. Alternative sources of energy would have to be used, which could be expensive in the setting-up stages but over the 30 years would mean savings in fuel costs.

Ideas and evidence: Acid rain
Answers
→ *Pupil's Book pages 159–161*

1 Considering the scale and the size of points plotted, the numbers need to be estimated, so this should be seen as an opportunity to develop estimation skills.

1st	2nd	3rd	4th	5th	6th	7th	8th	9th	10th	11th	12th	13th	14th	15th
250	310	330	300	400	600	900	905	800	540	530	480	495	470	445

2 Between 7th and 9th December.
3 **a)** 250 micrograms/cm^3
   b) 1100 micrograms/cm^3
   c) 1550 micrograms/cm^3
   d) 400 micrograms/cm^3
4 As the smoke and sulphur dioxide levels increase there is an increase in deaths per day. Later, as the levels of the two pollutants drop so does the number of deaths per day.
5 **SMO**ke and fo**G**.
6 **a)** Sulphur dioxide – 26%
   Nitrogen oxides – 51%
   Smoke particles – 47%
   b) Incomplete combustion takes place inside vehicle engines due to limited supplies of air/oxygen, so carbon monoxide is one of the products. In power stations complete combustion is more likely to take place, and therefore carbon dioxide is produced.
   c) Modern fuels are often low sulphur-content fuels (ULS = ultra low sulphur).
   d) Leaves covered in soot and dust will not have good access to sunlight for photosynthesis, which will restrict their growth.
   e) Sulphur dioxide – volcanic activity, domestic oil-fired boilers and coal fires, aeroplanes and ships.
   Nitrogen oxides – lightning activity, motor vehicle exhaust gases, aeroplanes and ships.
   Smoke particles – domestic fires, bonfires, forest fires.
   Carbon monoxide – domestic boilers.
7 Diesel cars produce less carbon monoxide and hydrocarbons on average when compared with petrol cars, and they have greater fuel economy, producing less CO_2 per km. However, diesel cars produce higher emissions of nitrogen oxides compared with petrol cars (with catalyst).

   Petrol cars produce virtually no particulate matter, but produce more CO_2 per km on average, and emissions of the regulated pollutants are higher than from diesel cars.

This lesson is supported by four worksheets which review and consolidate work from Book 2: Chapter 2 Rocks and weathering, and Chapter 10 The rock cycle. This topic still causes concern in the Key Stage 3 SATs, and teachers can also use the alternative activity sheets written to support *Thinking Through Science 3 Blue*.

Activity

| Worksheet 6.6R |

Reasoning: Rock cycle definitions game

➡ *Worksheet 6.6R: Rock cycle definitions game (S)*
This provides 20 definitions and key words to match up. Pupils can then create their own definitions for the extra words given.

Answers

1 – erosion	8 – weathering	15 – mineral
2 – lustre	9 – crystals	16 – marble
3 – gneiss	10 – igneous	17 – deposition
4 – rock	11 – cementation	18 – crystallisation
5 – cleavage	12 – sedimentary	19 – geologist
6 – streak	13– compacted	20 – hardness
7 – rock cycle	14 – sandstone	

Activity

| Worksheet 6.7R |

Information processing: Types of weathering

➡ *Worksheet 6.7R: Types of weathering (S)*

Answers

Physical weathering	Chemical weathering
gravity: rocks falling from high places	plant acid: lichens growing on rocks
frost action: formation of scree	carbonic acid: limestone caverns
plant roots: lifted pavements	acid rain: blurred inscriptions of grave markings

Activity

| Worksheet 6.8R |

Practical: Take a weathering walk

➡ *Worksheet 6.8R: Take a weathering walk (P)*

Equipment
- clipboards
- magnifying glasses

Pupils take a walking tour around the school campus to observe a range of physical and chemical weathering. There should be an opportunity for pupils to record their observations, making an accurate record of the location of the weathering so that the example could be photographed/videoed.

Attainment targets
Work in the previous section should provide evidence that pupils are working towards the following attainment levels.

Use word equations to summarise chemical reactions	Level 6
Use patterns of reactivity to predict the outcome of chemical reactions	Level 7

Activity

| Worksheet 6.9R |

Reasoning: Rock cycle sequence

➡ *Worksheet 6.9R: Rock cycle sequence (E)*
Pupils cut up each of the statements and in groups agree a suitable sequence. Cards should be placed on the blank rock cycle sheet, and the rest of the exercise completed.

Answer
Possible sequence:

I, E, H, A, D, C, F, B, G.

3 Reducing the effects of acid rain

Learning outcomes
Pupils:

- describe how emissions from a particular source of acid rain could be reduced
- identify a source of acid rain and its effect on living organisms within a particular environment

How can the pollution problems caused by acid rain be solved?

Answers
➡ *Pupils' Book pages 162–165*

10 They will lower the amount of nitrogen present, and the lower temperature will make it less likely that the nitrogen present will be able to combine with oxygen to produce oxides of nitrogen.

11

Method	Advantage	Disadvantage
change air:fuel ratio	less nitrogen oxides form	there will be incomplete combustion leading to more carbon monoxide
recirculate exhaust fumes	less nitrogen oxides form	there could be more incomplete combustion leading to more carbon monoxide
catalytic converters	nitrogen oxide changed to nitrogen; hydrocarbons changed to water and carbon dioxide; carbon monoxide changed to carbon dioxide	increases the emission of carbon dioxide which will contribute to global warming

12 **a)** Neutralisation.
   b) Calcium sulphate.
13 Europe, including Scandinavia, north east of the USA, India, China and Sumatra (Indonesia).

14

Region	Environment
central Europe	industrial and built-up areas
Scandinavia	widespread forestation
north east America	industrial and built-up areas
India	a mixture of rural areas and built-up city areas with associated industries
south east coast of China	industrial
Sumatra	forestation

(India has a large industrial sector although many live on the fertile plains of the Ganges and Brahmaputra and are poor farmers.

South east coast of China: most of the industrial development is on or near the coast. China has plentiful coal supplies and a wide range of other fuels.)

15 Pupils need to use the appropriate information from pages 162–163 depending on whether the area is built up (reduction in SO_2 and NOs levels in cars), industrial (reduction in SO_2 and NOs levels in power stations) or rural areas where effective treatment of damaged areas needs to be facilitated. Reduction in levels from vehicles and power stations could impact on the levels of pollution on neighbouring rural districts.

16 Build up of industries; increase in population leading to extra transport demands and use of cars, aeroplanes and other fuelled modes of transport; pollution carried by prevailing winds from nearby sources.

17 UK, Germany, Slovakia, Czech Republic and Switzerland.

18 a) Buildings and monuments, particularly those made of limestone (calcium carbonate), will be chemically weathered by acid rain; also corrosion of metals, paints and ceramics.

b) People's health will suffer, with increasing respiratory problems (such as dry coughs, headaches, eye, nose and throat irritation). Most at risk are asthma sufferers. (There is also an indirect link to Alzheimer's disease – acid rain causes the release of toxic metals, including aluminium, which is linked to Alzheimer's disease.)

c) Roots are damaged by acidic rainfall, causing death or stunted growth; soil nutrients are destroyed by the acidity; micro-organisms that release nutrients from organic matter are destroyed, reducing the availability of nutrients; acid rain damages leaves.

d) Acid rain causes the pH to drop. A pH less than 5.5 kills all trout, salmon, plankton, snails, clams, and a pH of less than 5.2 kills all bacteria.

19 a) Southern Scandinavia is downwind of Britain and western Europe.

b) Industrial parts of central and western Europe are downwind of Eastern Europe.

The sulphuric acid (rain) enters the atmosphere, and accumulates in the clouds, which are carried by the prevailing winds long distances.

Activity Practical: Treating polluted water

Worksheet 6.10R

→ *Worksheet 6.10R: Treating polluted water (P)*

Equipment

Crushed limestone is easily obtained from local garden stores or nurseries. The acid rain can be a 0.4 M solution of sulphuric acid.

- pH paper and colour chart (pH range 2–7)
- acid rain solution
- distilled water
- measuring cylinder
- spatula
- 2 stirring rods
- crushed limestone
- beakers
- water samples

Answers

4 Bubbling.

5 Neutralisation.

6 It has a larger total surface area so it reacts more quickly with the acid and ensures all the acid is neutralised.

7 More concentrated acid; higher temperature of acid.

8 limestone + acid $\longrightarrow$ a calcium salt + water + carbon dioxide

9 calcium carbonate + nitric acid $\longrightarrow$ calcium nitrate + water + carbon dioxide

$$CaCO_3 + 2HNO_3 \longrightarrow Ca(NO_3)_2 + H_2O + CO_2$$

Activity Practical: Heating limestone

Worksheet 6.11R

→ *Worksheet 6.11R Heating limestone (P)*

The properties of limestone will be compared with the properties of quicklime and slaked lime. Pupils have to decide which chemical is the most suitable for treating lakes and forests affected by acid rain.

Equipment
- small pieces of limestone
- tripod, gauze, Bunsen burner
- 2 watch glasses
- pipettes
- pH paper
- eye protection

Answers

1 Change in appearance (colour) between limestone and quicklime. The quicklime reacts vigorously with water, resulting in the slaking of lime. The reaction is highly exothermic – the solid swells, cracks, and there is steam produced due to the quantity of heat energy transferred. The pH test shows the product to be alkaline whereas the limestone shows no obvious effect.

2 Calcium oxide.

3 Slaking of lime.
calcium oxide + water $\longrightarrow$ calcium hydroxide

4 a) Producing quicklime would be more expensive; it is an alkali – it would react vigorously with the water, raising the temperature of the water and producing an alkaline environment.

b) The limestone has to be spread over large areas of water using aeroplanes – this is expensive; crushing, packing and transporting the limestone is expensive.

4 *What factors affect the pH of rainwater?*

Learning outcomes
Pupils:

- use secondary sources to develop and test hypotheses about factors that might affect the pH of rainwater
- explain why it is appropriate to use secondary sources, search for patterns in data and describe any patterns found
- analyse and evaluate their data in terms of the quality of the data and the limitations of the data collected
- search for patterns in data and describe any patterns found

Activity ## Enquiry: Acid rain investigation

➡ *Pupil's Book page 165*

➡ *Worksheet 6.12R: Testing water samples for pH levels (D)*

| Worksheet 6.12R |
Pupils can either use secondary sources or collect and test actual samples to answer the questions posed in Question 5 on page 165 of the Pupil's Book. The worksheet offers another approach. It is important for pupils to consider the advantages and disadvantages of each method of data collection.

Equipment for sample collection
- sample bottles and caps
- plastic pipettes
- Universal Indicator
- disposable gloves

Safety
- An adult must be present to establish the depth of the water.
- Plastic gloves must be used to protect against any infection, including Weil's disease.
- The Key Stage 3 strategy unit *Strengthening the reaching and learning of interdependence* contains advice on taking groups pond dipping. Another useful document is *Group Safety at Water Margins*, from the DfES CCPR.

Answers

→ *Worksheet 6.12R: Testing water samples for pH levels (D)*

1 Pure water has a pH of 7; the pupils have not considered the possibility of any dissolved substances affecting the pH.

2 Water samples.

3 pH measurement.

4 Volume of water, temperature, amount of indicator.

5 Pupils need to consider where they will collect samples from, and will need to be supervised if they are collecting water from streams, lakes, ponds etc.

6 Supervision; suitable clothing; wounds on hands should be covered, preferably by gloves; simple apparatus (plastic containers would be most suitable).

7 pH paper only allows measurement of pH to the nearest whole number. They might have used a pH meter.

8 Using the pH meter.

9 So that the data is more reliable; avoid anomalous results.

10 6.8

11 Check pupils' tables and graphs.

12 Rainwater is very slightly acidic, due to the presence of dissolved substances.

13 **a)** Bottled water needs neutralising with a suitable (non-harmful) weak alkali.

   b) Tap water is alkaline and needs neutralising with a suitable weak acid.

15 Investigate what substances may be causing the pH levels in the bottled water and the tap water. Further work could include contacting the water board and the water bottling company for further data and information.

Answers

→ *Pupils' Book page 165*

1 The question should include the variable they intend changing (the independent variable), and the variable they intend measuring/observing (the dependent variable). For example, 'How does the pH of the acid rain affect the growth of cress seedlings?'.

2 Other factors include: environment (rural, industrial, built up); proximity of busy roads/railways/airports; average rainfall; presence of heavy industries/motorways/power stations.

3 In this situation using a sufficiently large sample balances out the effect of extreme variations. There are often variables which are difficult to control and this investigation will not fit easily into the fair test model.

4 Testing rainwater samples:
Advantages – they can repeat the tests if necessary; they can choose when and where they will carry out the tests.
Disadvantages – they will only collect local data; the collection and testing will take a lot of time.
Using secondary sources:
Advantages – allows access to a wider range of data; quick.
Disadvantages – no way of checking how reliable or accurate the sources might be.

5 Pupils' answers based on the results of their own practical investigation or on what they have found from secondary sources.

Activity Enquiry: Analysing data

→ *Pupil's Book page 166*

Group 1

1 **a)** There is no obvious correlation.
   b) Weather conditions (wind direction), and type of location (countryside, town/city, industrial area).
   c) The numbers could be placed on a map of the UK and Ireland to indicate the spread of samples and volumes taken. This would provide further data for pupils to interpret.

Group 2 and Group 3

2 The group 3 sample is twice as big.
3 The data from group 2 is far from conclusive – the pH tends to decrease, although there are not enough results to be confident. The data from group 3 suggests the opposite, that as the volume of rainfall increases, there is an increase in pH.
4 Group 3.
5 Group 2 needs more results spread across the whole volume range.
   Group 3 needs more results above 30 cm^3 spread across to 80 cm^3.
   Both groups need to reconsider the range of rainwater volume used.

Attainment targets

Work in the previous sections should provide evidence that pupils are working towards the following attainment levels.

Identify key factors in complex contexts and in which the variables cannot easily be controlled	Level 7
Synthesise information from a range of sources, and identify possible limitations in secondary data	Level 7

5 *Is pollution worse now?*

Learning outcomes

Pupils:

- describe ways in which air and water pollution in their locality is monitored
- identify steps taken to reduce pollution
- know that indicator organisms, for example lichens and aquatic organisms, are susceptible to high levels of air acidity
- identify key trends in data and draw conclusions relating to the evidence supporting the issue of global warming

Activity

Worksheet 6.13R

Practical: Effect of soil pH on bean plant growth

→ *Worksheet 6.13R: Effect of soil pH on bean plant growth (P, E)*
This activity revisits and develops the CASE lessons 13 and 14 on bean sampling and growing broad beans. Broad beans grow best in the range pH 5.5–6.5. Key words are frequency, range, median and mean. The data collected by one group can be used by other groups. This then becomes a data analysis activity.

Equipment
- large numbers of broad beans
- labels
- pots with soil at each pH: pH 3 (vinegar), pH 5 (black coffee), pH 7 (distilled water), pH 9 (borax solution), pH 11 (limewater)
- pH paper
- rulers
- digital camera if available

Answers
1, 2, 3 Possible variables are colour; texture; shape; scar of attachment to pod; size.
6 6.5
7 8.0–4.1
12 a) 6.2; 9.1–1.1
 b) 5.7

Activity

Information processing: Global warming – fact or fiction?

A useful website for accessing data on water, ecology and soil pollution is:
 http://urgent.nerc.ac.uk/search_home.htm
 (URGENT – Urban ReGeneration and the ENvironmenT.)

Answers

Worksheet 6.14R

Worksheet 6.14R: Global warming – fact or fiction? (S)
This worksheet could be used as a homework activity.
1 33 °C lower.
2 $\frac{2}{3} \times \frac{1}{2} = \frac{1}{3}$
3

Evidence	Predictions
Since 1750 the atmospheric concentration of carbon dioxide has risen by one-third	Rising global temperatures are expected to further raise sea level
Land surface temperature has risen 0.45–0.6 °C in the last century	Scientists think that the daily addition of greenhouse gases to the atmosphere will raise the Earth's average temperature by several degrees in the next century
Sea levels have risen approximately 15–20 cm (6–8 inches) worldwide in the last century	Agriculture could be affected in a variety of ways due to changes in rainfall and temperatures
Rainfall has increased by about 1 percent over the world's continents in the last century	Increased rates of extinction are expected

4 a) This will assist in the recycling of carbon dioxide by the process of photosynthesis.
 b) The extraction and chemical processing of new materials is very expensive and uses a large amount of fuel, so this would reduce carbon dioxide emissions from fuel combustion.

c) This will reduce the amount of electricity used which has been generated in a power station by the combustion of a fossil fuel (coal, oil, gas), and so reduce the amount of carbon dioxide released into the atmosphere.

d) Same argument as b).

e) This reduces the production of carbon monoxide, carbon dioxide, oxides of nitrogen, unburnt fuels and smoke, which cause atmospheric pollution and contribute to the greenhouse effect.

5 This article states that there is still some uncertainty about the extent of climate change. Scientists believe that they need more data to make confident predictions. The data collected will be plotted on scatter graphs. They will extrapolate from the graphs and predict by how much the temperatures will change in the next hundred years.

6 The satellites will give accurate measurements of any changes to ice and land mass boundaries. This will be an indication of whether temperatures are getting warmer or colder.

Activity ## Information processing: Lichens as pollution indicators
Answers

Worksheet 6.15R

➡ *Worksheet 6.15R: Lichens as pollution indicators (S)*

1 Powdery (slightly leafy).

2 Use of quadrats.

3 Take quadrat measurements of a cluster of trees using a spinner to determine the direction. Repeat this at different distances from the town centre. Or, collect an Ordnance Survey map of the town. Mark lines on the map spreading out from the town centre. Walk outwards from the town centre, using a compass to keep on course. Take samples from trees every 100 metres. Different groups can follow different directions.

4 The density of lichens increases as the distance from the city centre increases.

5 Pupils need to find out how acidic the atmosphere is around their school. A lichen survey would give them an indication of the relative levels of acid pollution, and they could measure the pH levels of samples of rainfall in a number of places around the school.

How does acid rain affect fish and other aquatic organisms?
Answers

➡ *Pupil's Book page 167*

20 Smaller, lighter organisms may be more sensitive to lower pH conditions which would affect their health. This would make it less likely that they could find food and escape predators.

21 These animals are lower down the food chain so the accumulation of any toxins present would be at a lower concentration.

22 Below a pH of 6, the snail population would decrease, and this would impact on algae and aquatic plants. At 5.5 the mayfly population would decline, and this would impact on dragonfly and fish populations. At 5 and below both bass and trout numbers would decline.

What is happening to the environment? Answers

→ *Pupil's Book pages 169–170*

23 Each location has been graded as high or low in the following table. Pupils can grade within those categories as long as they can justify their classification.

Higher pollution (C–D)	Lower pollution (A–B)
Cities/towns in deep valleys	Cities/towns on hills
In summer, during sunny, still, weather, particularly ozone in suburban and rural areas	Windy or wet weather at any time of year
In winter, in cold, still, foggy weather, particularly vehicle pollutants in large cities	Rural areas away from major roads and factories (for most pollutants except ozone)
Busy roads with heavy traffic next to high buildings and busy road junctions	Residential roads with light traffic
High levels of solid fuel (for example, coal and wood) used for heating in the local area	Smoke control area or areas with high levels of gas or electric used for heating

24 A town park – leafy lichens (medium tolerance).
Trees along a busy main road – slightly leafy lichens (tolerant). Pupils may refer to the scarcity of the shrubby lichens along the busy main road, and the abundance of these and leafy lichens will be greatest in the village orchard.
A village orchard – shrubby lichens (highly intolerant).

25 The numbers of each species present would indicate the levels of acidity in the lake. Each has a different tolerance to acidity. As the pH drops due to pollutants, each species in turn will decrease in numbers.

Time to think

→ *Pupil's Book page 170*

Each activity allows pupils the opportunity to reflect on the extent of their understanding of these environmental issues. It would not be necessary to complete all three; it depends on the time available and the nature of the class.

These activities provide opportunities for peer assessment. Pupils can decide on criteria for quality in the products of the task and then advise one another on where they feel they have been done successfully and where improvements could be made.

6 *Green plants*

Green machine
Answers

➡ *Pupil's Book pages 171–172*

Pupils should be encouraged to look at the diagrams and discuss them with other pupils. They should then use these ideas to create a poster, a concept map or summary notes. From these discussions and products you should be able to pick up their starting point for understanding photosynthesis and plant structure.

26 Products will vary, but accuracy and understanding should be checked and challenged. Terms such as variegated, destarched plants and energy transfer process may be useful additions to their posters, concept maps or summary notes, to see how they incorporate them into their ideas.

27 A variety of answers may come up. For example, plants make their own food using CO_2 and H_2O while humans take in complex foods such as carbohydrates, proteins and fats. Plants utilise solar energy to make food, whereas humans take in chemically stored energy.

Humans need to grow, breed and kill, catch or collect their food, while plants can remain in place and produce it.

28 a) To get rid of the waterproof layer and to break down cell walls, to make it easier for chemicals to reach the insides of the cells.

b) C, A, B.

c) Iodine in potassium iodide solution, which we usually call 'iodine'.

d) Starch – turns blue/black.
Leaf in light – turns blue/black.
Leaf in dark – remains brown.
Potato – turns blue/black.
Seed – turns blue/black.

29 a) Leaves A and D did not affect the iodine, which means that they do not contain starch. This is because these leaves come from plants kept in the dark. Leaves B and C do contain starch, which is shown by turning the iodine blue/black. These were leaves from plants kept in the light. This means that light is needed for leaves to produce starch in photosynthesis.

b) In leaves A and D nothing happens.
In leaves B and C, the chlorophyll uses sunlight energy to combine CO_2 and H_2O to make sugar, which is stored in the leaves as starch.

Question 30 could be set for homework – see the notes for Pupil's Book page 173 in lesson 7.

Activity

| Worksheet 6.16R |

Practical: Testing leaves for starch

→ *Worksheet 6.16R: Testing leaves for starch (P)*
It would be a good idea to test some destarched leaves and leaves from plants kept in the light. There is often confusion with this practical as the heating stage is really only necessary to break down the leaf membranes and some cell walls in order that iodine can get into the leaf. Worksheet 6.16R tries to make this evident. It is better for pupils to use an electrically heated water bath than allow them to heat the water with a Bunsen when there are bottles of ethanol around. (The diagrams on Pupil's Book page 171 include a Bunsen for this purpose as this is the diagram they are likely to meet in examinations.)

7 *Use of plants*

Learning outcomes
Pupils:

- explore and categorise the various uses of plants and plant materials and products
- relate how farming, science and technology depend on one another to improve crop production
- check on function and details of photosynthesis

→ *Pupil's Book page 173*
Many pupils fail to realise that through photosynthesis green plants have the basic building block, glucose, which can then be converted into a whole range of other materials. For example, glucose units can be joined together to make starch or cellulose. If nitrates are added, glucose can be turned into proteins which make up the cytoplasm of cells. So wood, bark, oils, resins and fibres can all be made by plants. The photographs on page 173 of the Pupil's Book provide a starter for thinking about this. It may be useful to set Question 30 as a homework activity prior to lesson 7, or to do it as a group activity in the lesson. It must be made clear that plants make these materials for themselves, but humans have harvested them and now grow plants specially for these materials. In many cases, humans have carried out special breeding programs to select plants that produce certain materials in abundance or of high quality.

Answer
→ *Pupil's Book page 173*
30

Textiles	Wooden products	Paper products	Food	Other
cotton thread	fences	books	fruit, vegetables	rubber
cotton fabric	floorboards	newspapers	nuts, grains	oils
linen fabric	furniture	tissue	sugar	perfume
rope	pencils	writing paper	oils	medicines

Time to think

→ *Pupil's Book page 174*

This activity provides an opportunity for the ideas just described to be discussed, and it also provides a useful summary point to check on understanding of photosynthesis.

Ideas and evidence: The story of wheat

→ *Pupil's Book pages 175–176*

The story of wheat exemplifies how humans have cultivated a plant for its products. This activity provides a comprehension exercise.

Answers

1 Ancient Greek and Roman writings; preserved grains in Egyptian tombs.
2 To improve natural-growing varieties of wheat.
3 Produced stronger plants, higher yield, and varieties with resistance to drought and disease.
4 The amount of produce from a certain area of land.
5 Bread wheat has a higher gluten content; this makes the dough elastic and traps the bubbles of carbon dioxide, giving bread a light, airy texture.
6 North America, southern parts of South America, Europe, the Middle East, northernmost parts of Africa, South Africa, Russia, central Asia (Kazakhstan etc.), north-east China and Korea, Australia.

Activity Research: Cotton

→ *Pupil's Book page 176*

A useful homework activity is for pupils to research the cultivation and processing of cotton.

Plant drugs and poisons

→ *Pupil's Book page 177*

Plant drugs and poisons are another group of plants that are used – for health or for their toxicity.

Activity Creative thinking: The importance of plants

→ *Pupil's Book page 177*

Pupils make a poster, pamphlet or presentation on the importance of plants to humans.

8 What are the best conditions for photosynthesis?

Learning outcomes

Pupils:

- construct good questions to check understanding as well as comprehension of text
- evaluate approaches to investigative work in terms of sample size, reliability and validity of data

Ideas and evidence: van Helmont

→ *Pupil's Book page 178*

Most pupils will understand that photosynthesis produces new materials and that plants need mineral salts, particularly nitrates, to grow, but they may not link these together because they often learn these ideas separately. The van Helmont story helps stress the idea that most of the growth comes from the plant photosynthesising. Pupils are asked at the end of this piece to write 2 or 3 questions to check understanding. The types of questions that should be encouraged are:

Why did van Helmont decide not to add anything to the pot of soil apart from water?
Where had the materials for the growth of the willow plant come from?
Why was the increase in weight of the tree after 5 years much greater than the loss of weight of the soil over this time?
Why was there a decrease in the weight of the soil after 5 years?

Activity Evaluation: Mung bean experiment

→ *Pupil's Book page 179*

The mung bean experiment allows pupils to check on their understanding of van Helmont's ideas. They have to select the set-up that they believe most resembles that of the original experiment. As well as this, ideas such as sample size and fair testing are challenged.

Answers

1 Because there is only one plant, and any increase would be too small to be shown against the total mass of the pot and soil.
2 Group B retained the water by covering the dish with cling film, and conditions were much the same for all the seeds. With group C, different amounts of water could have been sprayed onto and transpired from the plants daily, and so this could have affected the mass.
3 Pupils may select group A, because only one plant was used. They may select group C, because nothing was added to the system apart from water, and so the method is very similar to van Helmont's.
They may select group B, because this achieved what van Helmont was trying to show.

Activity

Worksheet 6.17R

Information processing: Fertilisers

➡ *Worksheet 6.17R: Fertilisers (D)*
This is a data analysis sheet on plant growth. The idea developed is similar to that for the CASE activity in which the idea of correlation is developed. The idea of fair testing is also considered.

Answers

1 Comparison with previous years is a possible comparator, but comparing yields using the two different fertilisers in the same year allows control and comparison. Discussion about two halves of the crop field or alternate plots will draw out the variables that could affect the results (soil type, edge factor, vulnerability to grazing etc.).

2 Berrivite produces 151 kg while Growmore produces 136 kg. The results with Berrivite are much more erratic, with high and low values which pupils may recognise from data. You could plot cumulative scores for 10, 20, 30,40 and 50 plants with each fertiliser to focus on this.

3 This leads to discussion of 'high' and 'low' values for Berrivite. Growmore produces yields above on average 20 kg per bush in all cases; Berrivite does this in only two rows. Growmore is more consistent.

9 *The role of the leaf and the root in photosynthesis*

Learning outcomes
Pupils:

- recognise the structure and function of plant parts
- explore efficiency and comparative costings of biofuels
- use reasoning to look at proportionality

Looking inside leaves

➡ *Pupil's Book pages 180–181*
This section looks at leaves and roots from a structure/function viewpoint. It also explains how industry needs to consider input costs (both energy and financial) and output to judge efficiency of production.

Answers

31 Green plants and some bacteria.

32 Because they transfer light energy into chemical energy (food).

33 So that they can increase crop yields or develop crops that can grow in different conditions. This has economic and sometimes important humanitarian benefits.

34 Bioethanol: $0.1/0.9 \times 100 = 11.1\%$
Biodiesel: $0.44/0.56 \times 100 = 78.6\%$
Energy efficiency can be increased by processing at the source of growth, so that local production is encouraged.

35 A gigajoule is a thousand million joules.

36 Pest-resistance would mean that less plant material is eaten and damaged by pests and so efficiency is increased.

37 There is a strain on fossil fuel resources and also concerns over pollution from fossil fuels. Biofuels are renewable and less of a problem in terms of pollution.

38 They contain many chloroplasts. Palisade cells are also densely packed, so that there are more cells able to photosynthesise.

39 Carbon dioxide (CO_2) and water (H_2O).

40 Oxygen (O_2).

41 carbon dioxide + water $\xrightarrow[\text{energy}]{\text{light}}$ glucose + oxygen

Activity ## Information processing: Underwater photosynthesis

➡ *Pupil's Book pages 182–183*

The experiment shown on page 182 of the Pupil's Book can be demonstrated prior to the activity to improve pupils' understanding. This activity looks at the idea of inverse proportionality (compensation in CASE terms) and asks pupils to look at graphical data and make predictions.

Answers

1

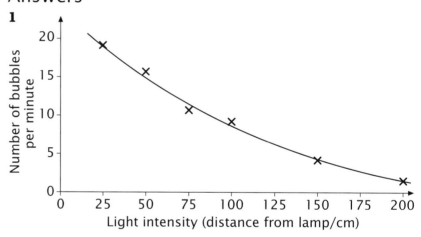

2 Distance from lamp (light intensity).

3 Amount and type of plant.

4 It is difficult to get light readings in this set-up.

5 a) 14 bubbles per minute (less than 16 at 50 cm).
   b) 12 bubbles per minute (greater than 11 at 75 cm).
   c) 1 bubble per minute.

6 Approximately 55 cm.

7 See if it will relight a glowing spill.

8 When CO_2 was added the rate of photosynthesis increased (for example, at a distance of 200 cm, 5 bubbles per minute were produced, compared to just 2 before the extra CO_2 had been pumped in). So CO_2 has an important role in increasing the rate of photosynthesis.

Ideas and evidence: The discovery of oxygen

➡ *Pupil's Book pages 183–184*

The 'Ideas and evidence' piece on Joseph Priestley's work is an extension activity that looks specifically at the way scientists can collaborate and develop ideas from one another's work. It can provide a useful homework activity. The phlogiston theory is also dealt with in Chapter 9.

Answers

1 The theory states that many chemicals contain a substance called phlogiston, which is released into the air on burning, so they lose mass when they burn.
2 Categorised as different types of 'air', with the 'goodness' of air equating to the amount of respiration it would support.
3 Priestley was able to use the gases produced from fermentation for his experiments.
4 Remove some of the oxygen from a bell jar of air by burning a candle in it. Have a mouse, plant or other organism in the jar to observe that the organism is still supplied with enough oxygen to respire.
5 'I have discovered a gas with five to six times the capacity to support respiration than air.'
'Animals and plants both remove oxygen from the air when they respire but plants also photosynthesise and so replace the oxygen.
6 He helped Lavoisier disprove the phlogiston theory since it is oxygen and not a substance inside a chemical that supports combustion and respiration.

Rooted to the spot
Answers
→ *Pupil's Book page 185*
42 **a)** C and D.
   b) C and D.
   c) A and B.

Activity Reasoning: Mineral salts
Answers
→ *Pupil's Book page 186*
1 The table should have one dependent (input) variable (growing medium), and one or two independent (outcome) variables (appearance or growth and development). For example:

Growing medium	Appearance	Development
complete culture	healthy	green leaves and good divided roots
no nitrogen	small	some leaf and root development
no magnesium	normal growth	yellow leaves

etc.

2 The same amount of solution has been used. The plants have all been kept in the same conditions.
3 For normal plant growth a range of mineral salts are needed. If any are deficient, there may be reduction in size, discoloration of the leaves, poor root growth or a combination of these problems.
4 Grow more than one plant in each condition.

10 *The importance of green plants to the environment*

Learning objectives

Pupils:

- review ideas developed in the chapter
- evaluate the parameters of a model for carbon dioxide input and output
- highlight areas to focus on for improvement or further development

Activity ## Reasoning: Atmosphere model

➡ *Pupil's Book page 187*

This 'Reasoning' activity and the following 'Time to think' activity are useful review activities for this chapter. Group work, peer assessment and support should be encouraged for these activities.

Answers

1 It does have an animal and a plant but the numbers are not representative.

2 Ideas generated from this question should be discussed.

Activity ## Review: Test on the environment

Worksheet 6.18R

➡ *Worksheet 6.18R: Test on the environment (R)*

Answers

1 Carbon dioxide; glucose. (2 marks)

2 All ticks except photosynthesis. (1 mark)

3 Sulphur dioxide; nitrogen oxide. (2 marks)

4 a) They produce sulphur dioxide.
b) Sulphur dioxide is released from the burning of petrol. (2 marks)

5 Lowers pH/makes it acidic; releases heavy metals from the soil. (2 marks)

6 Many industries moved out of London; catalytic converters on modern vehicles; fewer factories using fossil fuels; chimneys have to have filters to reduce pollution; chimneys built taller to prevent pollution affecting local area. (Any 3.) (3 marks)

7 Eliminates = kills off.
Biodiversity = wide range of species. (2 marks)

8 Some lichens are more tolerant of sulphur dioxide than others. There is more sulphur dioxide in Sheffield, so different types of lichen would be found there. (2 marks)

9 a) Palisade layer. (1 mark)
b) To allow gases in and out. (1 mark)
c) Increased light intensity leads to increased rate of photosynthesis. (1 mark)

10 Greenhouse effect. (1 mark)

7 Genes and inheritance

→ ## *Rationale*

This chapter provides up to 8½ hours of teaching materials. When teaching this chapter, teachers should make reference to their school's sex education policy and PSHE scheme. Teachers will be aware of the need for sensitivity to the personal circumstances of individual pupils and their families when dealing with genetic inheritance, characteristics and genetic diseases. It is unwise to do activities about personal family trees.

The key ideas explored through this chapter are interdependence and the cell. The idea of interdependence in and between biological and physical environments is fundamental. By the end of Year 6 most pupils will have some understanding of the links between life processes in animals and plants and the environments in which they are found. They will have some understanding of reproduction. They know that the wide variety of animals, plants and materials can be classified using their similarities and differences. They will have been taught that animals and plants are often adapted to their environment through differences in their structure.

In Year 7, pupils will have developed knowledge and understanding that humans depend on and affect living organisms and their physical environment. They will know that organisms that belong to the same species share many characteristics, and that variation is fundamental and inevitable. They learn how natural and artificial selection can affect an organism's success in living and growing in its environment. They will know that cells are relatively very small and that although 'typical' animal and plant cells have similarities and differences, the function of specialised cells depends on their structure. They will know how sperm and egg cells are adapted for reproduction. They learn that complex, multi-celled organisms, such as humans and green plants, need time to grow and develop, and have specialised organ systems; and that reproductive systems ensure that offspring are similar to their parents.

In Year 8 pupils will have looked at interdependence as a key idea in ecology, and explored cell structure in more depth when studying microbes and disease.

There are opportunities for three different types of scientific enquiry in this chapter. These are:

1 Pattern seeking in surveys and correlations – see lessons 2 and 6.
Objectives:

* to use preliminary work to decide what to measure and observe and whether the approach is practicable

- to consider what other factors, including those that cannot be controlled, might affect the results and how to deal with them
- to collect and record data appropriately
- to identify and describe trends in data
- to evaluate the limitations of the evidence by considering sample size and the possible effect of other factors
- to use scientific knowledge and understanding to interpret results

2 Using experimental models and analogies to explore an explanation, hypothesis or a theory – see lessons 3 and 5. Objectives:

- to use preliminary work with a model to decide what to measure and to determine the number of measurements to be taken
- to record measurements
- to record data on a graph and draw an appropriate curve/line to fit data
- to identify and describe patterns in graphs
- to evaluate the conclusion by considering how good the data is

3 Using secondary sources – see lessons 3, 4, 5 and 7. Objectives:

- to decide which factors may be relevant to an enquiry
- to identify when it is appropriate to use data from secondary sources
- to search for information
- to decide which sources of information are appropriate
- to select appropriate data from secondary sources
- to identify and describe patterns in data
- to present information appropriately
- to look critically at sources of secondary data
- to look critically at results to decide how strongly they support a hypothesis or prediction
- to interpret results using scientific knowledge and understanding

This chapter has plenty of opportunities to look at the development of ideas and evidence in inheritance, which compared with many other areas of school science has a relatively recent history. Pupils have access to lots of media stores and popular science TV programmes featuring these ideas.

→ *Overview*

The textbook sections, activities and worksheets have been arranged into 1 hour blocks to aid lesson planning. Clearly several of the activities and worksheets could form part of a homework session. The planning includes reading time for individual sections but some teachers may prefer to organise this as homework preparation for the following lesson. Worksheets are of six types – extension (E), support for an activity (S), practical (P), key skills (K), developmental (D) and review (R) – to allow for differentiation and flexibility to accommodate teachers' preferred practice. The actual timing and emphasis on different sections will depend on the current knowledge base of the pupils, the ability of the teaching group and the preferences of the teacher.

Lesson	Worksheets
1 Introducing inheritance	Worksheet 7.1R: True/false statements (R) Worksheet 7.2R: Flower structure (P)
2 Variation	
3 Genetics	Worksheet 7.3R: How does chance influence inheritance? (E) Worksheet 7.4R: Variations in pea growth (P)
4 Why the variation?	Worksheet 7.5R: Family inheritance: eye colour (S)
5 Genes	Worksheet 7.6R: Researching genetic disorders (S)
6 Selection	Worksheet 7.7R: How the wild cabbage became edible (S)
7 Mutation	
8 Genetic engineering	
Review	Worksheet 7.8R: Test on genes and inheritance (R)

➡ *Chapter plan*

	Demonstration	Practical	ICT	Activity	Word play	Time to think	Ideas and evidence
Lesson 1		Flower structure				What do you know?	Inheritance
Lesson 2			Data processing	Reasoning: Variation in populations Information processing: Mendel's peas Enquiry: Studying characteristics			
Lesson 3		Variations in pea growth	Use of word processing and graphics software Internet research	Enquiry: Investigating probability Reasoning: Same or different Creative thinking: Boy or girl Reasoning: Twins and siblings	Identical similar, different		
Lesson 4				Reasoning: Exploring probablility Reasoning: Family inheritance	'Luck' or 'chance' sayings	Environ-mental variation	DNA – life's spiral staircase

table continues

	Demonstration	Practical	ICT	Activity	Word play	Time to think	Ideas and evidence
Lesson 5			Internet research Word processing	Research: Genetic disorders Creative thinking: Gene map Information processing: Gene model Research: GM crops Creative thinking: Company identity		Article on genetic engineering Review	Stevens and Wilson
Lesson 6				Information processing: What do you know? Research: Natural selection Reasoning: Better breeds Reasoning: How the wild cabbage became edible	Adaptation		Evolution
Lesson 7				Enquiry: Peas			
Lesson 8		Choice of full investiga-tion	Internet research PowerPoint presentation	Research: Rare breeds		Review of chapter	
Review				Review: Test on genes and inheritance			

 # Expectations

At the end of this chapter

in terms of scientific enquiry

most pupils will: select and use secondary sources of information about inheritance and selective breeding; plan how to collect, store and use data about large numbers of individual organisms; use ICT to produce graphs and draw conclusions from these; evaluate the strength of evidence in relation to sample size and variations within the sample

some pupils will have progressed further and will: synthesise information about inheritance and selective breeding and identify limitations in the data; assemble and decide whether the data collected about individuals is sufficient for firm conclusions

in terms of life forces and living things

most pupils will: identify some characteristics and describe how they are influenced by environmental conditions; describe how sexual reproduction results in genetic information being inherited from both parents; identify desirable characteristics in a plant or animal that arise from selection (artificial and natural); outline how these characteristics are passed on and discuss social issues related to selective breeding

some pupils will have progressed further and will:
describe how selective breeding results in offspring with
desirable characteristics and that asexual reproduction
produces clones; know about genetic mutations and gene
manipulation

➡ *Links with CASE*

The main CASE reasoning patterns developed in this chapter
are probability, with some reference to correlation linked to
this, and modelling. Many biological investigations rely on
probability reasoning (lessons 3 and 4). Deductions and
inferences are often expressed as 'the most likely explanation'.
There are several places in this chapter where pupils need to
understand the use of sampling as a means of ensuring that
investigations are 'fair' and that variations can only be
investigated using representative sampling methods. It is
implicit that a representative sample assumes that any weak
correlation between two or more variables is likely NOT to be
due to chance (a null hypothesis). If a strong correlation is
found then it is not due to chance. In genetics, the importance
of ratios allows pupils to model the probable offspring of
parental crosses (lessons 2, 3 and 4). There is also a reminder
of how analogies make useful scientific models (lesson 5).

➡ *Pupils' misconceptions*

Misconception	Scientific understanding
Chromosomes only exist when a cell is dividing.	Chromosomes become visible as they thicken when the cell divides; they are too thin to be seen usually.
When any cell divides the two new cells have half the chromosomes.	Only sex cells contain half the chromosome numbers; all other cells contain a full set.
Chromosomes and genes are the same thing.	Chromosomes are made up of genes.
Apes are closely related to humans because 98% of their genes are the same as ours.	This is a media myth. We do not know the ape's genome so we cannot compare it with ours. So far only 30 to 40 basic proteins are similar in humans and apes.
Recent events influence the chances of the next event, for example, a couple who already have five sons are more likely to have a girl next time.	Probability theory states that each and every chance event has the same probability of occurring, whatever happened previously, unless that event itself directly changes the conditions (conditional probability).
Human cloning will result in lots of identical human beings, like robots.	A clone cannot be an exact copy of its DNA donor. The environment will modify it and non-nucleic DNA in the receiving organism will also influence the cloned organism.
Evolution is only a theory as it has not been proved, and creation theory is just as likely to be true.	A theory in science is based on a series of logical statements that can be used together to give an explanation that can be tested. The creation theory is not a scientific theory; it is based on belief and is not open to the same sort of scientific investigations as evolution.
GM foods will alter our genes if we eat them. They also kill insects.	Genes are proteins that are broken down during digestion, so they cannot directly influence our genome. So far surveys show that insect abundance and diversity is not affected by the growth of GM crops.

⇒ # *Literacy, numeracy and other cross-curricular links*

Several lessons encourage research on the internet, particularly where there are 'Ideas and evidence' sections. These could act as a basis for extended writing activities. There is some scope for using spreadsheets in the investigations about variations. Links with numeracy are provided by finding the range, mean and median of sets of data, and by working out proportions, ratios and probability, but mathematical calculations are routine and simple.

Language for learning

By the end of this chapter pupils will be able to understand, use and spell correctly:

- words and phrases relating to inheritance – for example, clone, gene, genetic information, genome, chromosome, gamete, genetically modified, selective breeding
- words with different meanings in scientific and everyday contexts – for example, inheritance, cell, variety, variation, model, probable, mean, average
- words with similar but distinct meanings – for example, variety, breed, species, adaptation
- words and phrases relating to scientific enquiry – for example, mean, mode, median, data sets, frequency tables, probability, correlation, sampling, representative, reliable.

Through the activities pupils will develop their skills in:

- appraising written and visual images quickly for their usefulness
- carrying out a web-search using relevant key words to research questions
- writing closely-argued text where precise links and connections are made within sentences
- asking questions to extend thinking and refine ideas.

1 *Introducing inheritance*

Learning outcomes
Pupils:

- assess their own understanding of the meanings of key words associated with inheritance – for example, chromosome, gene, DNA
- describe some ways in which sperm and egg cells are adapted to their functions
- summarise how sexual reproduction occurs in flowering plants
- summarise similarities and differences in fertilisation in flowering plants and animals
- explain the importance of Mendel's work in genetics

Worksheet 7.1R

What do you know?

→ *Pupil's Book pages 188–189*
→ *Worksheet 7.1R: True/false statements (R)*

It is essential in this first lesson to find out what pupils already know or do not know, as much of the work to come builds on knowledge that should have been acquired in Years 7 and 8. Spend 10 to 15 minutes on the quick quiz in the textbook on page 189 (groups can swap and mark each other's answers), or use Worksheet 7.1R (True/false statements). If you use the worksheet, set Question 7 (about what causes variation in wheat) as homework.

Answers

→ *Pupil's Book page 189*

1 'Inheritance' means the passing on of things from parents to offspring – in science it particularly refers to characteristics and genetic variations.

2 Sperm cells are small, mobile (with a tail), and carry half the genetic information found in a male's normal cells. They are made in the testes.

3 Egg cells are large, immobile and have a thick jelly covering. They too contain half the genetic information in the female's normal cells. They are made in the ovaries.

4 Any fertilised egg has obtained half its genetic materials from the mother and half from the father. By chance alone some of the genetic information found in brothers and sisters will be the same, so they will share some characteristics.

5 Identical twins are formed when the fertilised egg splits into two cells during early embryo development. Each new cell continues to develop into a baby, both with the same genetic material.

6 'Unique' means one of a kind, original.

7 Variations in wheat plants could have been caused by variations inherited from either parents (genetic factors) or by environmental factors such as lack of water, a windy site or poor soil. The two factors, genetic and environmental, may both together produce variation.

Answers

➡ *Worksheet 7.1R: True/false statements (R)*

Identical twins do not have to be the same sex	False
Genes are found in every living organism	True
DNA stands for Deoxygenaterhizome Nuclide Antacid	False
Genes are made up of DNA	True
Every living organism is made up of cells	True
Chromosomes are made up of genes	True
Mutation means the same as alien	False
All living cells contain a nucleus	True
Every fly in the world has the same number of chromosomes	True
In measuring height of people, mean, mode and median are all different types of averages	True
Genetically modified crops contain genes but normal crops do not	False
Brothers and sisters are similar because their cells have the same chromosomes	False
Flowers are the sex organs of plants	True
Sperm and egg cells have the same number of chromosomes as cheek cells	False
We already have the technology to clone a human baby	False
Two parents are needed for asexual reproduction	False
Some animals can breed across species, e.g. donkey and horse	True
Variations in human height are inherited	True
Giraffes have long necks because they gradually got stretched over many generations	False
'Unique' means 'the only one of its kind'	True

Ideas and evidence: Inheritance

➡ *Pupil's Book pages 189–190*
Pupils should do this activity on their own so they have an opportunity to appraise a written text quickly for its usefulness. Give them a time limit of 10 minutes. Make sure that they have understood the key words: genetics, inheritance, offspring, genes, heredity, traits, characteristics, generations.

Chromosomes

➡ *Pupil's Book page 191*
It is not essential that pupils have detailed knowledge of chromosomes, but they may have heard the word in news reports so it is useful at this stage to distinguish the difference between genes, genetic materials and chromosomes. The activity also encourages pupils to revisit the previous 'Ideas and evidence' section. You could show a short video clip of meiotic cell division so that pupils can see the movement of chromosomes and how they divide up into sex cells.

If you wish to do Worksheet 7.2R in this lesson then this Pupil's Book section can be left out or given as a homework.

Answers

→ *Pupil's Book page 191*

1 The characteristics we inherit from our parents are passed on to us, the offspring, inside the nuclei of the sex cells, as genes.

2 The word 'gene' comes from the Greek for 'descent'. Genes are the things that carry our characteristics from one 'generation' to another.

3 Perhaps a name that says it carries characteristics, for example, character particle or inheritance unit.

More about Mendel

→ *Pupil's Book page 192*

→ *Worksheet 7.2R: Flower structure (P)*

Worksheet 7.2R

Pupils need to know the structure and function of a typical flower. Here a link is made between the importance of sexual reproduction in flowers and Mendel's work on inheritance. If you have time, Worksheet 7.2R is a practical investigation into flower structure. You need at least 30 minutes to complete it.

Equipment

Each pair will need:

- 1 buttercup flower (or similar)
- 1 grass head (cocksfoot, rye, or ear of barley)
- magnifying glass
- white tile
- forceps
- lamp

A useful website for all plant-related resources is run by Science and Plants for Schools:

http://www-saps.plantsci.cam.ac.uk/

Their aims are to promote exciting teaching of plant science and molecular biology, to develop new educational resources and to interest young people in plants and molecular biology.

Answers

→ *Pupil's Book page 193*

4 Pupils should be able to identify the name and functions of: carpel, containing egg cells (female gametes) at its base (inside the swollen ovary), stamens, containing pollen grains (the male gametes), stem or stalk, petals, sepals. There is no need to look at the structure of anthers or the carpel in more detail at this Key Stage.

5 Cross-pollination is when the male gametes, the pollen, travel from one plant to another, where they will land on the carpel and fertilise that plant's ova; self-pollination is when the pollen lands on the top of the carpel of the same plant, so that the plant will self-fertilise.

6 Wind and insects can carry pollen from one plant to another.

7 To artificially cross-pollinate a flower, you could remove the stamens (male parts) of that flower so that only pollen from another plant lands on its carpel. Alternatively you could dust the carpel with a paintbrush full of pollen from another plant. This is done so that you can be sure which plant is providing the male gametes in the formation of the seeds (offspring).

8 Pupils can make up a quiz, a crossword, a true/false knowledge card game (see Chapter 2, page 36 of this Teacher's Book, for method), or make and cut out flower parts to rearrange and labels to go with them. This last question can be used as a homework activity or an extra activity at any time through the rest of this chapter.

2 *Variation*

Learning outcomes

Pupils:

- recognise the difference between continuous and discontinuous variation in populations
- describe similarities between parents and offspring in pea plants
- identify some inherited characteristics in plants and animals
- use modelling methods to develop their reasoning about probability and chance
- present data sets and frequency tables using ICT to make graphs
- use sampling methods to ensure data is representative
- make and record appropriate measurements
- explain how evidence supports conclusions
- relate characteristics to genetic information passed from both parents

The emphasis on variation and the factors that influence it builds on the work done in Year 7. The most important part of this lesson is to develop pupils' ability to use sampling to examine variation. You can use Worksheets 7.3R and/or 7.4R here. These are particularly useful if you have used the CASE materials in Year 8, as these lessons are similar to *Thinking Science* lessons 13 and 14 and are designed to develop probability reasoning. If they are not used here, they can be used at any time in this chapter as a bridging activity. Details of the worksheets can be found in the notes for lesson 3.

Activity ## Reasoning: Variation in populations

→ *Pupil's Book page 193*

This reasoning activity is a reinforcement of work done in Year 7 (see Book 1 Chapter 2 pages 48, 53–55). If you have not got time, leave out this activity and go on to the next section on variables.

Answers

1 Human height shows continuous variation; no two people are the same height. The pea plants are all either tall or short, so they show discontinuous variation.

a) The range of the human population's height is from 136 cm to 208 cm.

b) There are two very narrow ranges of the pea height, the small (dwarf) peas are around 36 cm and the tall ones range from 111 to 123 cm.

2 It would have been very difficult for Mendel to have worked out his ideas about inheritance if he had been looking at continuous characteristics (many characteristics are continuous in human populations). He could not have seen the genetic inheritance pattern from parent to offspring so easily.

Variables
Answers
➡ *Pupil's Book page 194*

9 Continuous variables are:

- length of a human hand
- width of a human hand
- number of people with blue eyes
- length of a worm
- length of pine cones
- number of people with grey eyes

Discontinuous variables are:

- number of peas in a pod
- number of flowers on a bluebell stem
- number of petals in a daisy head

Note that pupils have to guess about discontinuous variables. This can lead to a short discussion about how they would find out if they were right by sampling, measuring and looking for relationships.

Activity Information processing: Mendel's peas
➡ *Pupil's Book pages 194–195*

It is not important that pupils memorise this example of pea crosses. The diagram is to show them how a sequence of annotated diagrams can describe fertilisation and inheritance. Making it into an overhead projection transparency or projecting it onto a white board facilitates discussion and explanation.

Answers
1 In the second generation the ratio is 3 tall to 1 short plant (3:1).

2 For a human population use a continuous line graph, as this is a continuous variable; for a pea population use a bar chart as there are only two categories of height, tall and short. It is a discontinuous variable.

It is helpful to ask pupils about the type of variables they have been using to make graphs in maths.

Collecting data

→ *Pupil's Book Page 195*

This is an important data processing exercise about measuring and sorting characteristics into data sets and frequency tables to look at variations. It takes about 30 minutes, and it is helpful to bring in some real daisies for pupils to look at. Pupils could be asked to design a simple spreadsheet that could be used to tally and sum totals, as well as plotting the graph.

Answers

10

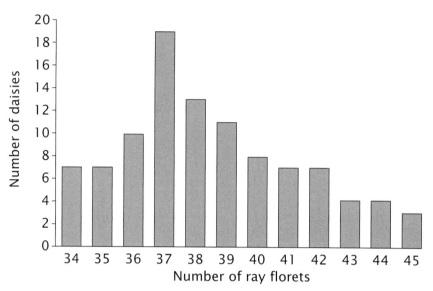

11 The numbers of ray florets fall into whole number categories; there are no half florets. Also, the range is between 34 and 45, so it is restricted.

12 34

13 45

14 34 to 45.

15 The median is the middle measurement, i.e. the 50th when the results are in order. The median here is 38.

16 The average number of ray florets is found by multiplying each category of ray florets by the number of flowers that have that number, adding these totals together and dividing by 100 (the total number of flowers examined). This gives 38.53 florets but since it is not possible to have part-florets, pupils should say that 39 is the average.

17 This is a question for class discussion. Ask pupils to work in pairs to suggest a number, then in groups of four. Write up each group answer for each organism and use these to discuss the difficulties of knowing how many is enough. It is worth re-introducing an OHT of the cartoon activity about sampling from Book 1 page 21. As a rule of thumb, measure and record characteristics from as many individuals in a representative sample as you have the time and resources for – the more you sample, the more accurate you are. Another way is to keep collecting and measuring individuals until you notice that you are not getting any new values for the variable you are recording.

Activity Enquiry: Studying characteristics

→ *Pupil's Book page 196*
This activity offers an opportunity for pupils to consider sample size, ways and accuracy of measurement, and how to present data clearly and systematically. Good examples to consider are:

• leaf length on small oak trees or holly
• body length in woodlice
• leaf width/length on plantain, daisy or geranium
• girth of trees of a particular species.

3 *Genetics*

Learning outcomes
Pupils:

• summarise how X and Y chromosomes determine the sex of humans
• compare genetic information in normal and sex cells
• discuss the ethical implications of genetic screening and counselling
• describe similarities between human parents and offspring
• read about some common genetic diseases and the amniocentesis test
• explain why individuals from the same parents may vary

This lesson applies to humans what pupils are learning about inheritance. The sex cell section reinforces Year 7 work on human reproduction (see Book 1, Chapter 8) so it should take no more than 20 minutes. The emphasis here is on probability reasoning. Use worksheets 7.3R or 7.4R if you have not already.

Activity Enquiry: Investigating probability

Worksheet 7.3R

→ *Worksheet 7.3R: How does chance influence inheritance? (E)*
This activity is based on modelling probability, using coloured beads and sampling to represent the possible combinations for gene pairing. It is for more able pupils because, although the modelling is at a concrete level, the explanations require abstract (formal) thinking, i.e. beyond Level 6. Find out from the Maths department how much work your pupils have done on probability at this stage and use this to link or bridge to this activity.

Equipment
Per group of four pupils:

• two opaque containers (milk cartons or similar)
• 100 red poppit beads
• 100 white poppit beads

(You could use different coloured beads or counters.)
Each group has two containers and each container has a mixture of 50 red beads and 50 white beads (200 beads in total).

Answers

1 Each bead represents a single gene.

2, 3 Each container represents one of the parents. A bead must be picked from each container to represent a gene inside the sperm cell (from the father) meeting a gene inside an egg cell (from the mother).

4 There are four possible combinations if a pair of beads is randomly taken from the containers:

Container 1	Container 2
red	red
red	white
white	red
white	white

5, 6 It is necessary to have so many beads and to select so many pairs to model probability because patterns are more likely to show up the larger the sample size.

7, 8 Each bead in each container has an equal chance of being selected, so initially there are four possible combinations that could be selected, assuming that each colour combination has an equal chance of being selected, i.e. 25%. The chances of selecting a gene pair with the same colour (red or white) is 50%. Selecting a pair of beads with one of each colour has a 50% chance, because red-white is the same as white-red (it does not matter which colour bead comes out of which container first).

9 This demonstrates the genetic principle that chance determines which gene pair is formed when two gametes fuse.

10 The chance selection of genes provides the basis for variation in organisms because each egg and each sperm contains thousands of genes, and as each sperm stands an equal chance of fertilising each egg, many combinations of genes are possible.

Summary and conclusion

The actual percentage of combinations for each pair will vary quite widely from group to group, as this is in fact a conditional probability model. Each time two beads are removed from the sample, the ratio of the remaining white to red is altered. To make a non-conditional probability model, each bead selection would need to be replaced before the next pair of beads is drawn.

Conditional probability describes what the chance is of something happening, given that something else has already happened. You do not have to explain this to pupils unless asked.

Display a class summary of each group's results. If you tally up the totals of each colour combination from each group, you will get nearer to the theoretical number expected. This shows that the larger the sample, the more reliable the conclusion you can draw from any trends or patterns.

Assuming that the red bead represents dominance over the white bead and that the beads represent the flower colour genes, the ratio of red-flowered plants to white-flowered plants in a group's and the class results is calculated by recognising that only a pair of two white beads will be white flowers, and all other combinations will be red flowers.

If the red-flowered plants were allowed to fertilise each other, the red-to-white flower ratio in their offspring is calculated by considering all types of possible crosses:

$Rr \times Rr \longrightarrow$ Red
$RR \times Rr \longrightarrow$ Red
$RR \times RR \longrightarrow$ Red

This is the same kind of problem as on page 194 of the Pupil's Book (Mendel's peas).

Activity

Worksheet 7.4R

Practical: Variations in pea growth

➡ *Worksheet 7.4R: Variations in pea growth (P)*
This alternative activity exploring probability is easier than that on Worksheet 7.3R, and can be done by all pupils following the *Thinking Through Science Red* course.

You will need to plant and grow yellow and green pea seeds 2 weeks before you want to use them. Soy beans are an alternative.

Pupils are asked to investigate if the colour of the seed affects the average length of root. Only by calculating frequency, median and range can pupils assess that there is no relationship. By plotting results on a frequency diagram, these can easily be compared. This is mostly a concrete exercise to produce a picture of median and range. Knowing the range is as important as knowing the mean. The activity reinforces the importance of taking large samples, and also provides a way of testing hypotheses about the effects of independent variables on dependent variables.

It helps to show pupils how to decide where the division is between root and shoot, to ensure that everyone uses the same measuring technique. There are no uniform values for shoot or root length; it varies from seed to seed as it is a continuous variable.

Activity

Reasoning: Same or different

➡ *Pupil's Book page 197*
This activity checks that pupils have read and understood the previous section on sex cells. It is best done by pupils individually (5 minutes), then pupils can work in pairs to compare and correct responses (another 5 minutes). Finally, lead a short summary discussion to make sure that everyone has the right answers.

Answers

Cells	Same or different genetic information?	Reasons
two cheek cells from the inside of Jane's cheek	same	Same, because these are both normal cells from the original fertilised egg cell
a cheek cell and a brain cell from Jane's body	same	Same, even though they are different types of cell. The genetic information is the same but the functions are different – you may need to explain that the cells switch on and off different parts of the genetic information to do different things because these are both normal cells from the original fertilised egg cell
a cheek cell and an egg cell from Jane's body	different	A gamete contains only half the amount of genetic information in a normal body cell. We cannot tell which genes are in the gamete
two egg cells from Jane's body	different	A gamete contains only half the amount of genetic information in a normal body cell. We cannot tell which genes are in each gamete

Determining the sex of a baby

➡ *Pupil's Book page 198*

These questions can be done in groups to check pupils' understanding. Give each group 10 minutes to complete all four questions in their exercise books.

18 100% of ova contain an X chromosome but only 50% contain a Y chromosome (50% are XX, 50% are XY).

19 The proportion of babies likely to be female is half, or a ratio of 1:1 female to male, or 'fifty-fifty' – make sure pupils understand that these expressions all mean the same thing.

Probability

➡ *Pupil's Book page 198*

A spinning coin is symmetrical, so there is an even chance of tails or heads.

20 You would prove this by spinning a coin a large number of times, probably about 100 times to see the pattern. Pupils may have already done this in maths.

21 This develops formal modelling ability. It can be done as a whole class discussion or as an individual homework. A coloured dot on one side of the coin could represent a particular characteristic that has only two forms (dominant and recessive) such as tongue rolling, pea seed colour, or pea flower colour. It is not a good model for characteristics that have more than one form, for example eye colour in humans, or variables that are continuous.

Attainment targets

Work in the previous sections should provide evidence that pupils are working towards the following attainment levels.

Describe the main stages in the human life cycle	Level 5
Describe some of the causes of variation in living things	Level 6
Use knowledge of cell structure to explain the functions of ova and sperm	Level 7

Activity Creative thinking: Boy or girl

→ *Pupil's Book page 198*
This 'Creative thinking' activity could be set for homework.

Tests/Some inherited diseases

→ *Pupil's Book pages 198–200*
Pupils should read through the sections on amniocentesis tests and inherited diseases. Some pupils may have direct experience of these topics, so sensitivity is required. Emphasise that amniocentesis tests are sometimes done as a routine precaution with older mothers, and that a clear result does not always mean that a baby will not inherit the genetic disease, as the tests are not 100% reliable. If you want to give pupils practice at research into secondary sources of information, use Worksheet 7.6R (see page 173).

Science and society

→ *Pupil's Book page 200*
You may want to use these questions as the basis for a classroom debate. Ask pairs of pupils to prepare some answers before you ask the whole class the questions. Give them 10 minutes to prepare and then have a 15-minute discussion.

Answers

22 Some advantages of choosing the sex of a baby could be to ensure that a gender-linked genetic defect is not passed on, or possibly to give a couple a child of the opposite sex when they already have a large number of children of the same sex.
Disadvantages include parents choosing a baby's sex for no medical reason. You may want to introduce the fact that in some societies boys are more desired than girls. This is a sensitive issue.

24 Currently (2004) the law allows sex selection of embryos where there are good medical reasons.

Activity Reasoning: Twins and siblings

→ *Pupil's Book page 201*
It is essential that all pupils learn the answers to these questions for SATs revision.

1 Identical twins carry the same set of genetic information because one egg cell is fertilised by one sperm. The fertilised egg splits into two cells which go on to form two individuals – identical twins.
Brothers and sisters including non-identical twins each carry a unique set of genetic material, even though they have inherited half the material from the father and half from the mother. This can be explained using two dice as a model.

Take a green and a red die. Explain that the green die represents genetic material from the mother and the red die is the genetic material from the father. Each throw of the two dice together represents a fertilisation process leading to a new offspring. Each offspring must have green and red material but they may have quite different combinations of numbers, for example, red 3 and green 6, red 6 and green 2, etc. (for a more detailed model of the reasoning behind this look at lesson 22 in *Thinking Science*).

2 No. Identical twins must be the same sex as the fertilised egg contains only one set of sex chromosomes, which replicate into two new cells that then split to form the basis of two new individuals.

3 If the eggs are from one woman and the sperm are from one man, the offspring produced will be similar.

Word play
➡ *Pupil's Book page 201*
This is an exercise in the use of the words 'identical', 'similar' and 'different' in relation to facial features.

Activity ## Creative thinking: Male or female
➡ *Pupil's Book page 201*
This activity requires time, so it could be set to cover several homework periods. It is useful to give the teams 10-minute classroom time slots to plan, co-ordinate and review their work. Ensure that they have access to art, design and word processing facilities.

4 *Why the variation?*

Learning outcomes
Pupils:

- explain that both environmental and inheritable factors influence organisms, causing variation
- explain why individuals with the same genetic information may vary
- identify some characteristics that are influenced by environmental factors
- identify environmental factors that influence the characteristics of an individual
- describe the structure of DNA
- understand what gene mapping is

This lesson is an opportunity for consolidation and assessment of understanding. It also introduces some details about DNA.

Begin the lesson by recapping what pupils think about probability and its role in inheritance. The 'Word play' activity on page 202 of the Pupil's Book is intended as a fun, quick start to the lesson and should take no more than 5 minutes. Lead into a short discussion about the 'Reasoning: Exploring probability' questions. You could link this with a consideration of astrology and see how many pupils believe that star signs influence luck.

The sections on DNA, the human genome project, gene mapping and cell division are extension activities for the most able or fast-working classes. These sections can also be set as reading and note-making activities. Pick and choose which sections you think are most suitable for your class. There are several research and creative activities for you to select for extended project work.

All pupils should do the section on GM crops. Note that all these sections feature highly in news reports. Make an area of your notice board into a section about genetics in the news, and ask pupils to contribute newspaper articles and pictures.

Activity

Reasoning: Exploring probability

→ *Pupil's Book page 202*

Pupils will highlight one event which makes them feel that they are lucky or unlucky. Thinking about the number of times you have won a raffle in terms of the number of times you have bought a raffle ticket relates to probabilities, and pupils should be encouraged to articulate luck in terms of probability. So, if you have never won a raffle and you have bought over 100 raffle tickets, then you are unlucky. A person who has won three prizes out of 100 raffle tickets is luckier. It is useful to get their reactions to winning twice with 50 tickets. Is this person even luckier? If so, how much luckier than the 3 out of 100 winner?

Question 4 involves consideration of a fair test – you can discuss the role of 'blind' trials, where the participants do not know what treatment or effect the researchers are looking at, so they cannot knowingly influence the outcome.

Answer

→ *Pupil's Book page 202*

25 The mother can only pass on an X chromosome but the father can pass on an X or a Y chromosome, so you could say it is the father's chromosome that determines the sex of a baby.

Activity

Reasoning: Family inheritance

→ *Worksheet 7.5R: Family inheritance: eye colour (S)*

Worksheet 7.5R

This is another opportunity for pupils to practise working out monohybrid crosses, this time about human eye colour. It can be set as a homework activity. It requires the same kind of reasoning as Mendel's peas (Pupils' Book page 194). Note that some eye colour genes (blue, green, grey) are continuous variables but brown is not.

Answers

1 The genes for the blue-eyed woman must be bb (recessive).

2 A cross between the two parents can be represented as:

Father Mother	B	B
b	Bb	Bb
b	Bb	Bb

The childrens' eyes are brown.

3 If a boy from this generation, Bb, had children with a girl with blue eyes, bb, the cross would be:

Boy / Girl	B	b
b	Bb	bb
b	Bb	bb

The chance of their children having brown or blue eyes is fifty-fifty.

It is important to check if pupils have really understood the principles and are not just recalling or repeating the Pupil's Book activity.

Environmental factors
Answers

→ *Pupil's Book page 202*

26 Environmental conditions such as the weather, for example, wind factor, temperature (often linked to altitude), water availability and the quality of the soil.

27 The environment is very important for child development. Children are affected by quality of nutrition, protection from the weather, and intellectual stimulus through talk and play.

28 This categorising activity can be used by pairs of pupils as a formative assessment exercise.

Likely to be environmental:

• Leaves of a beech tree growing in woodlands are on average larger but thinner than leaves of the same species of tree growing in a garden with no shade.
• Seedlings of beans grown in a dark cupboard are white. Seedlings of beans grown on the windowsill are green.
• Supermarkets ask farmers to plant their dwarf carrot varieties very close together so that they are uniformly small and so that each row of carrots has a larger number of carrots than when spaced apart.
• At about 6 months old, breast-fed babies are larger on average than bottle-fed babies.

Likely to be genetic:

• The banded snail shell has a range of different colours; they can be pink, yellow or brown, wherever the snails live.
• Upland sheep have shorter legs than lowland sheep.
• People today are on average taller than their grandparents. This could be in either category, (environmental and genetic) as nutrition is better today than in our grandparents' day, but there is also likely to be a genetic factor.

Time to think/Ideas and evidence: DNA – life's spiral staircase

➡ *Pupil's Book page 203*

These sections are for reading and discussion. It is not essential that they are done but many pupils find these fascinating topics. They could alternatively be used as homework activities.

5 *Genes*

Learning outcomes

Pupils:

- differentiate between a gene and a genome
- explore how analogies help us to understand scientific ideas and theories
- communicate what genetic engineering is using scientific terms
- research genetically modified crops
- understand how many scientists through history have contributed to the present-day understanding of genetics and evolution
- identify and select useful and relevant sources of information

Like lesson 4, this lesson has reading that relates to the sort of information pupils may be hearing about in the news and on popular science programmes. You can choose which sections on gene mapping, genetic engineering, and 'Ideas and evidence' are most relevant and interesting to your particular class but all pupils need to know about genetically modified crops, and the analogy (adapted from Book 1) is helpful to pupils in building an understanding of how genetic materials relate to each other. The 'Ideas and evidence' section gives an opportunity to look at how scientists often reach similar conclusions around the same time, and the story of Rosalind Franklin on page 203 and the photograph of Barbara McClintock on page 206 give recognition to pioneering women scientists.

Activity Research: Bar code

The bar code-like appearance of the chromosome is due to the differences between sections of genetic material. Bar codes on products carry information that scanners can read, for example, price, amount, and an instruction for reordering. Bar codes are similar to chromosomes in carrying information but different in that they are static pieces of information and do not change, whereas chromosome material is dynamic and changing. Pupils will spot obvious differences in the shapes of both.

Activity

Worksheet 7.6R

Research: Genetic disorders

➡ *Worksheet 7.6R: Researching genetic disorders (S)*
Lesson 5 provides a context for using Worksheet 7.6R to develop secondary research skills using the internet.

You could ask the careers adviser to provide some literature or sources about the careers listed on the worksheet, and about other related careers.

An alternative is to ask each pair of pupils to research just one disease, and then to combine all the research in a class book instead of making presentations which could take more time than you can allocate. This could be done in class time, by allowing three or four 20 minute sessions at the end of several lessons, or it can be given as a homework activity.

The skills developed include:

- asking appropriate questions
- using available resources outside of the school (health and research organisations)
- using critical thinking skills
- forming conclusions
- refining teamwork skills.

Activity

Creative thinking: Gene map

➡ *Pupil's Book page 206*

1 Pupils could list age, gender, personal medical history, and any diseases that relatives have died or suffered from.

2 This is an opportunity for some cross-curricular work on literacy – pupils can spend 10 minutes discussing their views in class in a group, and then write their letters as homework.

Time to think

➡ *Pupil's Book page 206*

Pupils will have made a mind map for the 'Creative thinking' activity on Pupil's Book page 198 when they were exploring myths about the sex of unborn babies. This is an opportunity to assess their understanding of the term 'genetic engineering'.

Activity

Information processing: Gene model

➡ *Pupil's Book page 207*

1   1 = genes, 2 = alphabet, 3 = chromosomes, 4 = inherit, 5 = analogy.

2, 3 An analogy is a model that states that one thing is like another, making it easier to understand.

Activity

Research: GM crops

➡ *Pupil's Book page 209*

Pupils research information and opinions about GM crops and make an informative display.

Activity Creative thinking: Company identity
→ *Pupil's Book page 209*
Your ICT department will tell you which software packages
pupils have been using to design letter templates and logos.
If pupils type 'company logo designs' into a search engine like
Google they will be able to look at all kinds of logos for ideas.

Ideas and evidence: Stevens and Wilson
→ *Pupil's Book page 209*
This is an interesting piece of history if time allows.

Time to think
→ *Pupil's Book page 210*
1 DNA, gene, chromosome, genome, nucleus, cell.
2 True:

- Genes are grouped together on chromosomes.
- DNA is a larger molecule than sugar.
- A double helix is shaped like a string of beads.
- All living things contain genetic information.
- A gene map would show what a genome contained.

False:

- Chromosomes are grouped together into genes.
- A genome is a large gene.
- DNA is found in the cytoplasm of a cell (pupils are entitled
  to think this is false, although there is some recent
  research to show it might be true).

6 *Selection*

Learning outcomes
Pupils:

- differentiate between artificial and natural selection
- explain how the characteristics of today's domestic animals
  and plants have been modified over time
- identify some characteristics that breeders wish to pass on
  and why they are desirable
- give specific examples of organisms modified by artificial
  and natural selection
- explain how evidence supports conclusions in the theory of
  evolution
- identify some inherited characteristics in plants and animals
- describe differences and similarities between parents and
  offspring
- plan an investigation to compare different characteristics in
  peas

Note that if you want to do the pea enquiry, it may take the
whole lesson. You could ask pupils to plan the investigation in
this lesson and hand their plan in for marking. Provide each
group with the necessary resources to carry out their
investigations in lessons 7 or 8.

If this investigation is not done then do the 'Information processing: What do you know?' and 'Word play' activities, both on page 211 of the Pupil's Book.

These are good formative assessment activities. If pupils are confused about what adaptations are, they will find the rest of this chapter hard to follow. It is worth recapping on adaptations and variation before proceeding any further.

Activity ## Information processing: What do you know?
→ *Pupil's Book page 211*
This is a revision activity about adaptions.

Word play
Answers
→ *Pupil's Book page 211*
The word 'adaptation' is used biologically for short-term reversible change:

- People who climb mountains at high altitudes for several weeks adapt to lower oxygen content in the air they breathe by producing more red blood corpuscles (cells).
- When you leave a dark room your eyes take a few seconds to adapt to bright sunshine.

The word 'adaptation' is used biologically for long-term non-reversible change:

- The leaves of a cactus plant are adapted to reduce water loss in the desert.
- Fish are adapted to live in water.

Non-scientific use of the word:

- Shakespeare's plays have been adapted for television.
- Old tractor tyres can be adapted to make containers to grow potatoes in.

Ideas and evidence: Evolution
→ *Pupil's Book page 210*
You could now return to the 'Ideas and evidence' section on evolution. The 'Research' activity on page 212 follows on from this.

Artificial selection
→ *Pupil's Book page 212*
Give pupils a few minutes to read through the text for themselves, and then get them to work in pairs to answer the questions.

Answers
29 Sharp pointed teeth, barking/snarling, pointed noses, eyes on side of head.
30 Shepherding sheep is unique to the collie; the body shape with very little fat and huge hind leg muscles for fast running is unique to the greyhound.

31 To make them useful to humans – the collie for agriculture, the greyhound for hunting food. Greyhounds also have far-sighted eyes and soft mouths, so they do not damage the prey.

32 By selective breeding, i.e. only letting suitable parents with favourable characteristics mate. Some breeders will, controversially, 'cull' puppies with undesirable traits.

You can use either the 'Reasoning' activity from Pupil's Book page 213 here, or Worksheet 7.7R, for pupils to explore artificial selection further, either in class or as a homework activity. The worksheet activity takes about 15 minutes to do.

Activity Reasoning: Better breeds
Answers
→ *Pupil's Book page 213*

1 From the Hereford parent the offspring has inherited a large head, short stocky legs and large hindquarters. From the Friesian parent it has inherited white patches and short body length. The cattle breeder would like a cow with enough muscle on to make good beef, but one that is also capable of producing a good milk yield.

2 Pupils are expected to get two or three characteristics for each organism. Some of your pupils may come from farms so this is their opportunity to share their knowledge. The characteristic and reason may overlap.

Organism	Characteristic	Why desirable/useful
pig	good muscle; fat; hardy; lots of piglets	make good sausages; able to live outside
sheep	lots of wool; hardy; producing twin lambs; fat/well-muscled	for good eating or wool for textiles; able to live in harsh conditions
cow	lots of milk; well-muscled; calf easily; hardy	some breeds such as highland cattle need to survive hard conditions; others are for either milk or beef; usually if they are for milk and beef, the yields of both are smaller than for specific milk/beef breeds
dog	affectionate/loyal; fierce; hardy; herding instinct; intelligent and trainable	pets; guard dogs; farm dogs; guide dogs for blind/deaf; drug detection; mountain rescue
wheat	fat seeds; lots of seeds on one head; short stems; disease resistant	high yield for farmers; not easily blown over
tomato	bright red; large (or small); sweet; slow to ripen; disease resistant; lots of fruit on one plant	attractive; nice flavour to eat; long storage on way to shops; high yield
lettuce	different shaped leaves and colour; slow to flower	attractive; nice flavour; high yield
daffodil	bright yellow; fancy shapes; strong stem	decorative cut or garden flowers

Activity Reasoning: How the wild cabbage became edible

Worksheet 7.7R

→ *Worksheet 7.7R: How the wild cabbage became edible (S)*
This worksheet provides a specific example of how humans have genetically manipulated plant species for their own use by selective breeding.

Answers

Characteristic matching: 1 – E, 2 – C, 3 – D, 4 – F, 5 – B, 6 – G.

1 'Hybridise' means to cross-breed or inter-breed.

2 Pupils may not know what 'close proximity' means. You could use this as a dictionary exercise to find out that it means 'close together'.

3 Insects pollinate the flowers. Growing some plants with muslin bags over the flowers so that insects cannot get to pollinate the flowers could test this. You would expect no seed production.

4 A list of other cultivated plants could include lettuce, tomato, potato, carrots; in fact the vast majority of the plant food we buy in shops today is created by selective breeding.

7 *Mutation*

Learning outcomes

Pupils:

- define the scientific concepts of mutation and mutant
- explain how bacterial resistance is a mutation
- summarise why there is a need to preserve variation in populations' gene pools
- identify some characteristics that breeders wish to pass on, and why they are desirable
- carry out and write up a full investigation

Activity ## Enquiry: Peas

→ *Pupil's Book page 214*

This activity will take a whole lesson if planned and carried out in the same lesson, or it could be spread over two lessons. This is a good assessment opportunity. Pupils are asked to design an investigation to compare the characteristics of the different pea varieties – for example, taste, texture, size, tenderness, cooking time. You need to provide a range of pea products, for example, canned mushy, processed, or garden peas, frozen peas, dried peas (you will need to allow time to soak and cook these for the investigation), fresh peas (these are usually hard to find but mangetout and sugar-snap peas are easier to obtain and can be used instead).

You may limit pupils' choice, for example by providing each group with a small sample of four sorts of pre-cooked pea. Unless you have easy access to facilities, tell pupils not to investigate cooking time but to use secondary information. You can draw their attention to the cooking instructions on the packaging, which you can have available in a display.

You might like to ask the Food Technology department to link with this as a cross-curricular investigation.

Answers

1 Suitable questions could include:

Do fresh peas taste nicer than preserved peas?
Which are the most tender peas to eat?
How does cooking affect texture and size?
Are all pea products from the same variety of pea? (This
may need secondary research.)

2 Pupils can compare as many as they like but this will have
an influence on their conclusions; the fewer the types, the
more restricted their conclusions, and fewer generalisations
can be made.

3 Sampling is made representative by making sure that the
samples are the same size portions, and by controlling the
other variables under investigation, for example, same
cooking time, same number of individual peas examined for
colour or shape so that variation is taken into account. It is
worth pointing out that supermarkets use quality control
methods to ensure that each tin or packet contains peas that
lie within the 'normal' range of variations so that they are
'average'.

Attainment targets

Work in the previous sections should provide evidence that
pupils are working towards the following attainment levels.

Describe some causes of variation	Level 6
Identify whether variation is likely to be genetic or environmental	Level 7
Explain how characteristics can be inherited by individuals	Level 8

8 *Genetic engineering*

Learning outcomes

Pupils:

- discuss ethical issues associated with genetics – for example,
  designer babies, gene therapy
- summarise the asexual process of cloning
- describe in terms of cells how desired characteristics are
  passed on

The last hour and a half allocated for this chapter gives an
opportunity to design your own lessons based on your
assessment of pupils' needs. You may decide to replace the
'Time to think' activity with one of the following options:

- Recap on previous sections that that you think have not been
  fully understood or that were not done in much detail due to
  lack of time.
- Return to worksheets not used to develop investigation skills
  or secondary research skills.
- Ask pupils to plan and carry out a full investigation into
  variation, referring back to examples given in the text.

Activity ## Research: Rare breeds

➡ *Pupil's Book page 215*

There are twenty approved conservation centres in the UK. These rare breed farm parks are regularly inspected by DEFRA and have to maintain very high standards. Useful websites include:

www.nccpg.com/
www.rarebreeds.org.uk
www.defra.gov.uk/Science/GeneticResources

Cloning

➡ *Pupil's Book page 216*

You need only spend 10 minutes on this section. If you want pupils to develop their observation skills you could provide them with lots of examples of asexual plant reproduction, for example bulbs, rhizomes, tubers, runners and trailers. Lay out the samples so that pupils can move around a 'circus' of observation stations and make notes and drawings of what they see. The availability of plant materials will depend on the time of year.

Time to think
Answers

➡ *Pupil's Book pages 216–217*

The photograph shows the chromosomes from a human embryo arranged in pairs. You can refer pupils back to the photographs on page 191 of the Pupil's Book, and the text about chromosomes.

1 It is the sex-determining pair.

2 It is male because the 23rd pair is an X and a Y chromosome.

3 No.

4 This report is unlikely to be true. If you want more of a debate about this, pupils can be referred back to the human genome project and do some secondary source research.

5, 6 These questions build on skills linked to 'Ideas and evidence' and 'Science and society'. This is an opportunity for classroom debate relating science to ethical issues and for developing pupils' respect for different viewpoints. Take care, as this can be a sensitive issue for many religions. Remind pupils there are no right answers here; opinions are matters of belief and values.

7, 8 These questions provide an opportunity for pupils who have not had much chance to use ICT to practise communicating scientific ideas by making an animated PowerPoint presentation to explain Mendel's work. This communication activity could be done after the SATs exams. Through this activity the following 'language for learning' skills can be developed:

- appraise written and visual images quickly for their usefulness
- carry out a web-search using relevant key words to research questions
- write closely argued text where precise links and connections are made within sentences
- ask questions to extend thinking and refine ideas.

The presentations can be evaluated using a 'traffic light' system.

Activity Review: Test on genes and inheritance

→ *Worksheet 7.8R: Test on genes and inheritance (R)*

Worksheet 7.8R

Answers

1 a) A = membrane; B = nucleus; C = cytoplasm.   (3 marks)
   b) In the nucleus.   (1 mark)
2 a) Unit of DNA that codes for a characteristic.   (1 mark)
   b) Pollen from one plant arrives at the carpel of
      another.   (1 mark)
   c) Nuclei of sex cells fuse.   (1 mark)
   d) Characteristics that have a range of values.   (1 mark)
3 Sex cells, zygote, embryo, fetus, baby.   (1 mark)
4 Males (XY) produce X or Y sperm.
  Females (XX) produce X eggs.
  These fuse to produce XX or XY.   (3 marks)
5 a) Cystic fibrosis; thalassaemia; sickle cell anaemia;
     Huntington's disease; haemophilia. (Any one.)   (1 mark)
   b) Description of the chosen disease.   (1 mark)
6 Double helix; hereditary material; found in the nucleus;
  full name is deoxyribonucleic acid; structure found by
  Crick and Watson with Franklin; contains four types of
  bases. (Any three.)   (3 marks)
7 a) Change in DNA/genes.   (1 mark)
   b) Replace mutated genes.   (1 mark)
   c) Evolution.   (1 mark)

8 Pressure and moments

→ Rationale

This chapter provides approximately 7½ hours of teaching materials. It covers the work in the QCA Scheme of Work Unit 9L Pressure and moments. It develops ideas from Key Stage 3 Unit 7K Forces and their effects, and links to Unit 9K Speeding up. Work on muscles as levers links to Unit 9B Fit and healthy.

→ Overview

The textbook sections, activities and worksheets have been arranged into 1 hour blocks to aid lesson planning. Clearly several of the activities and worksheets could form part of a homework session. The planning includes reading time for individual sections but some teachers may prefer to organise this as homework preparation for the following lesson. Six types of worksheet – extension (E), support for an activity (S), practical (P), key skills (K), developmental (D) and review (R) – allow for differentiation and flexibility to accommodate teachers' preferred practice. The actual timing and emphasis on different sections will depend on the current knowledge base of the pupils, the ability of the teaching group and the preferences of the teacher.

Lesson	Worksheets
1 Revision of forces and introduction to the concept of pressure	
2 The relationship between pressure, force and area	Worksheet 8.1R: Calculate your pressure (S) Worksheet 8.2R: Questions on pressure (S)
3 Pressure of liquids	Worksheet 8.3R: Hydraulic devices (S)
4 The particle theory for pressure	
5 Measuring gas pressure	Worksheet 8.4R: Pressure in the lungs (S)
6 The turning effect of a force	Worksheet 8.5R: Balancing see-saws (S)
7 Review of work	
Review	Worksheet 8.6R: Test on pressure and moments (R)

→ _Chapter plan_

	Demonstration	Practical	ICT	Activity	Word play	Time to think	Ideas and evidence
Lesson 1				Reasoning: Floating in water Research: Pascal Enquiry: Planning an investigation	Pressure	What do you know?	
Lesson 2		Measure your pressure	Use of spreadsheet Calculate your pressure	Consolidation: Questions on pressure Creative thinking: Sinking competition Enquiry: Force experiment Creative thinking: Three–legged chair Creative thinking: Sports products			
Lesson 3	Liquid pressure Pressure through a liquid	Hydraulics		Reasoning: Divers Data handling: Hydraulic calculations			
Lesson 4	Atmospheric pressure			Enquiry: Rubber suckers	'Pneu'	Particle theory of pressure	Experiments on the atmosphere and atmospheric pressure
Lesson 5	The water manometer		Use of spreadsheet or graphing package	Enquiry: Manometer Literacy: Pressure in the lungs Information processing: Air pressure Information processing: Altitude			
Lesson 6		Levers Moments Balancing	Use of spreadsheet on moments	Information processing: How the arm moves Information processing: Wire cutters Enquiry: Data analysis Information processing: Balancing see-saws Reasoning: Find the mystery data		Compound variables	
Lesson 7					Review of force, pressure and moments		
Review				Review: Test on pressure and moments			

➡ *Expectations*

At the end of this chapter

in terms of scientific enquiry

most pupils will: plan an investigation into balance, making sufficient observations with precision; identify a pattern in their results and use this to draw conclusions, relating these to the principle of moments

some pupils will have progressed further and will: account for anomalies in the observations of balance and evaluate their conclusions by reference to the principle of moments

in terms of physical processes

most pupils will: summarise key ideas about pressure; use the relationship between force, area and pressure between solids and within liquids and gases; explain the action of levers, including examples in the human skeleton in terms of the turning effect of a force; use the principle of moments to explain balance and give examples of its application, for example, crane counterweight

some pupils will have progressed further and will: use the definition of pressure in calculations to explain the operation of a range of devices; relate hydrostatic pressure in liquids and gases to density; apply the principle of moments to explain a range of situations, including the action of levers

➡ *Links with CASE*

In this chapter pupils are expected to deal with the compound variable pressure. A compound variable is one made up of two or more other variables. Pressure is defined as force per unit area (force/area). Pupils will also be familiar with density defined as mass per unit volume (mass/volume), and other compound variables, such as speed. To use the compound variable pressure effectively they will need to understand that the individual components force and area can change independently. So, if the force increases but the area remains the same then the pressure increases. Conversely, if the area increases and the force remains constant then the pressure decreases. The difficulty comes when both the force and the area change and pupils' thinking has to grapple with this. This requires formal operational thinking.

Work on floating and sinking could be linked to CASE 27, and divers (Pupil's Book page 229) links to CASE 29.

⮕ *Pupils' misconceptions*

Misconception	Scientific understanding
In a fluid, pressure acts only down.	Pressure acts in all directions in fluids.
The force in a collapsing can is due to a sucking force.	The force in the collapsing can is a pushing force due to pressure difference between the inside and outside of the can.
When an object is in equilibrium, the forces cease to act.	For a see-saw in equilibrium, the clockwise moments equal the anti-clockwise moments.

⮕ *Literacy, numeracy and other cross-curricular links*

There are some opportunities to encourage pupils to read and extract information from a variety of sources, but these feature less in this chapter than in others. Opportunities provided include researching information to write a paragraph to explain the action of artesian wells or large fountains.

There are a number of numerical calculations requiring pupils to rearrange the pressure, force and area formula and to calculate turning moments. There are ICT opportunities using spreadsheets.

Language for learning

By the end of this chapter pupils will be able to understand, use and spell correctly:

- words relating to pressure – for example, force, area, hydraulic, pneumatic
- words and phrases relating to balance – for example moment, pivot, lever, turning effect, counterbalance
- words and phrases relating to the human body – for example, antagonistic muscles.

Through the activities pupils will develop their skills in:

- presenting and listening to arguments based on scientific understanding.

1 *Revision of forces and introduction to the concept of pressure*

Learning outcomes

Pupils:

- explain the relationship between force and area – for example in terms of lying on a bed of nails
- apply the quantitative relation between pressure, force and area to a number of situations – for example, skis, sharp blades

What do you know?

→ *Pupil's Book pages 218–220*

This section recaps previous work and should help in identifying areas of misconception and/or misuse of terminology. It would be useful to have newton meters and beakers on hand so that pupils who need to physically try out some of the activities can do so. Alternatively, you may wish to demonstrate some of the activities as starters.

Answers

1 Check on the links as well as the main boxes selected.
2 Only the fourth and sixth statements are strictly true.
3 Change direction, for example a bat hitting a ball; change shape, for example two cars colliding; change speed, for example by pressing the accelerator in a car.
4 The reading on the newton meter goes down when the object is in water. This could be performed as a quick demonstration, and the pupils would be able to observe the apparent loss in weight when an object is suspended in a liquid.
5 The reading would be in-between the other two. This is a further quick activity that could easily be demonstrated. Pupils would be able to feel the force acting upwards.
6 The upthrust of water replaces the reaction force of your hand.
7 Gravity and upthrust.
8 The force is acting downwards. It is the resultant force.

Activity Reasoning: Floating in water

→ *Pupil's Book page 221*

Answers

1 As Peter moves into deeper water, upthrust pushes up more strongly on his body so he begins to float. He floats on his back easily because the upthrust acts on a greater area of his body.
2 500 N
3 Because of upthrust.
4 Salt water, because it provides more upthrust.

Word play

→ *Pupil's Book page 222*

This activity allows pupils to check that they are using terminology scientifically. It can provide assessment for learning opportunities as pupils can be asked to judge the accuracy of sentences and to suggest and explain improvements to their peers.

The relationship between pressure, force and area

→ *Pupil's Book page 222*

The relationship between pressure, force and area is introduced by referring to a number of pairs of pictures. It might be helpful to get pupils to decide on useful questions to ask one another about the pairs of pictures.

Answers

→ *Pupil's Book page 223*

1 area = force/pressure
2 pressure = force/area
3 **a)** A = 300 cm^2, B = 500 cm^2, C = 1500 cm^2.
   b) C should be at the base.
   c) A should be at the base.
   d) Smallest area surface = A or opposite end.
   e) The force is found by multiplying the mass (in kg) by 10 N/kg (gravity). Greatest pressure = 25 × 10/300 = 0.833 N/cm^2. Least pressure = 25 × 10/1500 = 0.167 N/cm^2.

Because pupils will come across a range of different units for measuring pressure this point should be made clear to the pupils, and the table of different units on page 224 of the Pupil's Book fully explained. Some discussion about why the various units, other than pascal, came about may prove useful here. (Finding out about the pascal is suggested as a research activity.)

Pupils should be able to perform simple calculations on pressure, force and area.

Activity ## Enquiry: Planning an investigation

→ *Pupil's Book page 224*

Pupils should plan a simple activity to model the idea that pressure is greater if the force is spread over a smaller area. At this stage they do not need to generate numerical data. It would be useful to decide on success criteria after considering initial ideas, before pupils work through and present their model to others.

2 *The relationship between pressure, force and area*

Learning outcomes

Pupils:

* show that they have grasped the key ideas of pressure

Calculating pressure

→ *Pupil's Book pages 224–225*

Answers

4 Pupils may write sentences such as: 'The weight is the mass multiplied by gravity,' as they want to show how to get weight from mass measurements. Alternatively they may say that mass is the 'amount of material' while weight is the 'measure on the scales as gravity pulls down'.
5 The girl wearing the stilettos, as the force applied is over a much smaller area, so the pressure is larger.

6 Pupils may refer back to their investigation. An alternative would be to model the stiletto and elephant's foot by using damp sand, clay or plasticine and doweling rods of different diameters and weights. This activity is looked at again later in the lesson (Enquiry, Pupil's Book page 226).

Activity

Worksheet 8.1R

Practical: Measure your pressure

➡ *Worksheet 8.1R: Calculate your pressure (S)*
Pupils measure the pressure they exert on the floor. The spreadsheet 'Shoe pressure' on the CD-ROM can also be used here to help with the idea of finding pressure from the force and the area variables. Pupils will need a weighing scale that measures in newtons, and a large piece of graph paper or squared paper to measure the area of their feet.
   Pupils need to be able to define mass as the amount of a substance – a measure of the number of atoms in it. Weight, on the other hand, is the pull on that mass by gravity.

Equipment
• newton scale
• squared paper
• access to a computer

Activity

Worksheet 8.2R

Consolidation: Questions on pressure
Answers

➡ *Worksheet 8.2R: Questions on pressure (S)*
1 A = force; B = pressure.
   Force = pressure × area
   Pressure = force/area
   Area = force/pressure
2 a) 350 N
  b) 350 N
  c) i) 0.58 N/cm^2
     ii) 0.39 N/cm^2
     iii) 0.15 N/cm^2
3 a) 0.15 cm
  b) 10 N
  c) 1 kg

Activity

Creative thinking: Sinking competition

➡ *Pupil's Book page 225*
Pupils could work in groups to agree on their own rules for the competition. These should then be agreed on by the whole class if the competition is carried out.

Activity

Enquiry: Force experiment

➡ *Pupil's Book page 226*
Pupils are asked to design a suitable investigation. This time it should generate numerical data. If the equipment is available, teachers could ask the pupils to actually perform the experiment. Pupils may need help in recognising the outcome variable – the depth that the rod sank into the clay – and also that there are two input variables because pressure is a compound variable.

Answers

1 Since the rod sank to exactly the same depth, the ratio force/area is a constant. Pupils may describe the relationship as proportional. As the area doubles so does the force.

2

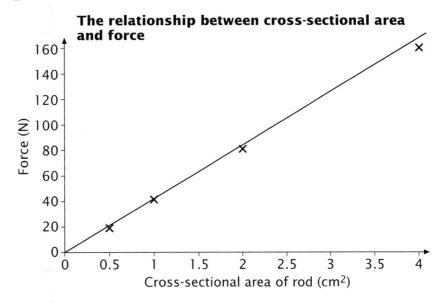

The relationship between cross-sectional area and force

3 Approximately 120 N.

Activity Creative thinking: Three-legged chair

➡ *Pupil's Book page 226*

Pupils may comment on the stability of the chair as well as the fact that the force is spread over a smaller area. They may want to increase the width of the legs to spread the force over a greater area.

Under pressure

➡ *Pupil's Book page 227*

For each set of pictures pupils should refer to the relative areas of the surfaces. It is important to encourage pupils to give a full explanation, and not to simply say high or low pressure.

7 A The surface area of the cheese wire in contact with the cheese is small, and so the pressure here is high. It is therefore easier to cut through cheese with a wire as less force is needed than with a knife.

B The bed of nails has many nails, although each individual nail has a small surface area. The total area in contact with the body is greater lying down than when standing, and the pressure is therefore reduced.

C The area of stones in contact with the foot is small compared to the area of the sand. On the stones your weight is pushing on this smaller area so the pressure is greater.

D The area of the high heel is smaller so the pressure on the floor is greater than for the boot. So high heels push more onto the floor.

    E The tip of the drawing pin is probably sharper than the tip of the nail so a smaller force is needed to give the required pressure to push the drawing pin in. Also, the head of the drawing pin is larger, so for a given force the pressure on your thumb is less than with a nail head. To apply sufficient force to the nail head without hurting your hand, you would need a hammer.

8 Any sensible examples. For example, low pressure – walking on soft surfaces such as snow; high pressure – cutting hard surfaces such as wood.

Activity
Creative thinking: Sports products

→ *Pupil's Book page 228*

Pupils should realise that ROLIF LOPA is an anagram. The features described are the opposite of those required.

Answers

1 Poor snow shoes – you want low density (light) snow shoes, with as large a surface area as possible. They should not sink. Poor ice skates – 'wide contact area and plastic' would give too much friction. This would be a poor investment prospect.

2 They should be light, with a large surface area to reduce the pressure on the snow.

3 You would want them to have a small surface area in contact with the ice. There should be a single, metal, sharp blade to create a high pressure which cuts the surface of the ice and reduces friction.

4 The article should show the points made in the answers to Questions 1–3.

3 *Pressure of liquids*

Learning outcomes

Pupils:

- apply the concept of transmission of pressure to predict the resulting force
- describe some effects and uses of liquids under pressure – for example, fire hoses, hydraulic systems
- describe an effect of atmospheric pressure or underwater pressure – for example, the danger to divers of 'the bends'

Pressure of liquids

→ *Pupil's Book page 228*

Activity
Demonstration: Liquid pressure

Teachers may want to show the traditional demonstration of how pressure in a liquid increases with depth (see diagram on next page). Pupils should be encouraged to predict the trajectory of the three water spouts.

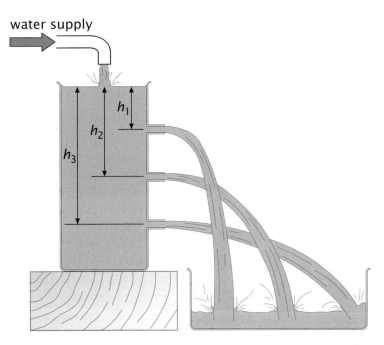

Pupils should be asked how and why an increase in density of the liquid would alter the trajectories of each spout.

Another demonstration that teachers may wish to show is the apparatus used to demonstrate that a liquid finds its own level.

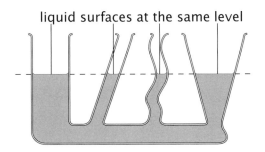

liquid surfaces at the same level

Activity Reasoning: Divers

➡ *Pupil's Book page 229*

This section looks at relative densities and how this can affect floating. It would be useful to demonstrate how divers float, swim and sink, before pupils attempt explanations.

Articulating ideas and comparing explanations is an important part of this activity.

Answers

1 Because the forces of upthrust and gravity are equal.

2 Float.

3 Floats, because salt increases the density of the water in the beaker and hence the upthrust.

4 By setting up the apparatus and performing the experiment.

5 By displacement, but it is easier to fill the test tube and empty the contents into a measuring cylinder.

6 It has the same overall density as water.

7 It is more dense than paraffin.

8 If its density matches or is less than that of the liquid, then the object will float. If the density is greater than that of the liquid, it will sink.

Liquid levels

➡ *Pupil's Book page 230*

Answers

➡ *Pupil's Book page 231*

The ideas relating to liquid levels and water pressure have applications for wells and fountains.

9 An artesian well and also the fountain at Witley Court depend on the increase of water pressure with depth. The artesian well spurts water because of the pressure of the water trapped deep underground between two layers of impermeable rock. At Witley Court water for the fountain was originally pumped by a steam engine from the nearby Hundred Pool to a reservoir at New Wood, well above the height of the Court. This was to maintain the pressure necessary to supply a fountain, which comprised 120 nozzles with a main jet capable of reaching about 35 metres. (A similar fountain may be seen in the gardens at Chatsworth House in Derbyshire.)

Time should be set aside for pupils to work on their own explanation of upthrust using the diagram on page 232 of the Pupil's Book. These should then be compared and any variations discussed.

Hydraulic systems

➡ *Pupil's Book page 232*

Activity ## Demonstration: Pressure through a liquid

Two syringes could be set up as shown on page 232 of the Pupil's Book, and used as a demonstration. A further demonstration of syringes filled with air would serve to demonstrate that gases can be compressed. This would allow for a discussion on the merits of a liquid, which is essentially incompressible, compared to a gas in, say, a robotic arm.

If the department has a model hydraulic jack this could be demonstrated.

Activity ## Practical: Hydraulics

It may be useful for pupils to try out a hydraulic system as shown in the diagram on Pupil's Book page 233, to get a sense of how it works.

Some applications of pressure

➡ *Pupil's Book pages 233–234*

Answers

10 15 cm
11 Pressure is the same throughout a liquid. If a force is applied over a small area it creates a large pressure, and this can be transferred through a liquid to create a large lifting force on the piston.

Activity
Worksheet 8.3R

Data handling: Hydraulic calculations
➡ *Worksheet 8.3R: Hydraulic devices (S)*
This worksheet provides practice at performing hydraulic calculations.

Answers
1 5 times.
2 Piston B is 6 times the cross-sectional area of piston A.
3 a) 6 N
b) 72 N
4 The pressure on each piston in a hydraulic jack must be the same, so the relationship between the areas is the same as the relationship between the load and effort.
5

Piston A area	Piston B area	Effort	Load
1 cm²	7 cm²	12 N	**84 N**
1 cm²	7 cm²	**9 N**	63 N
2 cm²	15 cm²	10 N	**75 N**
2 cm²	15 cm²	**9 N**	67.5 N
2.5 cm²	15 cm²	**8 N**	48 N
2 cm²	**24 cm²**	3 N	36 N
0.5 cm²	**2.5 cm²**	20 N	100 N

4 *The particle theory for pressure*

Learning outcomes
Pupils:

- apply the model of the particle theory of matter to explain the behaviour of gases under pressure
- apply the particle model of matter to explain why liquids are incompressible and gases are compressible

Activity ## Demonstration: Atmospheric pressure
There are a number of demonstrations on the atmosphere and atmospheric pressure which are worth performing if the pupils have not already seen them. These include:

- the collapsing can experiment
- inflating a balloon by removing the air from around it
- Magdeburg hemispheres.

Word play
➡ *Pupil's Book page 234*
1 Air bed.
2 A collection of air or gas in the space surrounding the lungs.

Ideas and evidence: Experiments on the atmosphere and atmospheric pressure

→ *Pupil's Book pages 235–236*

Answers

1 Air is removed from inside the can, reducing the air pressure inside the can compared to the outside air pressure. The pressure of the air on the outside of the can crushes it.

2 The pressure inside the balloon is greater than the pressure outside the balloon, and so the balloon inflates.

3 Half of a sphere.

4

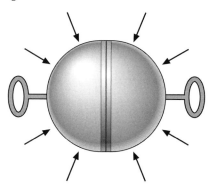

5 Nothing. It is a vacuum (although the complete removal of all air particles is difficult to achieve in practice).

Activity Enquiry: Rubber suckers

→ *Pupil's Book page 237*

Pupils should write clear instructions showing what they want to investigate, how they would carry out the investigations, and how they would make it a fair test.

Time to think

→ *Pupil's Book page 237*

This activity helps pupils find the language to explain the ideas they have met. Once they have worked through the matching exercise they should be encouraged to talk through what leads to increased air pressure and how the collapsing can experiment works.

Answers

Air consists of a mixture of particles moving all the time. The particles collide with each other and everything around them.

Different particles move at different speeds.

When the particles hit the side of a container they bounce back with the same average kinetic energy.

The air particles moving around inside the can will hit each other and the sides of the can.

As the particles get hotter they gain energy and move faster. They hit the sides of the container harder and the pressure inside the can increases.

In the collapsing can experiment, initially there is air inside the can exerting the same pressure as outside.

As the air is removed, there are fewer air particles hitting the outside of the can and the pressure inside the can decreases.

The pressure inside the can falls to zero because there are no air particles hitting the inside of the can.

The pressure on the outside of the can makes the can collapse.

5 *Measuring gas pressure*

Learning outcomes
Pupils:

- explain how a manometer works
- describe how air pressure decreases with height
- explain the decrease in terms of the distribution of the air particles

Activity ## Demonstration: The water manometer
This can be demonstrated by measuring the pressure of the gas mains.

Activity ## Enquiry: Manometer
➡ *Pupil's Book page 238*
Pupils should be reminded how to find lung capacity (see Book 2 Chapter 6, Enquiry (part 2), Teacher's Book page 143). An alternative is to use lung capacity bags.

Equipment to carry out the experiment will include:
- large 2 m water manometer
- mouthpieces
- disinfectant
- rule or tape measure
- bathroom scales calibrated in newtons
- large container to measure tidal volume
- lung capacity bags

A spreadsheet is provided for this activity on the CD-ROM. Only one computer is essential, however teachers may wish to collect all the data and allow pupils to spend a further lesson analysing the results in the IT room.

Activity ## Literacy: Pressure in the lungs

| Worksheet 8.4R |

➡ *Worksheet 8.4R: Pressure in the lungs (S)*
This is a cloze activity to encourage careful reading of text. Pupils should complete the worksheet in groups and then make their own notes or annotate a diagram of the thorax to explain inspiration and expiration.

Activity Information processing: Air pressure
➡ *Pupil's Book page 239*

Answers

1

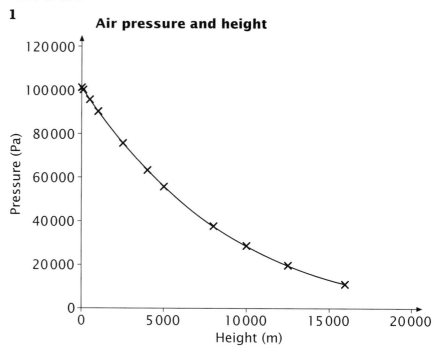

Air pressure and height

2 a) 86 000 Pa
   b) 58 000 Pa
   c) 34 000 Pa
   d) They will need to take oxygen with them, as the higher they go the less oxygen there is available to them.
   e) 11 100 Pa
   f) 22 000 Pa

Activity Information processing: Altitude
➡ *Pupil's Book page 240*

Answers

1 100 kPa
2 Approximately 1040 m from pupils' graphs.
3 Temperature, wind speed.
4 Altitude in 500 m steps and pressure in 10 kPa increments.

6 *The turning effect of a force*

Learning outcomes
Pupils:

- describe how to make a task easier by increasing the distance between the effort and the pivot
- identify levers in a number of household devices
- describe the arrangement of muscles in the arm and relate them to the parts of a lever

- explain how an antagonistic muscle pair works
- describe how an object can be kept in balance – for example, human body, crane
- apply the idea of the turning effect of a force to everyday situations – for example, lifting heavy objects
- recall the principle of moments and apply it to a range of situations

Simple machines

➡ *Pupil's Book page 242*

This section starts with a look at some examples of simple levers. It is important that pupils know and understand the terms effort, load and pivot before they attempt the questions.

Activity ## Practical: Levers

It would be useful if real practical examples of different types of lever were shown, as well as making reference to the pictures in the Pupil's Book on pages 242 and 243.

Equipment
- bottle opener
- screwdriver
- scissors
- tweezers

Answers

➡ *Pupil's Book page 242–243*

12 Longer one.

13 Down at the left hand end of the crowbar, in the direction of the effort.

14 Scissors – effort is closing the handles; pivot is the screw; load is the reaction of the cord against the blades.
Nutcracker – effort is closing the handles; pivot is the screw; load is the reaction of the shell against the nutcracker.
Paint tin – effort is the downwards force on the handle; pivot is the end of the blade under the lid; load is the lid of the tin.
Wheelbarrow – effort is the upwards pull on the handles; pivot is the centre of the wheel; load is in the centre of the hopper.
Bottle opener – effort is downwards on the end of the opener; pivot is the part of the opener touching the cap; load is the cap on the bottle.
Hammer – effort is at the top of the handle to the right; pivot is the part of the hammer touching the nail; load is the nail in the wood.

15 Between the load and the effort.

Activity Information processing: How the arm moves
➡ *Pupil's Book page 245*

Answer

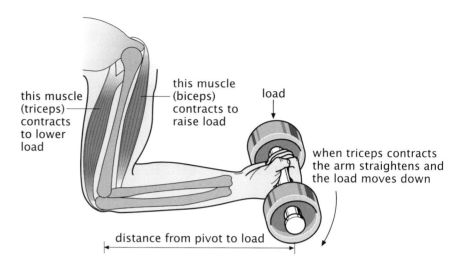

this muscle (triceps) contracts to lower load

this muscle (biceps) contracts to raise load

load

when triceps contracts the arm straightens and the load moves down

distance from pivot to load

Antagonistic muscles enable us to lift and lower objects. One set pulls the arm up and the other pulls it back down.

Turning moments

➡ *Pupil's Book page 246*

The term 'moment' is introduced here. Pupils are often confused by this term and associate it with an instant of time. Moments are turning forces. Both the size of the force and the distance between where the force is applied and the turning point (the pivot) affect the size of the moment, so moments are compound variables.

Activity ## Practical: Moments

The idea of the turning effect can be demonstrated using the example of a door. A practical activity would be to make a 'mobile' or show one to the class and get the pupils to identify the pivot points. Moving items on the mobile or altering their mass with paperclips gives an indication of moments and why they are compound variables.

Time to think

➡ *Pupil's Book page 246*

Answer

Pressure (force/area); density (mass/volume; speed (distance/time).

Balance

➡ *Pupil's Book page 246*

There are many toys and objects that rely on equilibrium. As many as possible should be demonstrated to the pupils.

Answers

16 The moments are equal.

17 If you change a variable on one side, you need to change the same variable on the other side by an equal amount.

Activity Information processing: Wire cutters

→ *Pupil's Book page 247*

Answers

1 $50 \times 9 = 450$ Ncm $= 4.5$ Nm

2 Force on wire $\times 1.5$ cm $= 50$ N $\times 9$ cm.
So force on wire $= 50 \times 9/1.5 = 300$ N.

3 $200/0.0005 = 400\,000$ N/cm^2

4 There is less resistance from the wire.

5 Force is applied 4 cm from the pivot, so calculations on moments and pressure should relate to this.

Activity Enquiry: Data analysis

→ *Pupil's Book pages 248–249*

Answers

1 (Holes are numbered from the pivot outwards.)

Left	Right
200 g at hole 1	100 g at hole 2
100 g at hole 2	200 g at hole 1
200 g at hole 2	100 g at hole 4
100 g at hole 4	200 g at hole 2

2 The mass on the left and on the right, and the distance of the mass from the pivot on the left and on the right.

3

Left		Right	
3 N	40 cm	4 N	30 cm
3 N	40 cm	6 N	20 cm
4 N	40 cm	5 N	30 cm
2 N	40 cm	4 N	20 cm
3 N	30 cm	3 N	30 cm

4 They are equal on both sides, with the exception of the third beam.

5 The third beam. To make it balance, one option is to remove a weight from the left hand side, leaving it at 40 cm, and add a weight to the right hand side and move the six weights to 20 cm.

6 The beams will balance if the mass $\times$ the distance has the same value on each side of the pivot.

Activity

| Worksheet 8.5R |

Information processing: Balancing see-saws

→ *Worksheet 8.5R: Balancing see-saws (S)*

Answers

1 It balances. The moment is the same on each side.
Left: $30 \times 3 = 90$, right: $45 \times 2 = 90$.

2 The moment is the same on each side. Left: $(35 \times 3) + (30 \times 1) = 135$, right: $45 \times 3 = 135$.

3 Left side went down, because the moment is now smaller on right side (Ruby is lighter than Anita).
Left: $(35 \times 3) + (30 \times 1) = 135$, left: $40 \times 3 = 120$.

4 Seat 2: Right: $(30 \times 3) + (45 \times 2) = 180$, left: $(40 \times 3) + ? = 120 + ?$, so 60 is needed. Therefore 30 kg must sit at position 2.

Extension

5 a) Left: $(35 \times 3) + (30 \times 2) + (30 \times 1) = 195$
Right: $(40 \times 3) + (45 \times 2) = 210$, so the right hand side goes down.

b) Pupils will select different examples.

c) Ruby on seat 3, Sam on seat 2, John on seat 5 and Anesh on seat 4;
or Ruby on seat 3, Anesh on seat 2, John on seat 5 and Sam on seat 4;
or Ruby on seat 4, Anesh on seat 5, John on seat 2 and Sam on seat 3;
or Ruby on seat 4, Sam on seat 5, John on seat 2 and Anesh on seat 3.

Activity ## Practical: Balancing

If the equipment is available pupils may perform the practical activity described to investigate the rules for balancing.

The data collected can be used in a spreadsheet activity to investigate moments. Rather than tell the pupils the rule, they should be encouraged to try alternatives to work out what the rule is.

Activity ## Reasoning: Find the mystery data

→ *Pupil's Book page 250*

Answers

1 11 000

2 At a distance of 50 (cm) the mass must be 220 (g).

3 $11\,000/50 = 220$. The moment (mass × distance) must be the same on both sides.

7 *Review of work*

Time to think

→ *Pupil's Book pages 250–253*

Pupils answer a number of different questions, including a definitions-matching exercise, to review the topics covered in the chapter.

Answers

1

force of gravity

2

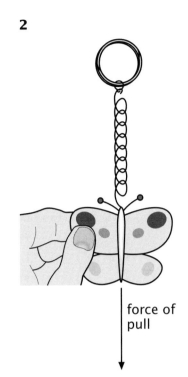

force of pull

3

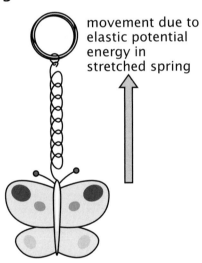

movement due to elastic potential energy in stretched spring

4 It stops moving because air resistance slows it down. All the other points need to be discussed to pick up misconceptions.

5 Where the arm joins the crane stand.

6 The long arm is needed to move objects into the construction.

7 The counterweight must be moved out from the pivot proportionally.

8 $6000 \times 8 = 48\,000$ Nm

9 $48\,000/11\,000 = 4.3$ m

10 The long arm would tip down.

11

turning effect of
one side of the
butterfly is
balanced by the
turning effect
of the other

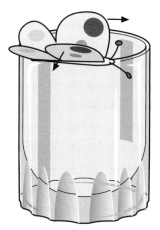

downward force of
gravity is balanced
by upward pull
by the thread

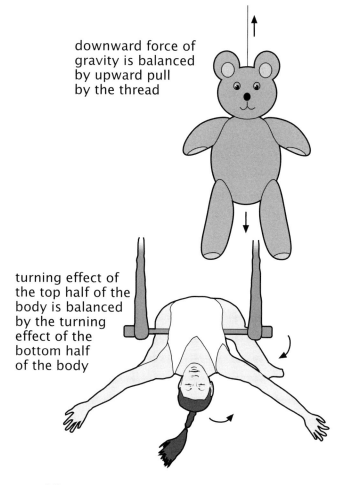

downward force of
weight of bottle and
liquid in it is
balanced by upward
force of liquid
surrounding it

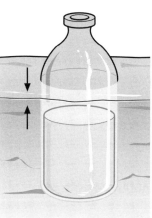

turning effect of
the top half of the
body is balanced
by the turning
effect of the
bottom half
of the body

12 air resistance – 10
balance – 16
barometer – 19
density – 11
floating – 9
force – 12
free fall – 13
hydraulics – 7
inertia – 4
lever – 3
manometer – 14
mass – 18
moment – 5
newton –1
pivot – 15
pneumatics – 2
pressure – 8
upthrust – 17
weight – 6

Activity

Review: Test on pressure and moments

➡ *Worksheet 8.6R: Test on pressure and moments (R)*

Answers

1 15 Nm	(1 mark)
2 D	(1 mark)
3 B	(1 mark)
4 D	(1 mark)
5 C	(1 mark)
6 C	(1 mark)
7 a) 300 N	(2 marks)
b) i) C	(1 mark)
ii) $300/1.5 = 200$ N/m^2	(2 marks)

8 a) Measures pressure differences/gas pressure; contains a column of water in two tubes; difference between two heights in tube equals the pressure difference/gas pressure. (3 marks)

b) Uses a lower force than load/used to lift heavy loads; because piston under load has larger area; this increases the pressure. (3 marks)

c) Can with lid with hole is heated, which forces out air, and the hole is blocked; reduced pressure inside; pressure outside the can is greater, and so it pushes the can in (can 'collapses'). (3 marks)

Using chemistry

→ Rationale

This unit provides up to 7 hours of teaching materials. It develops ideas from the Key Stage 3 Unit 9E Reactions of metals and metal compounds, and Unit 9F Patterns of reactivity. It links to other units, particularly to aspects of photosynthesis and respiration in Unit 8B Respiration, and Unit 9C Plants and photosynthesis, as well as to units on energy – Unit 8I Heating and cooling, and Unit 9I Energy and electricity.

This chapter aims to build upon the key idea of particles introduced in Year 7 and developed through Year 8. In this chapter, pupils consolidate and develop their understanding of essential aspects of chemistry by:

- Recognising that the atoms of some elements can become more permanently joined to each other as the elements combine to form simple compounds, and that mixtures are composed of constituents that are not chemically combined.
- Representing compounds by formulae, and understanding how the formulae are derived. There is a concerted focus on summarising and explaining chemical reactions using word and symbol equations. Pupil activities include the use of combustion flicker books and support for writing word and balanced symbol equations.
- Predicting the names and simple formulae of substances formed in chemical reactions. Considerable use is made of more sophisticated particle models to reinforce pupils' understanding of how chemical reactions take place and why mass is conserved in chemical reactions. Activities include a full science enquiry comparing the contrasting ideas on combustion of Georg Stahl and Antoine Lavoisier. The chapter considers how Lavoisier developed techniques for deriving more accurate and useful data to support his oxygen theory.

Applications of chemistry considered in this chapter include:

- Chemical reactions as energy sources: matches, fuel cells, fireworks, handwarmers.
- Generating electricity through the development of voltaic cells. This topic allows pupils to evaluate the contrasting views of Galvani and Volta.
- Plastics, including the development of biodegradable plastics.
- Medicines – consideration is given to how clinical trials are run.

➡ *Overview*

The textbook sections, activities and worksheets have been arranged into 1 hour blocks to aid lesson planning. Clearly several of the activities and worksheets could form part of a homework session. Lesson planning must allow sufficient review time for the learning outcomes to be clearly assessed. This forms a key element of the process of formative assessment. The planning includes reading time for individual sections but some teachers may prefer to organise this as homework preparation for the following lesson. The worksheets, which support the learning process, have been written to consolidate recall of key facts and the continued development of key ideas. Worksheets are of six types – extension (E), support for an activity (S), practical (P), key skills (K), developmental (D) and review (R) – to allow for differentiation and flexibility to accommodate teachers' preferred practice. The actual timing and emphasis on different sections will depend on the current knowledge base of the pupils, the ability of the teaching group and the preferences of the teacher.

Lesson	Worksheets
1 What do you know?	Worksheet 9.1R: What happens when copper is heated? (P) Worksheet 9.2R: Combustion flicker book (D)
2 What happens when fuels burn?	Worksheet 9.3R: How to write a symbol equation (S) Worksheet 9.4R: Atoms, molecules and formulae (S) Worksheet 9.5R: Atoms, molecules and formulae cards (S) Worksheet 9.6R: Test match special (P)
3 Burning ideas	Worksheet 9.7R: Which is the better theory of burning? (P)
4 Chemicals as energy resources	Worksheet 9.8R: Displacement reactions (S) Worksheet 9.9R: Handwarmers (P)
5 Generating electricity using metals	Worksheet 9.10R: Fruit and vegetable batteries (P)
6 Using chemicals to make useful products	Worksheet 9.11R: Picking the right plastic (D)
Review	Worksheet 9.12R: Test on using chemistry (R)

For pupils who have difficulty and need more support with their understanding of the key words, processes such as polymerisation and the use of word equations, worksheets that accompany the *Thinking Through Science Blue* course are available on the CD-ROM.

➡ *Chapter plan*

	Demonstration	Practical	ICT	Activity	Word play	Time to think	Ideas and evidence
Lesson 1		Heating copper	Spreadsheet to calculate the mass change/ Cu:O ratio when Cu is heated	Creative thinking: Flicker book		What do you know?	Considering different explanations for the effect of heat on copper metal
Lesson 2		Chemical reactions		Evaluation: Is hydrogen the best fuel? Review: Revising symbol equations Consolidation: Atoms, molecules and formulae Reasoning: Fireworks	Alternatives to the term 'decompose'	Review of word and symbol equations for complete and incomplete combustion of methane	How do matches work?
Lesson 3	Theory of conservation of mass	Which is the better theory of burning?	Spreadsheet to calculate the mass change/ Mg:O ratio when Mg is heated	Evaluation: Does the phlogiston or the oxygen theory best explain how things burn? Reasoning: Oxygen theory Enquiry: Making measurements Creative thinking: Letter to Georg Stahl			Burning ideas
Lesson 4	Handwarmers	Hand-warmers		Review: Displacement reactions Reasoning: Redox Information processing: Interpreting data: Patterns in displacement reactions	Origins of 'quicklime' and 'slaked lime'		
Lesson 5		Fruit and vegetable batteries		Reasoning: Electrolysis	'lysis'		New electricity
Lesson 6	Nylon rope trick			Reasoning: Properties of plastics	'Poly' 'Mono'		
Review				Review: Test on using chemistry		Review of chapter	

➡ *Expectations*

At the end of this chapter

in terms of materials and their properties

most pupils will: describe how chemical reactions are used to make new products and as a source of energy; use the particle model to explain how mass is conserved during chemical reactions and other changes; represent chemical reactions by word equations; describe chemical reactions that are used to produce energy (looking at displacement reactions, pupils could predict which combination of metal/metal oxides or salt solutions would bring about the highest temperature change); use simple voltaic cells to make predictions about the largest voltage produced and link metal/metal salt combinations with expected temperature changes

some pupils will have progressed further and will: be able to resolve observations in which mass appears to be lost with the principle of conservation of mass, and represent a wide range of reactions by symbol equations including state symbols; be able to relate the energy produced to differences in reactivity and demonstrate an ability to link quantitatively voltages and metal pairings; extend their ideas about energy from chemical reactions and use secondary sources to find out about 'chemical heaters' for meals or handwarmers for climbers and explorers; recognise that mass is conserved in reactions in which gases are produced, and explain the apparent loss in mass in reactions involving the production of gases; evaluate Lavoisier's contribution to the development of ideas about burning

in terms of scientific enquiry

most pupils will: make measurements of temperature and mass adequate for the investigation they are carrying out; describe some of the stages in development of a new product; carry out an experiment to support the oxygen theory of combustion

some pupils will have progressed further and will: explain the stages of development of a new product; consider how the particle model and knowledge of gases helped change earlier ideas about burning; plan, carry out and evaluate an experiment to test the oxygen theory of combustion

Links with CASE

This chapter allows for the development of the manipulation of key variables.

The combustion of hydrocarbon fuels links with CASE 25 (formal models) – use of concrete and abstract models to develop an understanding of chemical reactions. The 'Copper combustion' spreadsheet allows pupils to develop their skills in manipulating data and identifying simple ratios.

→ *Pupils' misconceptions*

Misconception	Scientific understanding
Particles are destroyed when a substance is burned, so it loses mass.	Mass is always conserved during a chemical reaction.
The name of a chemical is not systematically related to the constituent elements.	Chemicals are systematically named, for example, -ate indicates the presence of oxygen in the compound. Formulae indicate the numbers and types of atoms present.
When two elements react together the atoms from the reactants are transmuted into new atoms (of the products). The reaction is a 'magical' change.	During a chemical change, reactants are used up, products are formed and energy is exchanged with the surroundings.
Reactions where gases are formed result in a loss of mass.	Gases have mass and after a chemical reaction all the atoms of the original reactants are still there, but in new combinations: $A + B \longrightarrow C + D$
Compounds are mixtures. The elements can be mixed in any proportions.	Compounds consist of fixed combinations of different types of atoms that cannot be easily separated.

→ *Literacy, numeracy and other cross-curricular links*

Language for learning

By the end of this chapter pupils will be able to understand, use and spell correctly:

- the names of a range of compounds

and understand:

- the significance of prefixes – for example, mono-, poly-, electro- and suffixes – for example, –ate, -lysis.

Through the 'Word play' activities pupils will:

- learn alternatives to the term decompose and consider different contexts for its use
- learn the origins of the terms quicklime and slaked lime
- use word roots to explain the meaning of electrolysis, polymers, monomers.

The chapter contains various passages which require clear comprehension; these include 'New electricity' concerning the work of Galvani and Volta, a passage on biodegradable plastics, and a summary of the stages involved in a clinical trial. There is an opportunity for creative writing: pupils are required to write a letter to Georg Stahl persuading him to rethink his support of the phlogiston theory.

1 *What do you know?*

Learning outcomes

Pupils:

- review the combustion of a range of fuels, including hydrocarbons, charcoal and hydrogen
- recall the conditions required for complete and incomplete combustion
- identify that elements are made from atoms of one kind
- explain the difference between compounds and mixtures

What do you know?

➡ *Pupil's Book pages 254–257*

Check that pupils are secure in their understanding of the key words – combustion, atom, molecule, element, compound and mixture. There are a number of activities in the book which will allow you to assess their knowledge and understanding. The review of fuel combustion recalls work covered at Year 7 in Book 1 Chapter 11, Simple chemical reactions.

There is a variety of exercises for pupils to engage with, including writing their own questions and producing concept maps.

Answers

➡ *Pupils Book pages 255–257*

1 a) Carbon dioxide.
  b) The clear solution goes cloudy/milky.
  c) Water/water vapour.
  d) Change from blue to pink.
  e) Carbon dioxide and water.
  f) Hydrogen, because it only produces water, and charcoal, because it only produces carbon dioxide.

2 a) Water.
  b) To condense the water vapour into a liquid.
  c) To ensure that the water has been derived from candle combustion and not from water in the limewater.
  d) The funnel is too close to the flame and is allowing incomplete combustion, hence the production of soot.
  e) Increased surface area increases the chances of complete combustion.

3 a) The stored chemical energy in the gas is transferred as heat (mainly) and light to the surroundings.
  b) Stored chemical energy is transferred mostly as heat, also light, and some sound.
  c) Stored chemical energy is transferred as less heat, more light, no sound. The diagram may be smaller, as less fuel is likely to burn due to the lack of air/oxygen.
  d) Fireworks/explosions/flares – chemical is energy transferred as light, sound and heat to the surroundings. Fluorescent tube – stored chemical energy is transferred as light and some heat to the surroundings.

4

Physical changes	Chemical changes
easily reversed to simple separation	difficult to reverse
no new chemicals are produced	new chemicals (products) are produced

5 1–C; 2–D; 3–A; 4–E; 5–B.

Activity

Worksheet 9.1R

Practical: Heating copper

➡ *Worksheet 9.1R: What happens when copper is heated? (P)*
This could be used as an activity-based 'What do you know?' to elicit any misconceptions that pupils may have regarding combustion as a chemical reaction. It would be useful to keep data from another class for pupils to analyse and evaluate. Question 6 is written with more able pupils in mind.

Equipment
- eye protection
- copper turnings or reduced copper wire
- sand
- test tube and holder
- heatproof mat
- spatula
- balance (the activity requires balance readings to 2 decimal places)

ICT
The spreadsheet allows pupils to compare the mass of copper before and after heating. There is the opportunity to compare the combining ratios for each group in the class, allowing pupils to suggest the likely formula for copper oxide. The derivation of an empirical formula using the spreadsheet would be more appropriate for the higher level pupils.

Answers
1 Copper only – black. Copper in sand – reddish/brown.
2 Copper only – gain in mass. Copper in sand – no/slight gain.
3 Air (oxygen).
4 The gain in mass by the copper in contact with the air suggests that copper is gaining something from the air. The copper atoms are combining with oxygen atoms.
5 copper + oxygen ⟶ copper oxide
6 Water would not allow any oxygen to make contact with the copper metal; the metal would not get hot enough to allow any possible reaction to take place.

Activity

Worksheet 9.2R

Creative thinking: Flicker book

➡ *Worksheet 9.2R: Combustion flicker book (D)*
A flicker book provides an excellent animation of the combustion reaction between methane and oxygen. This idea can be extended to all key chemical reactions.

Attainment targets

Work in the previous section should provide evidence that pupils are working towards the following attainment levels.

Recognise that atoms of elements can be represented by symbols	Level 6
Explain the differences between elements and compounds in terms of their constituent particles	Level 7

2 *What happens when fuels burn?*

Learning outcomes

Pupils:

- recognise a wide range of fuels and describe fuels as substances that release energy when they burn
- generalise about the products of burning fuels that contain hydrogen and carbon
- balance the advantages of hydrogen and methane as fuels against their disadvantages

This lesson begins with an exercise to classify fuels. It then develops the use of both word and symbol equations for complete and incomplete combustion of hydrocarbon fuels. This is consolidated in a 'Time to think' section.

Pupils compare the energy transfers in fuel cells and power stations and compare the efficiency of both. This will consolidate the teaching of the key idea of Energy in Year 9, which considers energy conservation, dissipation and efficiency.

Pupils learn about safety matches and fireworks as common applications of burning. Pupils investigate the chemical composition of fireworks and consolidate their understanding of chemical formulae.

Answers

→ *Pupil's Book pages 257–258*

2 Wood/kindling/peat/coal.

3 Crude oil derivatives: natural gas; oil; paraffin.

5 Grey = carbon; white = hydrogen; red = oxygen.

6 propane + oxygen $\longrightarrow$ water + carbon dioxide

$$C_3H_8 + 5O_2 \longrightarrow 4H_2O + 3CO_2$$

Activity

Worksheet 9.3R

Review: Revising symbol equations

→ *Worksheet 9.3R: How to write a symbol equation (S)*

This summarises the essential stages in writing a balanced symbol equation, including the use of state symbols. This is a higher order skill (HOT) and it is essential that pupils studying science and in particular chemistry, are able to both understand and apply the process of balancing equations in more complex and unfamiliar situations. Balanced symbol equations show clearly the idea of conservation of mass and eliminate many common misconceptions regarding chemical changes.

Answers

1 $2H_2(g) + O_2(g) \longrightarrow 2H_2O(l)$
This reaction is sometimes described as a synthesis reaction because two elements are joining together to make/ synthesise the compound water.

2 $C_2H_4(g) + 3O_2(g) \longrightarrow 2CO_2(g) + 2H_2O(l)$

3 $2Al(s) + Fe_2O_3(s) \longrightarrow Al_2O_3(s) + 2Fe(s)$ (Thermit reaction)

Activity

Worksheet 9.4R

Worksheet 9.5R

Consolidation: Atoms, molecules and formulae

➡ *Worksheet 9.4R: Atoms, molecules and formulae (S)*
➡ *Worksheet 9.5R: Atoms, molecules and formulae cards (S)*
This is a definitions-matching game.

Incomplete combustion

➡ *Pupil's Book pages 258*

Answers

7 natural gas + oxygen $\longrightarrow$ carbon + water
(methane)

8 petrol(l) + oxygen(g) $\longrightarrow$ carbon monoxide(g) + water(l)

Hydrogen as fuel

➡ *Pupil's Book pages 259–260*

Answers

9 $2H_2 + O_2 \longrightarrow 2H_2O$

Extension

10 Products of complete combustion: carbon dioxide; water vapour. Products of incomplete combustion: carbon monoxide; carbon (soot); water vapour.

a) Soot will irritate the delicate lining of the respiratory system, causing us to cough. Particles will get trapped in the cilia of the cells lining our respiratory system.

b) Incomplete combustion produces carbon monoxide, which combines with haemoglobin in the blood in place of oxygen to form carboxy-haemoglobin. This prevents the circulation of oxygen and so there is less available for respiration. Conservationists would argue that burning hydrogen does not produce large quantities of carbon dioxide.

c) Carbon dioxide increases in the atmosphere lead to global warming through the greenhouse effect.

d) Pupils need to refer to the release of carbon dioxide from methane, whereas the combustion of hydrogen only releases water vapour.

11 Soot on top of leaves prevents leaves from absorbing light, which is necessary for photosynthesis.

12 Hydrogen only produces H_2O, whereas methane may produce carbon, carbon monoxide or carbon dioxide. If complete combustion takes place, then the carbon dioxide emissions will further exacerbate the problems of global warming.

13 The fuel cell has only one stage whereas the power station has several stages. At each stage only a given percentage of the energy is transferred as useful energy. In the power station hot waste gases come from the furnace, and cooled steam from the turbine eventually returns to the boiler, but this will not be 100% efficient. Overall, the smaller the number of stages the more efficient the system is.

Ideas and evidence: How do matches work?

➡ *Pupil's Book pages 260–261*

After reading the text pupils should try to describe the role of the sulphur, carbon and potassium chlorate in the match head, and explain how the match produces a flame.

1, 2

Elements	Compounds	Elements contained in compounds
phosphorus sulphur oxygen	potassium chlorate phosphorus sulphide	potassium, chlorine, oxygen phosphorus, sulphur

3 Phosphorus oxide and sulphur (di)oxide:
phosphorus sulphide + oxygen ⟶
phosphorus oxide + sulphur (di)oxide

4 Both the oxides produced by the combustion of phosphorus sulphide are non-metal oxides (Book 1, Chapter 11) and are strongly acidic.

5 He separated the flammable chemicals: matchbox – red phosphorus, match head – potassium chlorate, sulphur.

Activity

Worksheet 9.6R

Practical: Chemical reactions

➡ *Worksheet 9.6R: Test match special (P)*

This activity offers a practical to consolidate key skills, and pupils' knowledge and understanding of simple combustion, acids and indicators, and fair testing.

Equipment
- eye protection
- Universal Indicator
- test tubes
- test tube holders
- tongs
- timers
- matches

A wide range of brands of matches should be available, to ensure that there is a wide range of match length, thickness and material (wood, cardboard).

Answers

1 Find out whether they need to be struck on the actual container or any rough surface.

2 Match length; thickness; material (wood, cardboard).

3 A survey; further research.

Thinking Through Science Teacher's Book 3 Red

Time to think

→ *Pupil's Book page 262*

1 Cobalt chloride paper – blue to pink; or anhydrous copper sulphate – grey-white to blue in the presence of water vapour.

2 Limewater; turns from clear to milky in the presence of carbon dioxide.

3 Reaction products are carbon dioxide and water (hydrogen oxide). The carbon and hydrogen in both products had to be derived from the hydrocarbon.

4 The amount of available oxygen determines whether carbon, carbon monoxide or carbon dioxide is produced.

5 $CH_4(g) + 2O_2(g) \longrightarrow CO_2(g) + 2H_2O(l)$ (plenty of air, complete combustion)

$2CH_4(g) + 3O_2(g) \longrightarrow 2CO(g) + 4H_2O(l)$ (some air)

$CH_4(g) + O_2(g) \longrightarrow C(s) + 2H_2O(l)$ (little air) Now balanced.

Activity Reasoning: Fireworks

→ *Pupil's Book page 263*

1 Pupils should look at the colours produced by the fireworks, and use the table on Pupil's Book page 263 to answer this.

2 magnesium + oxygen $\longrightarrow$ magnesium oxide
$2Mg + O_2 \longrightarrow 2MgO$
The symbol equation has been included in case you consider that pupils could manage this.

3 Strontium or lithium, and copper.

4 Magnesium, strontium, calcium, barium are all in group 2 (alkali earth metals), lithium and sodium are in group 1 (alkali metals), and copper is a transition metal.

5 Lithium nitrate; lithium chloride; lithium sulphate.

6

Compound	Formula	Number of elements	Number of atoms
lithium carbonate	Li_2CO_3	3	6
strontium carbonate	$SrCO_3$	3	5
sodium nitrate	$NaNO_3$	3	5
copper chloride	$CuCl_2$	2	3

Answers

→ *Pupil's Book page 264*

14 **a)** The rapid release of gases out of the end of the rocket propels the rocket in the opposite direction. It is similar to an inflated balloon being released, only with much more force. (This can be demonstrated in the classroom.) You are creating a small explosion inside the firework, and when that explosion occurs, all of its energy and momentum are directed one way.

b) The mass of the rocket will decrease.

15

Component	Ingredient
oxidiser	potassium nitrate
binder	starch
fuel	sulphur, charcoal
metal to produce sparks	e.g. iron, steel, aluminium

Background information – Sparklers

A sparkler consists of a chemical mixture that is moulded onto a rigid stick or wire. These chemicals are often mixed with water to form a slurry that can be coated on a wire (by dipping), or poured into a tube. Once the mixture dries, you have a sparkler. Aluminium, iron, steel, zinc or magnesium dust or flakes may be used to create the bright, shimmering sparks. The metal flakes heat up until they are incandescent and shine brightly or, at a high enough temperature, actually burn. Chemicals can be added to create colours. The fuel and oxidiser are proportioned, along with the other chemicals, so that the sparkler burns slowly rather than exploding like a firecracker.

Answer

➡ *Pupil's Book page 264*

16 Banger – firework which explodes because the reaction takes place very quickly, with the rapid release of gases in a very short period of time.
Rocket – fast reaction which propels the firework forwards at a rapid rate.
Sparkler – safe to hold at arm's length.

Attainment targets

Work in the previous sections should provide evidence that pupils are working towards the following attainment levels.

Know that combustion is an oxidation reaction involving oxygen and resulting in oxides	Level 6
Recognise that compounds can be represented by formulae	Level 7
Represent chemical reactions by balanced symbol equations	Level 8
The routine use of balanced equations for chemical reactions	Exceptional performance

3 *Burning ideas*

Learning outcomes

Pupils:

- use experimental models to find out whether the oxygen or phlogiston model best explains how magnesium burns
- use preliminary work with a model to decide what to measure and to determine the number of measurements to be taken
- record measurements

- record data on a graph and draw an appropriate curve/line to fit data
- identify and describe patterns in graphs
- evaluate the conclusion by considering how good the data is
- state that the mass of magnesium oxide is greater than the magnesium, and explain this in terms of combination with oxygen
- use models to describe the conservation of mass in a reaction
- recognise that mass is conserved in reactions in which gases are produced and explain the apparent loss in mass in reactions involving the production of gases

The main emphasis of the lesson is the 'Ideas and evidence' section, 'Burning ideas'. This looks at the development of modern theories of burning. Pupils are required to compare different sets of data on the burning of magnesium in air, and are asked to judge whether the data supports the phlogiston or the oxygen theory of combustion. Pupils should be encouraged to think about the results of the spreadsheet activity that links with Worksheet 9.1R *What happens when copper is heated?*.

Ideas and evidence: Burning ideas
Answers
→ *Pupil's Book pages 264–265*
1 The changes in masses involved were very small but still highly significant. Very small increases and/or decreases in mass needed to be quantified.
2 Very small changes in mass need to be detected in reactions involving gases.
3 Materials that contained phlogiston should lose mass. Substances with no phlogiston would remain at constant mass.
4 Approximately four-fifths (79%).

Activity Evaluation: Does the phlogiston or the oxygen theory best explain how things burn?
Answers
→ *Pupil's Book pages 266–267*
1 During the combustion of magnesium the most common observations are a very bright white flame and the silver metal changing into white ash.
2 Overall pattern is an apparent loss of mass.
3 Phlogiston theory.
4 Pupil error; possibly used a balance that was not sensitive enough.
5 Set 2; misreading the balance which may have been incorrectly tared.
6 There is an increase in mass.
7 The magnesium may have only melted, and not ignited.
8 Oxygen theory.
9 The method used allows the actual mass changes to be measured. Apparent loss of mass due to escaping smoke and fumes is avoided. Using a balance that measures to 2 decimal places allows much smaller mass changes to be detected.

10 The phlogiston theory was not supported by the increasing evidence showing actual increases in mass when substances burned in air.

Activity Reasoning: Oxygen theory
Answers
➡ *Pupil's Book page 267*
1 Substances gain mass when they burn because their atoms combine with atoms of oxygen.
2 A candle goes out in a gas jar because the supply of oxygen runs out.
3 Charcoal leaves hardly any ash because the main products, carbon dioxide and water vapour, escape into the air leaving very little solid residue.
4 A mouse would die in an airtight container because there is a limited supply of oxygen available for it to breathe.

Activity Enquiry: Making measurements
Answers
➡ *Pupil's Book page 267*
1 A crucible lid.

The plan should include:

• measuring the mass of the crucible plus lid and the length of magnesium ribbon
• heating the crucible and lid and magnesium ribbon in a strong blue flame
• carefully lifting the lid just enough to allow air into the crucible, but so that no fumes escape
• after the magnesium has burned, allowing the apparatus to cool down before re-weighing.

Activity Practical: Which is the better theory of burning?
➡ *Worksheet: 9.7R: Which is the better theory of burning? (P)*

Worksheet 9.7R

Equipment
• eye protection
• crucible and lid
• tripod
• Bunsen burner
• pipe clay triangle
• heatproof mat
• tongs
• balance
• magnesium ribbon

This can be a full investigation. The worksheet provides a help sheet. There are some spreadsheets available on the CD-ROM for use with this investigation.

Answers
1 Any moisture will vaporise on heating and may affect any mass increase produced by the burning magnesium.
2 **a)** This removes any corrosion, to ensure the magnesium can oxidise.
   b) The oxygen needs to reach all the surfaces of the metal.
   c) This allows sufficient air to enter the crucible without letting any fumes escape.

5 magnesium + oxygen ⟶ magnesium oxide
   $2Mg(s) + O_2(g) \longrightarrow 2MgO(s)$

6 A magnesium atom (particle) has been joined through a chemical reaction with an oxygen atom (particle). The resulting substance is the compound named magnesium oxide.

7 By heating the contents further, pupils will achieve the maximum mass possible, as the magnesium will have been completely oxidised into magnesium oxide. This should allow them to derive a more realistic empirical formula for the oxide. Incomplete oxidation would result in a lower final mass for pupils to calculate the formula.

Attainment targets

Work in the previous section should provide evidence that pupils are working towards the following attainment levels.

Level	Planning	Obtaining and presenting evidence	Considering evidence	Evaluating
5	Identify the key variables to be considered. Produce a prediction which begins to use the particle model in terms of the expected mass change	Chose to use a 0.01 g balance because it is more precise, even though it is more difficult to use. Repeat anomalous results because they do not seem to fit the pattern	Recognise which results do and do not support their prediction	Suggest any improvements to the method
6	Plan to take enough measurements for the investigation. Use books and preliminary work to assist in their predicting and planning	Measure a variety of quantities accurately, even if the divisions are fine. Make enough measurements for the given task	Anomalous results are explained by, e.g. accuracy or sufficiency	Stronger evidence could have been obtained by changes to procedure (which are included)
7	Detailed scientific knowledge is used by referring to the balanced symbol equation for the oxidation of magnesium. Decide to heat to constant weight as an appropriate approach. Care is taken to account for any potential loss of mass by the escaping of oxide vapours	Use of spreadsheet on CD-ROM to derive an empirical formula for the oxide	Derive a formula for the oxide by interpreting the patterns in the data they have collected	Consider whether the data collected on the spreadsheet is sufficient to draw confident conclusions

Activity Creative thinking: Letter to Georg Stahl

➡ *Pupil's Book page 268*
This activity could be given as homework.

Activity Demonstrations: Theory of conservation of mass

Safety
• Lead nitrate – use a concentration lower than 0.01 M (harmful)

Possible demonstrations

1 Use a plastic soft drinks bottle, half full of water. Add an Alka-Seltzer tablet, tighten the stopper and place on a top-pan balance.
2 Measure the mass before and after a simple displacement reaction.
3 Use lead nitrate solution and potassium iodide solution. Place lead nitrate solution into the bottom of a small conical flask. Have potassium iodide solution in a small test tube suspended by a thread and held upright by being tightly fixed by a rubber bung. Weigh the apparatus, invert it, allow precipitation to take place and then reweigh.

Answers

→ *Pupil's Book pages 268–269*

17 copper sulphate + zinc $\longrightarrow$ zinc sulphate + copper
   $CuSO_4$ + Zn $\longrightarrow$ $ZnSO_4$ + Cu

18 This is a displacement reaction. The zinc replaces the copper to form zinc sulphate. The total number of particles (atoms) is exactly the same both before and after the reaction.
   reactants (7 particles) $\longrightarrow$ products (7 particles)

19 Each reaction produces a gas as a product (hydrogen; carbon dioxide). The gas escapes into the air resulting in a loss of mass of the container.

20 He developed a balance for measuring mass that could weigh to 0.0005 g so that he could accurately measure changes in mass during chemical reactions.

Experiment 1: Mass of mercury oxide then mass of remaining mercury.

mercury oxide $\longrightarrow$ mercury + oxygen
$2HgO \longrightarrow 2Hg + O_2$

Experiment 2: Mass of mercury oxide after heating the mercury remaining from Experiment 1.

mercury + oxygen $\longrightarrow$ mercury oxide
$2Hg + O_2 \longrightarrow 2HgO$

21 Hydrogen and chlorine.
22 Non-metals.
23 Hydrobromic acid; hydrofluoric acid.

4 *Chemicals as energy resources*

Learning outcomes

Pupils:

- describe chemical reactions that are used to produce energy
- relate the energy produced to differences in reactivity
- describe ways in which some chemical reactions can be used, for example, handwarmers
- investigate which combination of calcium chloride and water produces the best handwarmer pack

This lesson includes a brief review of displacement reactions using Worksheet 9.8R and then investigates how the combination of metals/metal salt solutions determines the maximum temperature change. Pupils investigate the best conditions to produce a handwarmer with an optimum maximum temperature rise.

Activity

Review: Displacement reactions

➡ *Worksheet 9.8R Displacement reactions (S)*

This is a short starter activity to review pupils' understanding of displacement reactions.

Answer

From most to least reactive: magnesium, zinc, lead, copper.

How else are chemical reactions used as energy resources?

Answers

Pupil's Book pages 269–270

24 Oxygen.

25 Aluminium, because it has removed the oxygen from the iron.

26 Competition by organisms within an ecosystem for shelter, food, water, light, space (biology/ecology).

27 $2Al + Fe_2O_3 \longrightarrow Al_2O_3 + 2Fe$

28 Aluminium is oxidised; it is the reducing agent.
Iron oxide is reduced; it is the oxidising agent.

Activity

Reasoning: Redox

➡ *Pupil's Book page 270*

W is more reactive than Y, but less reactive than X.
Order of reactivity, from most to least reactive: X, W, Y.
Y and XO – no reaction. Y and WO – no reaction.

Activity

Information processing: Interpreting data: Patterns in displacement reactions

➡ *Pupil's Book page 270*

1 Change in appearance of metals; solutions change colour; iron becomes coated with copper in copper nitrate.

2 Magnesium, zinc, iron, copper, silver.

3 Iron does not react with zinc nitrate – no temperature increase recorded.

4 magnesium + silver nitrate $\longrightarrow$ magnesium nitrate + silver
magnesium + zinc nitrate $\longrightarrow$ magnesium nitrate + zinc
magnesium + copper nitrate $\longrightarrow$ magnesium nitrate + copper
iron + silver nitrate $\longrightarrow$ iron nitrate + silver
iron + copper nitrate $\longrightarrow$ iron nitrate + copper

5 There are 30 possible combinations. These include magnesium vs. silver nitrate and silver vs. magnesium nitrate. The 30 combinations will include 15 that will not react. Pupils will not need to duplicate every combination, therefore 15 combinations will be sufficient. Pupils will either detect a reaction or not.

6

Metal \ Salt solution	AgNO$_3$	Zn(NO$_3$)$_2$	Cu(NO$_3$)$_2$	Fe(NO$_3$)$_2$	Sn(NO$_3$)$_2$	Al(NO$_3$)$_3$
magnesium	4 °C	1 °C	3 °C	2 °C	2–3 °C	1 °C
iron	3 °C	——	2 °C		1 °C	——
aluminium	3–4 °C	——	3 °C	1 °C	1–2 °C	
tin	1–2 °C	——	0–1 °C	——		——

7 $Zn(s) + 2AgNO_3(aq) \longrightarrow Zn(NO_3)_2(aq) + 2Ag(s)$
$2Al(s) + 3Cu(NO_3)_2(aq) \longrightarrow 2Al(NO_3)_3(aq) + 3Cu(s)$

Comparing handwarmers
Answers

→ *Pupil's Book page 271*

29

Physical change	Chemical change
the crystallisation of supersaturated sodium acetate solution	the combination of calcium oxide in water
dissolving calcium chloride in water	

The physical changes here are reversible dissolving events where no chemical reaction has taken place. Adding calcium oxide to water results in the formation of a new chemical which cannot be reversed.

30 In the absence of undissolved solid a supersaturated solution may be obtained – this contains an amount of solid in excess of its true solubility. Such solutions can occur when a saturated solution is cooled in the complete absence of solid or dust particles. There is no nucleus round which the crystals can form. For example, if crystals of sodium thiosulphate are heated in a boiling tube with a few cm^3 of water until they all dissolve, a saturated solution forms. The sodium thiosulphate does not crystallise out when the solution cools. If the liquid is seeded with a very small sodium thiosulphate crystal, crystals will once again begin to separate, starting from the seedling crystal as centre, and growing steadily downwards into the solution.

Activity Demonstration: Handwarmers

Equipment
- eye protection
- mass balance
- beaker
- measuring cylinder
- thermometer
- calcium chloride (8 mesh)
- stirring rod
- spatula
- 2 sealable freezer bags – large and small

1 Add approximately 200 cm^3 of distilled water to the large bag. Place the bag inside a beaker to keep it upright.

2 Add 4.5 g calcium chloride to the small bag. Partially close the bag, leaving some of the seal open.

3 Place the small bag containing the calcium chloride into the large bag.

4 Seal the large bag.

5 Activate the heat pack by squashing the inner bag to release the calcium chloride, and shaking the water and calcium chloride together. Observe what happens.

Activity Practical: Handwarmers

Worksheet 9.9R

➡ *Worksheet 9.9R: Handwarmers (P)*

Pupils are provided with background chemical data, such as the energy transferred per gram of dissolved calcium chloride and the solubility of calcium chloride at room temperature and at 100 °C.

The task is:

'You are working for a company that wants to develop a heat pack. Each pack is to contain 100 cm^3 of water. Your job is to determine how much calcium chloride must be present in a heat pack to achieve a maximum temperature of 40–50 °C.'

The equipment is the same as for the demonstration above. The pupils should use what they have seen demonstrated to plan their investigation.

Word play

➡ *Pupil's Book page 271*

We drink water/other drinks when we are thirsty (quenching our thirst). Slaking is the old fashioned word for quenching. Here water is added to the calcium oxide (quicklime) until the reaction is complete and calcium hydroxide (slaked lime) is produced.

$$CaO + H_2O \longrightarrow Ca(OH)_2$$

If further water is added, milk of lime is produced, which when filtered gives a clear, dilute solution of calcium hydroxide ('limewater') which can be tested with carbon dioxide.

5 *Generating electricity using metals*

Learning outcomes

Pupils:

- find out about the chemical reactions in some cells
- find out how electrical energy is produced from certain reactions

Chemical cells are also covered in Unit 9I Energy and electricity (Chapter 3).

The activity 'Fruit and vegetable batteries' requires pupils to investigate the key factors in determining the voltage of fruit or vegetable batteries and to measure the voltage with as many combinations of metal/fruit as possible. The Pupils' Book includes a related 'Reasoning' activity, and the 'Ideas and evidence' section 'New electricity' gives an opportunity for extended reading and to evaluate the contrasting conclusions of Galvani and Volta. The work of Davy is also considered; this shows how the voltaic cell was developed to facilitate the discovery of a number of new metallic elements through electrolysis.

Activity

| Worksheet 9.10R |

Practical: Fruit and vegetable batteries

→ *Worksheet 9.10R: Fruit and vegetable batteries (P)*

The challenge is to investigate the key factors in determining the voltage of fruit or vegetable batteries. Autumn would be a good time to carry out this practical as there will be copious quantities of apples and other fruit available. Potatoes are cheap and are available all year round. Refer back to Pupil's Book page 80, where there is a diagram of a potato clock. The clock could be used as an alternative to the fruit or vegetable batteries in determining what factors affect the voltage.

Equipment
- several pieces of fruit and vegetables which pupils bring from home (only one from each pupil)
- distilled water
- salt water
- four types of metals: copper, iron, magnesium, zinc
- voltmeter, connecting wires

Answers
1 Distilled water will not produce a voltage. Salt will produce a strong electrolyte, which will allow a current to flow.
2 Using the same metals produces no voltage. Different metals will produce a voltage.
3 This will depend the data they have collected.
4 Exact concentrations; use pure chemicals; test chemical combinations carefully to produce the desired voltage.

Extension
Distance between metals; surface area of metals.

Activity

Reasoning: Electrolysis
Answers
→ *Pupil's Book page 272*
1 Combination of metal electrodes.
2 Voltage (V) measured.
3 Electrolyte; concentration/temperature of electrolyte; distance between electrodes; size of electrodes (surface area).
4 Magnesium, zinc, iron, lead, copper.
5 Metals further apart in the activity series produce the highest voltage.
6 **a)** 0.31 V
  b) 1.93 V
7 Approximately 1.9 V (actual value 2.0 V). Aluminium is between magnesium and zinc in the activity series (Mg/Cu is 2.71 V; Zn/Cu is 1.10 V).

Ideas and evidence: New electricity
Answers

→ *Pupil's Book page 273*

1 water ⟶ hydrogen + oxygen
$$2H_2O \longrightarrow 2H_2 + O_2$$

2 It was Galvani's assistant (often reported as his wife) who observed that a frog's legs violently contracted if a metal scalpel were touched to a certain leg nerve during dissection.

3 He thought that it was the muscles that contained the electricity.

4 Fresh muscle may work better than older muscle; heart muscle would generate electricity better/faster than other muscle; larger muscles would contract more and produce more electricity.

5 He tried non-metals instead of metals, and used a combination of an iron plate for placing the frog on and a brass hook for making simultaneous contact with the nerve and the iron.

   His published paper stated that the leg twitched more with wires made from certain metals than others. Galvani thought that humans and animals have something called 'animal electricity' produced in their brains, and that this travels down the nerves to make the muscles twitch.

6 Volta used his electrometer to detect electric charge. He did not detect any electric charge in animal tissue. He repeated Galvani's experiment but replaced animal tissue with papers soaked in salt water and used silver and zinc discs. His electrometer detected electric charge.

7 Wood, bone, pottery, various minerals, rocks, gemstones.

8 Pure water is a poor conductor but the addition of acid, which fully ionises, will produce a solution that is a strong electrolyte.

Word play

→ *Pupil's Book page 274*

Plasmolysis – the shrinkage/breakdown of the cytoplasm away from the cell wall.

Haemolysis – the breakdown of red blood cells with the release of **haemo**globin.

Humphry Davy
Answers

→ *Pupil's Book page 274*

31

Properties of potassium	
Typical of a metal	**Unusual for a metal**
high lustre (shiny)	soft
malleable (easily shaped)	reacts violently with water

32 Some of the globules of potassium burned with an explosion and bright flame as soon as they were formed.

33 Potassium hydroxide.

34 Molten salts would only produce the metal and the non-metal with which it was combined, for example, sodium chloride (NaCl) would break down into sodium and chlorine. If a solution of sodium chloride was used the cathode would release hydrogen.

Pupils might suggest that as soon as any metal such as potassium, sodium, lithium was produced during the electrolysis of an aqueous solution it would react immediately and violently with the water present.

Attainment targets

Work in the previous sections should provide evidence that pupils are working towards the following attainment levels.

Describe evidence for some accepted scientific ideas and explain how the interpretation of evidence by scientists leads to the development and acceptance of new ideas	Level 6
Use the patterns of reactivity of metals to make predictions about other chemical reactions	Level 7

6 *Using chemistry to make useful products*

Polymers

Pupils compare the chemistry of natural polymers (proteins, starch, cellulose and DNA) with synthetic polymers, and consider the stages in the development of biodegradable plastics. The lesson is concluded by looking at how modern medicines are developed through clinical trials.

Activity

Worksheet 9.11R

Reasoning: Properties of plastics

➡ *Worksheet 9.11R: Picking the right plastic (D)*

This activity looks at the properties of plastics, and contrasts their properties with those of the metal copper.

Answers

2 Easily shaped; economical to make; unreactive, so chemicals can be easily stored; do not crack/shatter when dropped; light/low density.

Extension

3 Hard; dense; good electrical and heat conductor; malleable; shiny; low reactivity.

Similarities	Differences
easily moulded, flexible	metals are conductors
most not easily scratched	metals have high melting points (thermoplastics are easily melted but thermosets are not)

4 a) Copper is very near the bottom of the series and so is unreactive, as are plastics. It will not react with the air or water.

b) Copper is too expensive and is becoming more and more limited in supply.

c) Iron rusts (corrodes) whereas plastic will not. This is a particular disadvantage for guttering. Plastic is cheaper.

Activity ## Demonstration: Nylon rope trick

Pupils should watch the nylon rope trick as a visual starter activity.

Equipment
- small beaker
- hexanediol chloride
- 1,6 diaminohexane
- forceps
- glass rod
- eye protection, gloves

Safety
- The acid chlorides are corrosive.
- 1,6 diaminohexane is an irritant.
- Cyclohexane is highly flammable.
- Wear eye protection and gloves when pulling out nylon thread.
- Use a well ventilated room and avoid all sources of ignition.

Preparation
- Dissolve 2.2 g of 1,6 diaminohexane in 50 ml of distilled water (beaker A).
- Dissolve 1.5 g of decanediol chloride or hexanediol chloride in 50 ml of cyclohexane in a separate beaker, labelled B.
- Carefully pour solution A into a small beaker.
- Gently pour solution B into solution A down a glass rod. The two liquid phases do not mix.
- With forceps, grasp the polymer film that forms at the interface of the two solutions and pull it carefully from the centre of the beaker.
- Wind the polymer thread on a stirring rod.
- Wash the polymer thoroughly with water or ethanol before handling.

Disposal
Any remaining reactants should be mixed thoroughly to produce nylon. The solid nylon should be washed before being discarded in a solid waste container. Any remaining liquid should be discarded in a solvent waste container or should be neutralised with either sodium hydrogen sulphate (if basic) or sodium carbonate (if acid) and flushed down the drain with water.

Word play

➡ *Pupil's Book page 275*

Polygon: many sided shape.
Polygamy: being married to more than one person.
Polypod: insects have many legs.
Polyunsaturated: long carbon chain molecule with many double bonds.
Monocle: single lens for correcting defective vision.
Monocycle: another name for a unicycle.
Monologue: a long speech made by one actor.

Monorail: a single track railway.
Monopoly: exclusive control of the market supply of a product or service.
Monoculture: farming practice where large areas of land are given over to one type of crop.
Monohybrid inheritance: inheritance of a single pair of alleles.

Polymers

Answers

➡ *Pupils' Book pages 275–276*

35 Proteins – used for growth and repair of cells.
DNA – provides the genetic code which controls the chemistry and determines the features of the cell.
Starch – stored food source in plants.
Cellulose – polymer used by plants to support cell structure.

36

Natural polymers	Synthetic polymers
proteins, DNA, starch, cellulose, fats, pectin	polystyrene, polythene, PVC, PVA

37

	Ethene	Propene
formula	C_2H_4	C_3H_6
total number of atoms in formula	6	9
total number of elements in formula	2	2
element/compound	compound	compound
atom/molecule	molecule	molecule

38 Linking loops to make Christmas decorations; links in a bicycle chain.
39 Hydrocarbon monomers.
40 Carbon dioxide and water.
41 Ethene: $C_2H_4 + 3O_2 \longrightarrow 2CO_2 + 2H_2O$
Propene: $2C_3H_6 + 9O_2 \longrightarrow 6CO_2 + 6H_2O$
polyethene + oxygen $\longrightarrow$ carbon dioxide + water
polypropene + oxygen $\longrightarrow$ carbon dioxide + water

Biodegradable plastics
Answers

➡ *Pupil's Book pages 277–278*

42 Any substance that can be broken down by micro-organisms would be described as biodegradable.
44 Simulate conditions under which biodegrading would take place – warm, moist, presence of micro-organisms.
Compare the rate of decomposition of different polymers.
45 Synthetic polymers are very inert (chemically unreactive); micro-organisms are not capable of breaking down/digesting man-made polymers.
46 To test the tensile strength it is necessary to compare equal-sized pieces of plastic or plastic bags. Add masses until destruction, and compare results.

Thinking Through Science Teacher's Book 3 Red

47 a) Carrier bags – cheap; light; does not rip/tear easily; handles do not stretch; carries a large load.

b) Plastic plates – heat resistant; rigid; strong; not brittle; keep their shape; light.

Medicines
Answers

→ *Pupil's Book page 279*

48 An agent that looks, feels and smells like the drug under review but has no real effect.

49 It would be unfair on the cancer sufferers if they were being deprived of a potential treatment/cure.

50

Stage	Main activities
1	Check how safe the drug is and how best to administer it to patients
2	Continue safety checks and assess its effect on patients
3	Increase number of patients involved, compare with other treatments
4	Monitor the drug over a longer period of time including possible side effects

51 It is unfair for those suffering not to have access to effective treatment. Perhaps increase the numbers involved and move into stage 3 for more data.

Time to think

Pupil's Book page 280

This activity is intended as an opportunity for pupils to identify with their teacher their improvements and learning needs. It presents useful review activities for the chapter.

Activity

Worksheet 9.12R

Review: Test on using chemistry

→ *Worksheet 9.12R: Test on using chemistry (R)*

Answers

1 a) Used up in burning; reacted with fuel/petrol; formed carbon dioxide/carbon monoxide. (Any one.)　(1 mark)

b) i) Water.　(1 mark)

ii) It is poisonous/toxic.　(1 mark)

2 a) More air/oxygen; better mixing gives more　(1 mark)
combustion/more efficient burning. (Any one.)　(1 mark)

b) Oxygen; carbon dioxide + water.　(2 marks)

3 a) i) Oxygen; magnesium oxide.　(2 marks)

ii) The oxygen had mass; oxygen was added to the magnesium; the magnesium has reacted with oxygen. (Any one.)　(1 mark)

b) Oxygen.　(1 mark)

c) Zink oxide.　(1 mark)

d) A – chemical; B – chemical; C – physical.　(1 mark)